FOLKTALE THEMES AND ACTIVITIES FOR CHILDREN, VOLUME 2

Learning Through Folklore Series

Norma J. Livo, Series Editor

Who's Endangered on Noah's Ark? Literary and Scientific Activities for Teachers and Parents. By Glenn McGlathery and Norma J. Livo. 1992.

Who's Afraid . . . ? Facing Children's Fears with Folktales. By Norma J. Livo. 1994.

Of Bugs and Beasts: Fact, Folklore, and Activities. By Lauren J. Livo, Glenn McGlathery, and Norma J. Livo. 1995.

Folktale Themes and Activities for Children, Volume 1: Pourquoi Tales. By Anne Marie Kraus. 1998.

Folktale Themes and Activities for Children, Volume 2: Trickster and Transformation Tales. By Anne Marie Kraus. 1999.

Folk Stories of the Hmong: An Activity Book. By Dia Cha and Norma J. Livo. 1999.

Folktale Themes and Activities for Children

Trickster and Transformation Tales

Volume 2

Anne Marie Kraus

Calligraphy by Susan K. Bins

1999
Teacher Ideas Press
A Division of
Libraries Unlimited, Inc.
Englewood, Colorado

For Dad—You've always been there for all of us.

TEACHER IDEAS PRESS
A Division of
Libraries Unlimited, Inc.
P.O. Box 6633
Englewood, CO 80155-6633
1-800-237-6124
www.lu.com/tip

Library of Congress Cataloging-in-Publication Data

Kraus, Anne Marie.
    Folktale themes and activities for children / Anne Marie Kraus; calligraphy by Susan K. Bins.
    xviii, 225 p. 22x28 cm.
    Includes bibliographical references and index.
    Contents: v. 2. Trickster and transformation tales.
    ISBN 1-56308-608-5
    1. Tales--Study and teaching (Elementary)   2. Folklore and children.   I. Bins, Susan K.   II. Title.
GR45.K73 1999
372.64--dc21

Contents

TRANSFORMATION TALES

Preface

The explosion in the number and variety of folktales has been a welcome trend in the publishing of books for children. Libraries and bookstores increasingly enrich their holdings with lavishly illustrated single-tale picture books and thoughtful, illustrated collections for children. Teachers, school media specialists, public librarians, recreation specialists, storytellers, and parents are eager to use these multicultural stories with children. *Folktale Themes and Activities for Children, Volume 2: Trickster and Transformation Tales* is a resource guide for planning children's folktale experiences. This guide offers annotated bibliographies and suggestions for grouping tales with common motifs, activities, and school curriculum connections. Whereas many of the activities focus on the school setting, anyone interested in folk literature will find this resource helpful as an organizational tool, a selection or purchasing tool, and an activity guide. Overall, *Folktale Themes and Activities for Children, Volume 2,* may be used as a guide for choosing stories based on a culture or country or based on a topic, motif, or theme.

In my years as a school library media specialist, I have come to use and view these tales with wonder and ardor. Students respond to trickster tales with laughter, with eager predictions, and with urgent requests for more. They listen wide-eyed and sober to transformation tales in which the characters follow their hearts and overcome daunting obstacles. Students also respond to these tales through creative outlets: writing, illustrating, and designing multimedia projects or puppet theater. This body of literature engages students in ways that link them to one another and to the past.

Today, society in general displays a new awareness of cultural diversity. Educational and recreational institutions are infusing their programs with multicultural concepts. With a rich body of folk literature available, the incorporation of multiculturalism flows naturally. These tales teach life lessons in a gentle way, expanding our view of humanity with their connections to the past and to other cultures, and they help us learn to cooperate, on both personal and global levels. I hope that those who sample folktales from this guide find refreshment and delight, akin to a dipper of cool water on a hot day.

Acknowledgments

I would like to acknowledge the people who shared their time and talents, enabling this book to take shape. Many thanks to Paula Brandt of the University of Iowa Curriculum Lab for her initial and sustained encouragement, her discriminating ideas, and her invaluable knowledge of children's literature. Paula thoughtfully read the text and provided insightful feedback. I am fortunate to have worked with creative teachers who shared their classrooms and ideas with me, allowing us to explore folktales in collaboration: Chris Gibson, Wendy Deutmeyer, Chris Shope, and Andrea McGann Keech. Busy and talented author Robert D. San Souci also took the time and care to pass on valuable information and experience.

I am grateful to the following artists who made contributions to this book. Susan K. Bins added visual style with her calligraphy and accompanying art. Artist Judy Moss spent hours sharing her expertise with sliding images for the transformation tales activities. Lauren Reece helped develop the accordion-fold transformation pictures for use in the classroom. Author/illustrator Gavin Bishop and North-South Books graciously granted permission for me to use Mr. Bishop's illustrations for the shadow puppet activity (from the book *Māui and the Sun: A Maori Tale* retold and illustrated by Gavin Bishop. Text and illustrations © 1996 by Gavin Bishop. Used by permission of North-South Books, Inc., New York). Andrea McGann Keech drew the silhouette pictures for the shadow puppets based on Gavin Bishop's book.

I could not embark on a folklore project without an affectionate nod to the staff and participants at Folklore Village Farm, a community that keeps the joy of folk traditions alive and offered me the opportunity to field-test some of the activities in this book.

I am grateful for the kind help of Deb Green and Craig Johnson at the Iowa City Public Library, and Carol Sokoloff at Prairie Lights Bookstore. I thank Ann Holton for her mentoring on all aspects of school librarianship. Thanks to Jan Irving for helping me to connect with Libraries Unlimited. Thank you to my son, Mike, who assisted with computer graphics and indexing, and to my daughter, Jenny, who provided encouragement and support in many forms. And thanks to the children in my classes in the Iowa City Schools, for their bright-eyed enthusiasm. It keeps me going and firms my continued belief in the sustenance provided by folk literature.

introduction

In recent years, there has been a renaissance in the art of storytelling and a surge in publishing new, illustrated tellings of old tales for children. *Folktale Themes and Activities for Children, Volume 2: Trickster and Transformation Tales* is a resource guide to help in the selection and planning of folktale-related experiences for children aged six through eleven. Folk literature, in single-tale editions and in collections, offers rich opportunities for read-aloud experiences, independent reading, group interactions, and individual activities.

Why is it important to provide planned experiences with folktales for children? Folktales constitute some of the world's oldest literature; they embody the concept of "story" while passing on the wisdom of a culture. Because these stories are so old, they provide a grounding upon which more contemporary experiences can be built. Familiarity with folktale themes is a measure of cultural literacy. Educationally, children benefit from these tales in many ways: They experience the sheer enjoyment of story, they predict consequences, they apply critical thinking skills by comparing tales, they embrace gentle lessons taught through the tales, they create their own imaginative fantasy stories or plays based on these tales, and they experience multicultural contexts. In addition, they learn that ever since ancient times, people all over the world have passed on wisdom and a sense of humor and wonder through these tales.

Because folk literature is embedded in a cultural context, teachers need to understand some basic issues before using folktales. The background information in this introduction examines these issues and assists with choosing and presenting tales to children. Several criteria for selecting tales are provided. Finally, this introduction explains how this guide is organized, with suggestions for ways to use it.

BACKGROUND ON THE USE OF FOLK LITERATURE

The publishing of folktales raises issues of sensitivity to the originators of the stories. These storytellers are unknown. Their modern "authors" participate in a long tradition of "retelling." Some of these authors-retellers come from within the culture of the tales—for example, Native American storytellers Gayle Ross and Joseph Bruchac. Not every tale is published by someone from within the culture of origin, especially in language that speaks to children. Other retellers have emerged, such as authors Robert D. San Souci, Howard Norman, and Verna Aardema, who dig stories out of dusty tomes or get them directly from the oral tradition, and bring them alive for children. Children should be made aware that these stories have been passed down in the oral tradition over many, many years. They should understand that the "author" is someone who found or heard the tale and wrote or rewrote it so that we, too, can enjoy the story.

There is a strong need for sensitivity toward the cultural context of each story, which is often different from the background or cultural milieu of the author, reader, storyteller, or listeners. Every tale is tied to a culture's belief system and traditions. For example, among Native American groups, certain tales are told only in a particular season, a fact that may be lost on non-Natives. Also, some aspects of a tale may have sacred significance unknown to a non-Native. In an African trickster/ pourquoi tale, the "how and why" elements may be part of the religion of that people. When possible, adults should research the culture from which the story comes and take note of any background information provided by the author. But even when additional research is not possible, the adult's reverence and respect for the story will enhance the learning experience for children.

Representation of Native American culture in children's books has long engendered emotional discussion. For too many years, Native peoples have been stereotyped as intellectually inferior or as noble, vanishing environmentalists. Fortunately, an increase in general awareness and in the number of Native authors is helping to turn this situation around. However, with folktales coming from an old oral tradition, there are opportunities for misrepresentation. Many published folktales for children have come from written versions in English that were compiled by Euro-American anthropologists and other collectors in the latter nineteenth and early twentieth centuries. Translation is fraught with complexities because mere words are only part of the story; there are also vocal inflections, facial cues, idiomatic expressions, and the entire body of culture and belief systems embedded in the story. Children's versions of folktales are also criticized for the manner in which the tellers alter events to resemble those in familiar European fairy tales or to soften the edges of controversial issues (Stott 1995, 82–85).

Therefore, the selector relies on authors with a reputation for their research and familiarity with the field and on the documentation of authenticity in their books. In the 1990s, publishers are requiring retellers of folktales to research as many documented sources of a tale as possible and to locate the earliest known version if they can (Shepard 1996b, 5). Betsy Hearne (1993a, 25) urges librarians to use more stringent standards in evaluating folktales published for children. She is critical of vague source notes, preferring "the truly exemplary source note [which] cites the specific source(s), adds a description for cultural context, *and* describes what the author has done to change the tale, with some explanation of why." Distinguished Native American author Joseph Bruchac (1995, xiii) states, "My point is *not* that only Native people can write about Native Americans, but that deep knowledge is necessary for anyone (Native or non-Native) to write well about those essential building blocks of Native American cultures—the words of their elders, the traditional stories told to their children." Graciela Italiano (1993) agrees that scholarship and experience with a culture's traditions are more important in writing for children than being a member of that culture. Adults working with this body of literature would benefit from reading sections of Hearne's articles (1993), Slapin and Seale's *Through Indian Eyes* (1992), or Jon C. Stott's *Native Americans in Children's Literature* (1995) for additional background on this aspect of the literature.

While being mindful of these sensitivities to cultural contexts, we must also remember the children (and adults!) who are eager to hear these multicultural tales. We must also remember the spirit of the oral tradition in which these stories were conceived: the spirit of listening, sharing, and retelling the tale. The act of retelling implies a constant evolutionary process. Author-storyteller Aaron Shepard explains: "Stories originate with individual tellers and spread through a culture. Travelers carry them from that culture to another, where storytellers adopt them, adapt them, and spread them through their own cultures. Then travelers carry them on again. Few stories belong exclusively to the culture where they are found. Most are told in different versions all over the world." He goes on to say, "There should be room for retellings both by those within a culture and those without. Each brings different knowledge, perspectives, and insights" (Shepard, 1996a, 11). Betsy Hearne (1993b, 33) proposes that when tales are adapted by authors outside the culture, "text adapted from folklore [should] be judged for its balance of two traditions: the one from which it is drawn and the one that it is entering." She warns against "fakelore," in which illustrations may imitate Native art in a superficial way. These unresearched folk art designs may disregard cultural symbolism. She prefers new, original art for illustrations by non-Natives, rather than generic "folk art."

In conclusion, I have used an inclusive approach tempered with care in selecting titles for the bibliographies in this guide. Because I am a librarian and an educator with a philosophy of open access to literature, I have been as inclusive as possible while focusing on respect for the material, documentation of sources, background contextual notes, and authors' reputations. I have included stories in the same spirit that they originated: the spirit of sharing and spreading these tales. Because I love this literature, and because children respond to it with wonder and enjoyment, I believe it should be shared in a respectful and generous way. Children are fertile ground for planting the seeds of multicultural awareness and appreciation. As stated in a traditional ending to many African tales, "This is my story. If it be sweet, or if it be not sweet, take some and let the rest come back to me" (Aardema 1994, 30).

TRICKSTER AND TRANSFORMATION TALES

A study of trickster and transformation tales reveals a broad array of plots, motifs, and characters, and yet there is an astonishing amount of commonality as well. The phenomenon of recurring themes is one reason that folktales are so fascinating. Both trickster and transformation elements are often found in the same story. In fact, the trickster characters Raven, Glooskap, and Coyote have the power to transform themselves or the beings around them. And a transformation is often the key to a trickster's escape. Conversely, often in transformation tales, a princess or prince is transformed into a frog or a beast, and then by solving a riddle or pursuing a quest, he or she tricks the evil enchanter. These tale types are delightfully intertwined for the fascination of children and the adults who work with them.

BOOKS INCLUDED IN THIS GUIDE

The books included in this guide were selected for their usefulness and appeal to children in first through fifth grade (ages six through eleven); in some cases, teachers may find the titles of use for kindergarten through sixth grade. Inclusion of books is based on their potential as read-alouds and for independent reading by children; most annotations include suggestions for age appropriateness. The teacher or librarian may assume that stories suggested for third- and fourth-grade independent reading are often good choices for reading aloud to younger children. However, the final decision of whether plot complexities or particular subject matter is suitable should rest with the adults who best know their groups of children. Suggestions for grade-level readability are approximate and are usually expressed as "primary grades" (first and second), "middle grades" (third and fourth), and "upper grades" (fifth and sixth). Again, these indications of readability are intended to give teachers a general idea of reading levels as a starting point, but the ultimate judge is the teacher.

Most of the books in the annotated bibliographies are relatively recent publications; a few were published prior to 1988. Although there is a focus on illustrated, single-tale editions, several folktale collections have been included for their usefulness. A majority of books in the bibliographies are in print at the time of this writing, but the availability of books increasingly varies from year to year. Some titles are available in paperback editions, making multiple copies affordable for whole language reading classes.

In keeping with the foregoing discussion on authenticity, the included books, to the best of available knowledge, contain authentic, well-told traditional stories. Evidence of authenticity includes written documentation of story sources, the author's credentials or experience in the field, the illustrator's credentials, and recommendations in other selection guides or children's literature reviews. The annotated bibliographies are intended to assist in selecting stories for use with children. The book lists are not necessarily definitive or comprehensive but rather practical, reflecting a sincere effort toward presenting quality literature.

WAYS TO USE THIS GUIDE

This guide is divided into two main sections, by the genres of trickster tales and transformation tales. Each section begins with background information about the genre. Next, a chapter of activities provides teaching plans, curriculum connections, art and drama suggestions, and other related activities for children. Following the activities chapter is a series of charts titled "Story Themes and Topics," in which tales from different cultures are listed in groups according to similar topics, themes, or motifs. Each section concludes with an annotated bibliography, arranged by continent, and further divided by country or culture. Some tales fit into more than one category; for example, the same story can be both a trickster tale and a transformation tale. In these cases, the title and its annotation appear in both bibliographies and charts. The index helps in the location of full information on any book with topical needs.

Folktale Themes and Activities for Children, Volume 2: Trickster and Transformation Tales may be consulted in a variety of ways. A person planning for topics such as animals, food, weather, survival, and sky phenomena may browse the story themes and topics charts (Chapter 3 and 7) or use the general index. Someone wanting a story from a particular geographical area may consult the annotated bibliographies, which are arranged by continental area and further subdivided by individual cultures. One of the most fascinating aspects of folk literature is the occurrence of similar motifs (or similar plots, tricks, characters, origin explanations, or transformational events) across cultures. For example, the "briar patch" trick and the mermaid transformation motif are themes found in many cultures. Telling or reading two or more stories containing similar elements makes for cohesive programming for storyhours or for compare-and-contrast skill activities for students. To plan a series of stories with similar elements, consult story themes and topics chapters (Chapter 3 and 7). To provide students with a whole language reading or literature unit, the activities chapter in each section offers lesson plans and student activities for language arts or social studies classes (Chapters 2 and 6). Those seeking artistic extensions (for example, multimedia projects or shadow puppet theater) will also find ideas in the activities chapters.

"I'd like some stories to integrate into our unit of study on weather"; . . . or . . . "I'm fascinated with stories that have similar themes, especially the Cinderella theme, and would like to put some together and compare"; . . . or . . . "Our summer recreation program is focusing on magic, and I need to come up with some books and activities that go beyond magic tricks"; . . . or . . . "There are a lot of neat folktale books out, and I'd like to have my students use them for reading class, but I don't have the time or resources to get everything organized and find enough different reading levels"; . . . or . . . "I need some ideas for infusing multiculturalism into my curriculum." These are some possible scenarios just ripe for the introduction of folk literature and for integrating multicultural awareness into the curriculum.

A FINAL THOUGHT

These stories come from a time before electricity and modern transportation, when one of the main channels for passing down wisdom was the telling of stories. The gentle lessons of these tales, the wisdom, the conflicts, the humor are all old and yet still ring true today. In today's world, where everything moves so fast and technology reigns, folktales can ground us in our ancient past. There are reasons that these tales endure through the millennia. The characters, both the monsters and the innocent protagonists, are archetypal of the inner struggles we all face. The twists and surprises of plots represent the life-paths we are on as we seek fulfillment. They give us hope that we can find our own magic and happy endings. There is a need to listen to the voices from the old times, to counterbalance our lives. There is a need to hear these stories that come from people who were closer to the rhythms of the earth and the power of nature than we are today. A folktale "reminds everyone that we are all connected, like the strands of Grandmother Spider's web" (Caduto and Bruchac 1989, 50).

REFERENCES

Aardema, Verna. 1994. *Misoso: Once Upon a Time Tales from Africa*. New York: Apple Soup Books.

Bruchac, Joseph. 1995. "Foreword." In Jon C. Stott, *Native Americans in Children's Literature*, xi–xiv. Phoenix, AZ: Oryx Press.

Caduto, Michael J., and Joseph Bruchac. 1989. *Keepers of the Earth: Native American Stories and Environmental Activities for Children*. Golden, CO: Fulcrum.

Hearne, Betsy. 1993a. "Cite the Source: Reducing Cultural Chaos in Picture Books, Part One." *School Library Journal* 39 (July): 22–27.

———. 1993b. "Respect the Source: Reducing Cultural Chaos in Picture Books, Part Two." *School Library Journal* 39 (August): 33–37.

Italiano, Graciela. 1993. "Reading Latin America: Issues in the Evaluation of Latino Children's Books in Spanish and English." In *Evaluating Children's Books: A Critical Look*, ed. Betsy Hearne and Roger Sutton, 119–132. Urbana-Champaign: University of Illinois Graduate School of Library and Information Science.

Shepard, Aaron. 1996a. "A Dozen Answers to the Multicultural Heckler." *Once Upon a Time* (Summer): 11.

———. 1996b. "Researching the Folktale." *SCBWI (Society of Children's Book Writers and Illustrators) Bulletin* (February/March): 5–6.

Slapin, Beverly, and Doris Seale. 1992. *Through Indian Eyes*. Philadelphia: New Society.

Stott, Jon C. 1995. *Native Americans in Children's Literature*. Phoenix, AZ: Oryx Press.

Chapter 1

Brer Rabbit escapes again, with a satisfied chuckle. Raven transforms himself, steals the sun through deceit, and brings sunlight to all living things. Anansi gets himself another good meal, without the effort of gardening or cooking. These trickster characters and others fairly leap out of the pages of picture books and folktale collections, ready to bring us laughter, nods of recognition, and hints of tricks yet to come. Trickster tales are part of the folk tradition of nearly every culture of the world, full of common themes and motifs, yet unique in their ingenuity and seemingly endless plotting for yet another trick. These entertaining stories are loved by all ages, and they offer countless opportunities to plan meaningful experiences in storytelling, reading aloud, school literature units, thinking skills, puppetry, drama, and cultural literacy.

A trickster is a character who uses wit and cunning to outsmart someone else, tricking him or her to achieve a particular goal. Tricksters' characteristics span a wide range of personality traits. They are known to be cunning, greedy, and wily; they are pretentious and given to deceit. They are lazy and prefer to procure food and other goods through trickery rather than through honest work. Their tricks are sometimes motivated by sheer prankish intent. Yet sometimes they act in a helpful manner in response to the needs of their fellow creatures. Tricksters are usually male characters. Although there are several tales about clever females, there is no body of folktales based on a female trickster (Del Negro 1996, 43). Tricksters are usually smaller and physically weaker than their opponents, and they gain their advantage by using "brains over brawn."

Tricksters are complex characters. They reflect the wide spectrum of personality traits and motivations found in human behavior, both positive and negative. They are alternately self-centered and generous. Storyteller Barbara Schutz-Gruber notes, "[The trickster] has all our virtues—creativity, wit, mercy, compassion. He also has all our faults—sloth, gluttony, deceit, lechery. The trickster is a caricature of ourselves—he has it all—good and bad, but in larger-than-life proportions" (Schutz-Gruber and Buckley 1991, 3). Sometimes tricksters play harmless pranks, just to escape, as in the story of "Brer Rabbit and the Tar Baby," when Brer Rabbit dupes his captor into throwing him into the briar patch, right where he wants to be. The mischief can be a bit more malicious, as in "Brer Rabbit Gets Brer Fox's Dinner" (Lester 1988, 3). Other times, the damage is extensive, as when Spider Ananse steals an old woman's entire garden crop in *The Dancing Granny* (Bryan 1977). Yet tricksters often play pranks to care for their communities' welfare. In *Brer Tiger and the Big Wind*, Brer Rabbit tricks a selfish bully into sharing his food and drink with all the famished animals during a drought (Faulkner 1995).

This dualistic personality is noted by Roger Abrahams: "Trickster [is] a figure who, at one and the same time, represents primal creativity and pathological destructiveness, childish innocence and self-absorption" (Abrahams 1983, 155). To distinguish between these paradoxical qualities, the Navajo have two different names for Coyote in their stories. "Coyote" is the name of the helpful character, and "Trotting Coyote" is the selfish one who can be malicious or foolish (Clarkson and Cross 1980, 285). Erdoes and Ortiz note that Native American tricksters do not follow the familiar system of characterization seen in European folktales. In Euro-Western fairy tales, the characters are typically one-dimensional, either good or bad. By contrast, the trickster exhibits a more complex and unpredictable mix. "To try to apply conventional (Western) logic is not only impossible but unnecessary" (Erdoes and Ortiz 1984, xii). And just to make events seem even more chaotic, the trickster's prank is often paid back by another trick in which the trickster is bested by the trickee.

Because a trickster often behaves badly, these tales, while primarily entertaining, also communicate lessons about moral values in society. By laughing at a trickster, we recognize common human foibles and remind ourselves in a humorous way that this is not acceptable behavior. In *African Folktales*, Abrahams states, "Trickster is the figure who most fully illustrates how not to act within society. . . . His antics represent just what sane and mature people do not do" (Abrahams 1983, 23, 155). Some Coyote tales were used by Native Americans to show children the path to acceptable behavior (Jones 1995, 125). Yet Julius Lester, reteller of Brer Rabbit tales, observes that "Trickster tales are not moral. . . . The reward for

[Trickster's] trickery is not punishment, but, generally, victory" (Lester 1988, x). Virginia Hamilton, in her collection *A Ring of Tricksters*, believes that "the animal tricksters were invented by the community to cast away acts of human misbehavior from more suitable deeds. These animal characters . . . performed outlandish tricks because the people needed them to. We're glad they did. . . . They seem very human, very much like ourselves" (Hamilton 1997, 73).

Some tricksters are considered culture heroes, legendary characters who have powers beyond their peers. They are given credit for providing essential elements to the cultural group, such as the sun, land formations, fire, weather, and even cultural values. Many stories of Raven, Coyote, and Glooskap show these characters in semi-creation roles, bringing the sun, shaping animals and the land, creating humans and animals. Yet these tricksters are not gods. They have some superhuman powers, but they are not deities.

Part of the appeal of the trickster is that he is often smaller, or in a position of less apparent power, than the trickee. We immediately identify with this position, having ourselves felt unempowered in various situations. This phenomenon is observed in *Funk & Wagnalls Standard Dictionary of Folklore, Mythology and Legend*: "Psychologically, the role of the trickster seems to be that of projecting the insufficiencies of man in his universe onto a smaller creature who, in besting his larger adversaries, permits the satisfactions of an obvious identification to those who recount or listen to these tales" (Leach 1972, 1123). John O. West remarks simply, "Oh, what fun it is to read or hear about the guy . . . who pulls off a trick on the folks who are in charge of things—or who think they are!" (West 1996, 9). To witness a trickster gaining the advantage gives its own sense of empowerment. It is even more fun when we are "in" on the trick unfolding in the story. Jane Yolen notes, "Every culture seems to treasure the cunning of the underdog" (Yolen 1986, 5).

This aspect of the underdog takes on special significance in the case of Brer Rabbit and other African American tales, such as stories of High John the Conqueror. Africans captured and brought to America under the brutal conditions of slavery took their stories with them, and despite their oppression, they continued to nurture their storytelling traditions. This creativity led to the creation of Brer Rabbit tales, which, to the casual notice of white oppressors, were simple stories of entertainment. But to the storytelling community of African Americans, they were stories that embodied the spirit of the trickster: the triumph of the oppressed. The enduring spirit of these people was remarkably kindled through the telling of a wily rabbit who could make a fool of Brer Fox, Brer Wolf, and Brer Bear, bigger in bulk but not in wit.

The Brer Rabbit character became a metaphor for the slave who was tricking the so-called master with his superior wit. This outlet allowed slaves to have a secret laugh, while outwardly complying with the so-called master. Clarkson and Cross observe that Brer Rabbit "was no less than the slave himself who could secretly delight in overcoming his master—if only in his imagination" (Clarkson and Cross 1980, 275). *The Encyclopedia of Black Folklore and Humor* describes these tales as "veiled protests against enslavement."

The very use of the term "Brer" for brother is an indication of a strong sense of community among African Americans. Oppression during and after slavery worked to make African Americans "an even more cohesive community" (Spalding 1972, 6–7). The storytelling tradition is one manifestation of that community. Virginia Hamilton, in her *Ring of Tricksters*, eloquently honors the phenomenon of

African American trickster tales: "Bruh Rabbit is the emblem and culture hero who symbolizes freedom for all those held in bondage. . . . Moreover, these animal trickster tales demonstrate the abiding faith and confidence early African Americans had in themselves, and their remarkable storytelling abilities" (Hamilton 1997, 13).

The most familiar tricksters are Coyote, Brer Rabbit, Anansi, and Raven, but many more exist, and even the most famous characters have their variants. Anansi is also known as Kwaku Anansi or Ananse, and he may appear as a spider or as a man. In the southeast United States he is known as Miss Nancy (South Carolina Sea Islands) and Aunt Nancy (among the Gullah). Brer Rabbit is also found as Bruh Rabby, Son Bunny, Cunnie Rabbit (a Creole character, actually a little deer), and Compère Lapin (Cajun). In African tales, we see trickster rabbit as Zomo the Rabbit and Shulo the Rabbit. Among Native American tales Rabbit makes an appearance as Great Hare. We also find Rabbit in Asian cultures. Turtle and Tortoise are tricksters in African and Native American tales. Māui is the trickster of Polynesian tales. Native American tales include trickster/culture heroes such as Glooskap (or Gluskabe) and Manabozho (or Nanabozho), who have certain creator characteristics. Some folklore collections include Jack among their tricksters, especially those from England and Appalachia. Molly (English) and Boots (Norwegian), who are associated with the Cinderella tale, are counterparts to Jack. Tricksters in the category of "Little Folk" include leprechauns (Irish), the Menehune (Hawaiian), and the nisse (Norwegian). New collections bring new trickster characters to our attention every year. Their characteristics are both universal and unique.

The age-old trickster tales have not only endured, but are becoming more widely known and appreciated. They continue to embody some basic universal basic needs: the need for recognition, the desire for things to be different than they are, the need to relieve stress with a good laugh. We identify with the spirit of the trickster tale. We identify with the character at an initial disadvantage, and we take heart in the knowledge that he or she can gain the edge through cleverness. We recognize good humor, and our spirit feels lighter in appreciation of it. We acknowledge that, like the trickster, we have both virtuous traits and traits that can lead to trouble. Trickster tales are for all ages and all cultures, dramatizing themes common to the human condition.

REFERENCES

Abrahams, Roger D. 1983. *African Folktales: Traditional Stories of the Black World*. New York: Pantheon Books.

Bryan, Ashley. 1977. *The Dancing Granny*. Illustrated by the author. New York: Aladdin Books.

Clarkson, Atelia, and Gilbert B. Cross. 1980. *World Folktales: A Scribner Resource Collection*. New York: Charles Scribner's Sons.

Del Negro, Janice M. 1996. "Trickster Tales." *Book Links* 5 (March): 43–47.

Erdoes, Richard, and Alfonso Ortiz. 1984. *American Indian Myths and Legends*. New York: Pantheon Books.

Faulkner, William J. 1995. *Brer Tiger and the Big Wind*. Illustrated by Roberta Wilson. New York: Morrow Junior Books.

Hamilton, Virginia. 1997. *A Ring of Tricksters: Animal Tales from America, the West Indies, and Africa*. Illustrated by Barry Moser. New York: Blue Sky Press.

Jones, Alison. 1995. *Larousse Dictionary of World Folklore*. New York: Larousse.

Leach, Maria, and Jerome Fried, eds. 1972. *Funk & Wagnalls Standard Dictionary of Folklore, Mythology and Legend*. New York: Funk & Wagnalls.

Lester, Julius. 1988. *More Tales of Uncle Remus: Further Adventures of Brer Rabbit, His Friends, Enemies, and Others*. Illustrated by Jerry Pinkney. New York: Dial Books.

Schutz-Gruber, Barbara G., and Barbara Frates Buckley. 1991. *Trickster Tales from Around the World: An Interdisciplinary Guide for Teachers*. Ann Arbor, MI: Barbara G. Schutz-Gruber.

Spalding, Henry D. 1972. *Encyclopedia of Black Folklore and Humor*. Illustrated by Rue Knapp. Middle Village, NY: Jonathan David.

West, John O. 1996. "Introduction." In *Trickster Tales: Forty Folk Stories from Around the World*, by Josepha Sherman. Illustrated by David Boston. Little Rock, AR: August House.

Yolen, Jane. 1986. *Favorite Folktales from Around the World*. New York: Pantheon Books.

Chapter 2

USING TRICKSTER TALES WITH CHILDREN

Trickster tales are a natural with children. The stories are entertaining, and children take to them eagerly. Children readily catch on to the playfulness of a trickster plot. They can see the trick in the making, and they are eager to make predictions about the trickster's intent and the outcomes. They quickly come to know the characters of Anansi, Brer Rabbit, Raven, and Coyote, and they ask for more stories with their favorite tricksters. As additional tales are presented, children begin to recognize recurring themes. They identify with the characters, sometimes rooting for the trickster if he is plotting against a bully, and sometimes pulling for the victim who, in return, tricks the trickster. The plot and characters in a trickster tale provide intrinsic motivation for children to focus on and participate wholeheartedly in the story and its related activities.

Trickster tales can by used and enjoyed at many levels. Beyond entertainment, these tales can provide many opportunities for learning and exploration at a deeper level. They provide a vehicle for recognizing universal human character traits and desires. Trickster tales also provide the material for students to develop thinking skills of prediction and comparison and contrast. They provide high motivation for independent reading, and they are a catalyst for creative expression in writing, storytelling, drama, and art. Finally, they offer an immersion into diverse cultures, allowing for the recognition of both unique and common themes across cultures. However they are encountered, trickster tales are ready and waiting, as are the tricksters themselves, ready for the next opportunity for fun.

The activities on the following pages can be adapted for use in a variety of settings. The stories are successful read-alouds just as they are, and a storyhour is even more fruitful when several tales with similar features are presented. The activities, while designed as part of a reading/language arts curriculum unit, can be used for a variety of purposes and age groups. A public librarian or recreation leader could use the stories as the bases for plays and shadow puppet theater. An after-school program could develop stick-puppet retellings of favorite tales. A storyteller could consult this guide for new stories to add to his or her repertoire. Programs working to develop storytelling by children could consult this guide; these stories are good ones for beginning storytellers. A school library media specialist could collaboratively explore this literature with a classroom teacher in the context of the reading curriculum. The plans could also be used as a model, with the teacher or librarian selecting different titles from the annotated bibliography (Chapter 4) or from the chart of story themes and topics (Chapter 3).

The following plans for a whole language literature unit on trickster tales have been developed for students in first and second grade, since many of the tales have been written in language accessible to readers in that age group. Also, several of the tales are available in paperback editions, making multiple copies for reading groups more affordable. However, the whole-group activities and read-alouds are successful with third, fourth, or fifth graders. If using a trickster tales unit of study with this older group, consult the annotated bibliography for additional titles for independent reading.

Following is a sequence of activities as presented in this chapter:

1. Read aloud a cluster of two or three stories that have a common element (i.e., stories in which the trickster outwits others to steal food; consult Chapter 3 for other ideas).

2. Conduct a whole-group discussion comparing the stories using a graphic organizer, such as a Venn diagram. Estimated time: 30 to 40 minutes, during the same week the stories are read.

3. Repeat steps 1 and 2 with new clusters of stories as time allows (i.e., stories in which the trickster plays a trick to help others, stories in which the trickster is tricked). Both the classroom teachers and the library media specialist can read stories and guide the Venn diagram discussion.

4. Students read selected tales independently. Suggestions are given for titles to purchase in multiple copies for reading groups.

5. Students participate in small group and independent response activities, including journal writing and small group discussion.

6. Students participate in a culminating whole-group discussion, contributing story titles to a web graphic organizer.

7. Students participate in creative extension projects: storytelling, stick puppet retelling, shadow puppet theater, singing, graphing, and a trickster party.

FOCUS AND GOALS FOR TRICKSTER TALE LITERATURE STUDY

Focus statement: Since times of old, people of different cultures have created and passed on stories in which a trickster character outwits others. Sometimes the trickster acts for his own gain, sometimes purely for mischief, and sometimes to help others. These stories allow us to laugh and help us to learn.

Goals:

- The learner will listen to and read a variety of trickster tales from different cultures.

- The learner will name prominent trickster characters, including Coyote, Raven, Brer Rabbit, and Anansi.

- The learner will recognize and identify common traits of the trickster character.

- The learner will develop the thinking skill of prediction and will participate in discussions to predict what the trickster character will do in the story.

- The learner will participate in compare-and-contrast activities, comparing the similar elements in two or more tales. The learner will also identify the unique elements in these stories and show his or her understanding in some graphic way.

- The learner will participate in discussions of common themes across different cultures.

- The learner will respond to these stories with a creative project, such as making stick puppets, singing, dramatizing the story, presenting a shadow puppet theater, or writing an original story.

STARTING UP: GROUP READ-ALOUDS AND ACTIVITIES

To give students a feel for the genre of the trickster tale, start with a whole-class read-aloud and discussion. Reading selected titles aloud gives everyone the same starting point. Selecting titles that show the different facets of the trickster character provides a foundation upon which students can build, eventually reading individual titles of their own choosing. The teacher-reader can find natural points in the story to stop and question students, or simply to give them the chance to make predictions.

The read-aloud plan below provides clusters of stories with common connections. Each cluster features an important thematic element typical of trickster tales. Children will be able to see the two sides of a trickster's personality and motivations: Sometimes he acts for his own greedy purposes; sometimes he acts to benefit others. Children will also be able to recognize a motif that occurs in tales from different cultures. Begin a study of trickster tales with read-alouds from these three categories:

- Tales in which the trickster outwits others to steal their food. Sometimes the trick ultimately fails, and a trick is played on the trickster.

- Tales in which the trickster plays a trick for the benefit of others.

- Tales in which a common motif occurs across stories from different cultures.

Tales in Which the Trickster Outwits Others to Steal Their Food

Before reading one of these tales to children, provide a short introduction and some cultural information, and give children opportunities to make predictions. Prediction is an important thinking skill, and trickster tales provide fertile ground for this activity. There are natural moments in the story when the reader can pause briefly and ask, "What do you think Anansi will do next?" or "Why has Raven turned himself into a baby?" Children are eager to offer solutions, and it is important to recognize all answers as good predictions, even if they don't actually come true in the story. For each story, a few suggested questions are given as models. However, the individual reader often determines the best questions to ask and the best times to ask them.

■ Story 1: *Anansi and the Moss-Covered Rock* by Eric Kimmel
Introduction to the story: This is a special kind of folktale, known as the trickster tale. A trickster likes to play tricks on other people or animals. And a trickster is often hungry, but he is not very interested in working for his own food. He would rather take it from others. In this story, the trickster is a famous one named Anansi. He is a spider. There are many stories about Anansi the spider. He can look like a spider or a man. Anansi stories come to us from West Africa. But we don't know who exactly made these stories up because folktales are passed on from one person to another, year after year.
Prediction question suggestions: When Anansi figures out what made him faint, ask the children, "What could Anansi do with this rock?" and "What does Anansi always want?" After Anansi plays his trick the first time, ask, "What is he going to do next?" If children don't already see it, point out Bush Deer hiding behind the foliage. Tell them to keep track of him through the rest of the story. When Anansi starts to try the trick on Bush Deer, give the children time to predict what will happen. Will Bush Deer fall for the trick? What could Bush Deer do to Anansi? At the end, discuss the final trick by asking "Who plays the final trick, and who gets tricked?" and "Does Anansi get what he was after?"

■ Story 2: *The Dancing Granny* by Ashley Bryan
Introduction to the story: This trickster tale is also about Ananse, but this time, he is portrayed as a man called Spider Ananse. Anansi stories came from West Africa. Some of these stories were brought by Africans slaves across the ocean to the West Indies in the Caribbean Sea. (Point out these locations on a map.) In this part of the world, singing and dancing are important, as you

will see. Look at the illustrations in this book. Notice how Ashley Bryan uses just a few pencil strokes to make Granny look like she is whirling and twirling in a dance.

Prediction question suggestions: At the beginning, when reading about Granny and her garden, ask the children to predict why Ananse will be playing his tricks. When Ananse gets Granny to dance, ask the children to predict what will happen. After the second time Granny dances away, ask the children to predict how many miles she will dance the next time, and the next, and which direction she will go. At the end, ask the children, "Who plays the final trick and who is tricked? Does Ananse get what he wants? What *does* he get in the end?"

■ Story 3: *Ma'ii and Cousin Horned Toad* by Shonto Begay

Introduction to the story: Now we meet a new trickster named Coyote. Coyote is a famous character in many Native American folktales. This story is Navajo, and so is the author/illustrator. The Navajo people live in the southwest United States, and they still tell Coyote stories. The Navajo word for Coyote is "Ma'ii." Like Anansi, Coyote loves to eat. He is going to visit his cousin Horned Toad, and guess what he wants? In some of the illustrations, Shonto Begay has hidden images of Horned Toad. See if you can find him as we read. The Navajo people give respect to a horned toad when they see one.

Prediction question suggestions: When Ma'ii rudely asks Horned Toad for more and more food, ask, "How would you feel if you were Horned Toad?" (Try to elicit responses beyond "mad.") As the story goes along, stop periodically and ask such questions as "When Ma'ii pretends to have a toothache, what is he trying to do? When Horned Toad tells Ma'ii he is having a great time in Ma'ii's belly, what is he trying to do? What kinds of things could Horned Toad do next? Ma'ii says he is going to burn Horned Toad out, but what do you think will happen? Who is getting tricked now?"

Compare-and-Contrast Activities for Stories About Stealing Food

Now that students have been introduced to three stories illustrating a common trickster trait, have them make some comparisons among the three. Children will have already noticed similarities, and this is a good time to formalize the thinking skill process of comparing and contrasting. By using a Venn diagram, you can illustrate the process for children.

Prepare your Venn diagram on a large piece of chart paper and attach it to the wall or board. Label each circle with a story title. Explain to students that each component of the stories will be written somewhere in the diagram. If the component exists for two of the stories, it will be written in the space where the two circles overlap. If it exists in just one story, it will be written in the space belonging only to that one story. If it exists in all three stories, it will be written in the space where all three circles overlap. (Hint: It may help to start with just two circles, and then add the third once the activity is in full swing.)

To start the process, have students retell parts of the story. Each time a child identifies a major component of the story, have the students determine which area of the diagram to write it in. Note the following components on the Venn diagram, and use them as points for guiding the discussion if necessary:

- Name of the trickster

- Culture of origin

- What the trickster wants

- Why the trickster is playing the trick

- The trick

- Highlights of the plot

- Who is being tricked

- Setting

- Illustrations

See a sample Venn diagram of the above stories (fig. 2.1). It is the result of actual Venn diagramming discussions among first and second grade students.

Tales in Which the Trickster Plays a Trick for the Benefit of Others

■ Story 1: *Fire Race* by Jonathan London
Introduction to the story: Here's another story about Coyote from the Native American Karuk people of California. Remember Coyote (Ma'ii) in *Ma'ii and Cousin Horned Toad*? He was rude and selfish in that story, but Coyote can sometimes act differently. The animals have a problem in this story; see what Coyote does about it.

Prediction question suggestions: When Coyote tells the Yellow Jacket Sisters that he will make them pretty, what will Coyote do? When Eagle snatches the fire stick in his talons, what will happen next? When Frog spits the hot coal out and it is swallowed by the tree, is there a way to get fire from the tree?

■ Story 2: *Brer Tiger and the Big Wind* by William J. Faulkner
Introduction to the story: Now we meet another famous trickster: Brer Rabbit. Brer Rabbit is a clever trickster from African American stories. In these stories, "Brer" means "Brother," and "Sis" means "Sister." Just like *Fire Race*, this story starts with a problem: There is a drought in the land. What does that mean? What do you think Brer Rabbit will do about it?

Prediction question suggestions: When all the animals arrive at their posts and Brer Rabbit calls out that there is a big wind coming, what are the animals doing? When they make all that noise, what kind of trick is it? How do you think Brer Tiger will respond to it? What is Brer Rabbit's rope for? When Brer Tiger asks Brer Rabbit to tie him up and Brer Rabbit refuses, how do you think Brer Tiger will respond? Why does Brer Rabbit refuse to tie up Brer Tiger the first two times he asks? What do you think will happen? In this story and in *Fire Race*, the trickster gets all the animals together before the trick. Why? How is the trick accomplished?

Trickster Characteristics: Stealing Food
in *Anansi and the Moss-Covered Rock, The Dancing Granny,* and *Ma'ii and Cousin Horned Toad*

Anansi and the Moss-Covered Rock (Kimmel)

The Dancing Granny (Bryan)

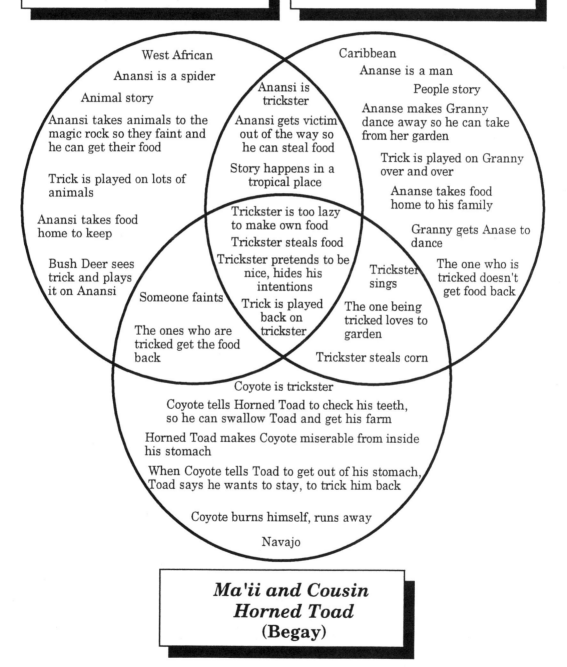

West African

Anansi is a spider

Animal story

Anansi takes animals to the magic rock so they faint and he can get their food

Trick is played on lots of animals

Anansi takes food home to keep

Bush Deer sees trick and plays it on Anansi

Anansi is trickster

Anansi gets victim out of the way so he can steal food

Story happens in a tropical place

Caribbean

Ananse is a man

People story

Ananse makes Granny dance away so he can take from her garden

Trick is played on Granny over and over

Ananse takes food home to his family

Granny gets Anase to dance

Trickster is too lazy to make own food

Trickster steals food

Trickster pretends to be nice, hides his intentions

Trick is played back on trickster

Trickster sings

The one who is tricked doesn't get food back

Someone faints

The ones who are tricked get the food back

The one being tricked loves to garden

Trickster steals corn

Coyote is trickster

Coyote tells Horned Toad to check his teeth, so he can swallow Toad and get his farm

Horned Toad makes Coyote miserable from inside his stomach

When Coyote tells Toad to get out of his stomach, Toad says he wants to stay, to trick him back

Coyote burns himself, runs away

Navajo

Ma'ii and Cousin Horned Toad (Begay)

Fig. 2.1.

■ Story 3: *Raven* by Gerald McDermott

Introduction to the story: Now we are going to meet yet another great trickster: Raven. The Native Americans of the Pacific Northwest tell stories about Raven, a big black bird. This story also starts with a problem: The world is new, and it is completely dark. Notice the illustrations in this story. The Native Americans of the Pacific Northwest have a special artistic style of making their pictures. Gerald McDermott is imitating this art style to give the feel of their culture.

Prediction question suggestions: When Raven changes himself into a pine needle and floats into the water, what happens to him? Why does he let himself get swallowed; what does he want? What do you think will happen next? Who is the baby? When Baby Raven is playing, what is he trying to do? How do you think he will get the light? How can he escape with it?

Compare-and-Contrast Activities for Stories
About a Trick to Help Others

Using the same process described in the section on stories about stealing food (pp. 13–14), take the students through a second Venn diagramming activity. The process will be familiar, and students should generate ideas more quickly this time. See the sample Venn diagram (fig. 2.2), the result of actual Venn diagramming discussions among first and second grade students.

The Folk Process

Now that the children have discussed stories from different cultures and noted ways in which the same themes or motifs occur across cultures, discuss with them the nature of folktales and how remarkable it is that the same story elements appear across continents and cultural groups. When reading folktales with children, take a few moments to discuss what a folktale is. Children need to understand the difference between a recently authored story and an original folktale. Folktales were created and passed on in the oral tradition. We don't even know the names of the people who started these stories! Most folktales were created hundreds of years ago—before electricity and television, before cars and trains, and before books were plentiful. Often stories were told around a fire or a table or hearth in the evening among friends and families. Those listeners then repeated the stories to other friends and family members. Usually, when people repeat a story they have heard, they tell it in their own way, changing some things, adding some things, making it their own version of the story. This is the folk process: the oral passing on of stories and songs, with the contents changing and evolving over time.

With a map or globe, point out where the folktales you read are from. Remind children that these stories came from people who didn't travel in cars and jets and that most people never left their home village or region. And yet, somehow, the same kinds of stories have turned up in all these places on the map! Anthropologists and folklorists spend their lives documenting and puzzling out this phenomenon. While we can discuss how this transference of tales around the globe might have happened, the important thing is to note the similarities and differences and to celebrate the wonder of the folk process.

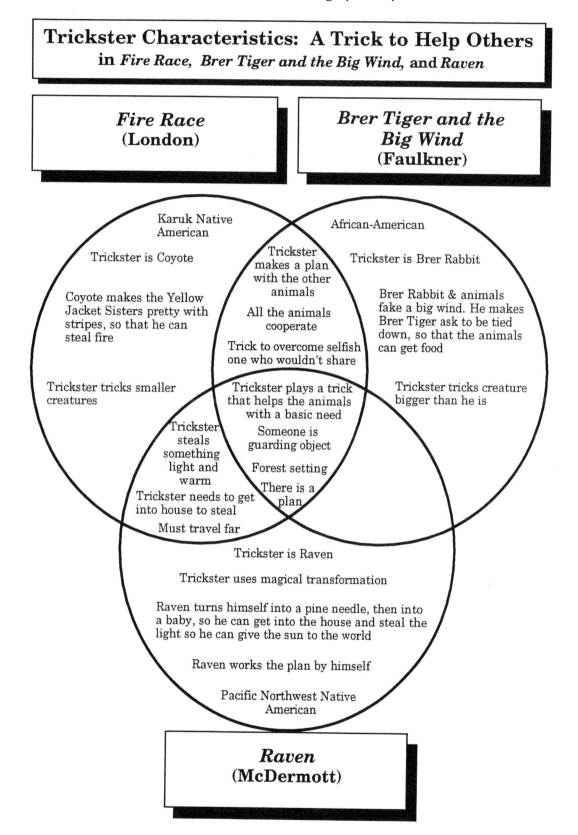

Trickster Characteristics: A Trick to Help Others
in *Fire Race, Brer Tiger and the Big Wind,* and *Raven*

Fire Race (London)

Brer Tiger and the Big Wind (Faulkner)

Karuk Native American

Trickster is Coyote

Coyote makes the Yellow Jacket Sisters pretty with stripes, so that he can steal fire

Trickster tricks smaller creatures

Trickster makes a plan with the other animals

All the animals cooperate

Trick to overcome selfish one who wouldn't share

African-American

Trickster is Brer Rabbit

Brer Rabbit & animals fake a big wind. He makes Brer Tiger ask to be tied down, so that the animals can get food

Trickster tricks creature bigger than he is

Trickster plays a trick that helps the animals with a basic need

Someone is guarding object

Forest setting

There is a plan

Trickster steals something light and warm

Trickster needs to get into house to steal

Must travel far

Trickster is Raven

Trickster uses magical transformation

Raven turns himself into a pine needle, then into a baby, so he can get into the house and steal the light so he can give the sun to the world

Raven works the plan by himself

Pacific Northwest Native American

Raven (McDermott)

Fig. 2.2.

Through these stories born of unique cultures, we can meet, enjoy, and, for a brief time, enter the world of other peoples. The stories, rich in their cultural heritage, give us a way to know and appreciate another culture. Folktales give us strands that help tie us all together. Stories and motifs common across cultures are one way we can celebrate similarities. At the same time, the tales showcase cultural distinctions, which should also to be recognized and appreciated. Pointing these wonders out to students in short, informal discussions will plant seeds of cultural appreciation and awareness of the folk process.

Additional Compare-and-Contrast Activities

The chart of story themes and topics (Chapter 3) provides ideas of other ways stories can be linked. Consider keeping a large chart on the wall similar to fig. 2.3 on page 19 to track all the stories the class reads. This chart identifies components of stories in a matrix format. A blank chart for this activity is provided. Such a chart can be used for a teacher's tracking purposes and for students' individual story tracking, as well as for a wall-sized chart.

Feel free to duplicate the matrix chart (fig. 2.3), as well as the blank Venn diagrams (figs. 2.4 and 2.5) on pages 20–21 for your classroom use. Figure 2.6 on page 22 gives two examples of two-circle Venn diagrams.

What Goes Around: Another Graphic Organizer

"What goes around, comes around" is an expression that applies to the trickster experience. For good or for ill, what a person "dishes out" to others often comes back to him or her. In trickster tales, a trickster is often paid back by the victim with another trick. When children recognize this reversal in a tale, they can use the graphic organizer on page 23 (fig. 2.7) to illustrate it. Some tales well suited to this activity are as follows:

Ananse's Feast by Tololwa M. Mollel

Anansi and the Moss-Covered Rock by Eric Kimmel

"Coyote and Mice" in *Coyote Goes Walking* by Tom Pohrt

"Crocodile! Crocodile!" in *Crocodile! Crocodile!* by Barbara Baumgartner

A Flea in the Ear by Stephen Wyllie

The Flying Tortoise by Tololwa M. Mollel

Ma'ii and Cousin Horned Toad by Shonto Begay

"Manners for True," in *Bo Rabbit Smart for True* by Priscilla Jaquith

The Mean Hyena by Judy Sierra

Monkey-Monkey's Trick by Patricia McKissack

Text continues on page 24.

Trickster Tales Chart

Title	Reteller (Author)	Culture	Name of trickster	What does trickster want?	Who is tricked?	Trick	How it works out in the end

Fig. 2.3.

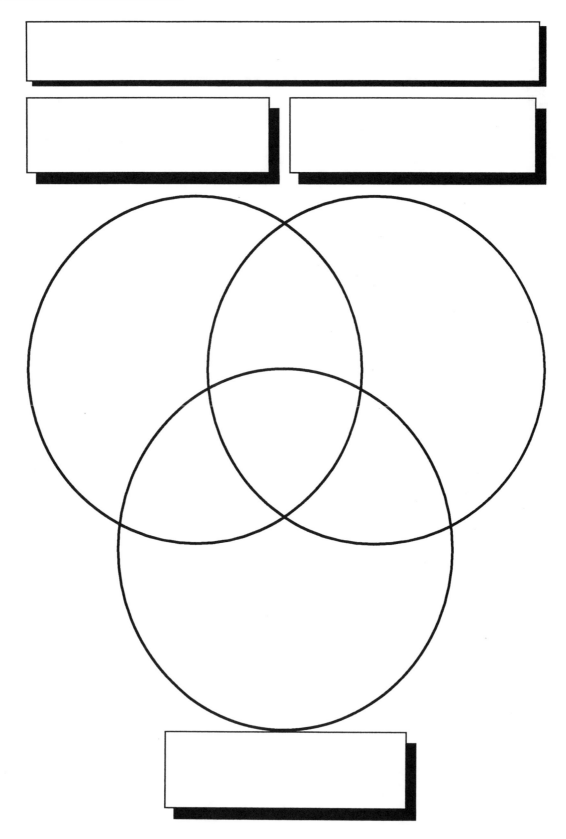

Fig. 2.4.

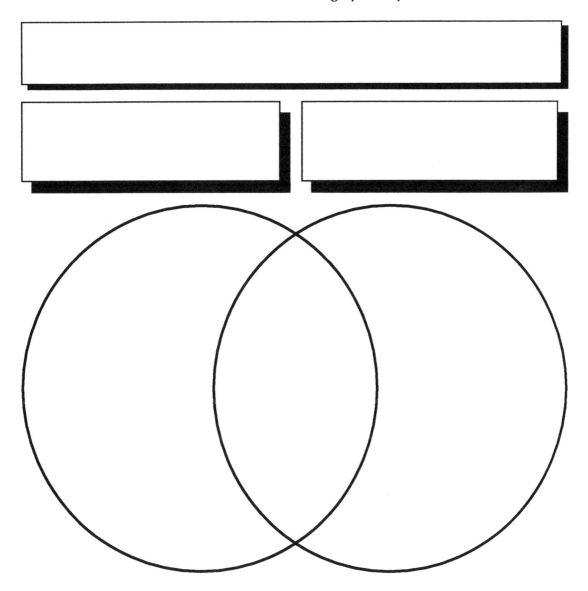

Fig. 2.5.

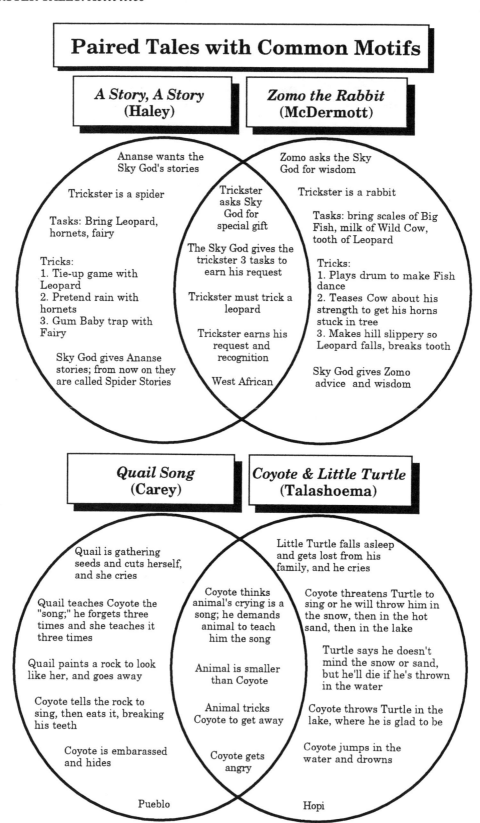

Paired Tales with Common Motifs

A Story, A Story (Haley)

Zomo the Rabbit (McDermott)

Ananse wants the Sky God's stories

Trickster is a spider

Tasks: Bring Leopard, hornets, fairy

Tricks:
1. Tie-up game with Leopard
2. Pretend rain with hornets
3. Gum Baby trap with Fairy

Sky God gives Ananse stories; from now on they are called Spider Stories

Trickster asks Sky God for special gift

The Sky God gives the trickster 3 tasks to earn his request

Trickster must trick a leopard

Trickster earns his request and recognition

West African

Zomo asks the Sky God for wisdom

Trickster is a rabbit

Tasks: bring scales of Big Fish, milk of Wild Cow, tooth of Leopard

Tricks:
1. Plays drum to make Fish dance
2. Teases Cow about his strength to get his horns stuck in tree
3. Makes hill slippery so Leopard falls, breaks tooth

Sky God gives Zomo advice and wisdom

Quail Song (Carey)

Coyote & Little Turtle (Talashoema)

Quail is gathering seeds and cuts herself, and she cries

Quail teaches Coyote the "song;" he forgets three times and she teaches it three times

Quail paints a rock to look like her, and goes away

Coyote tells the rock to sing, then eats it, breaking his teeth

Coyote is embarassed and hides

Coyote thinks animal's crying is a song; he demands animal to teach him the song

Animal is smaller than Coyote

Animal tricks Coyote to get away

Coyote gets angry

Pueblo

Little Turtle falls asleep and gets lost from his family, and he cries

Coyote threatens Turtle to sing or he will throw him in the snow, then in the hot sand, then in the lake

Turtle says he doesn't mind the snow or sand, but he'll die if he's thrown in the water

Coyote throws Turtle in the lake, where he is glad to be

Coyote jumps in the water and drowns

Hopi

Fig. 2.6.

From *Folktale Themes and Activities for Children, Vol. 2*. © 1999 Anne Marie Kraus. Libraries Unlimited. (800) 237-6124.

Tricking the Trickster Back

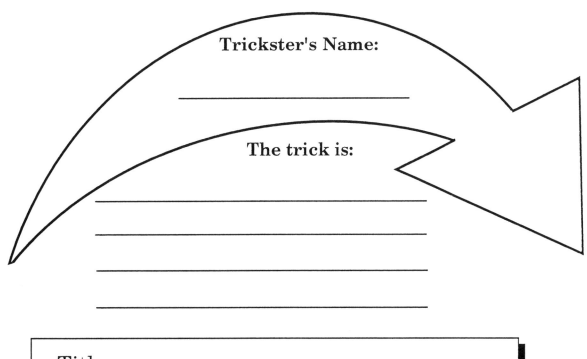

Trickster's Name:

_____

The trick is:

_____

_____

_____

_____

Title:

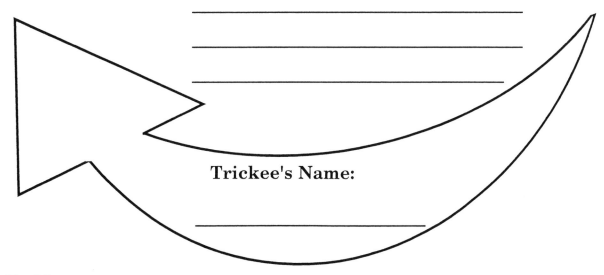

The trick is: _____

_____

_____

_____

Trickee's Name:

_____

Fig. 2.7.

INDEPENDENT READING: TITLES FOR READING GROUPS WITH DISCUSSION QUESTIONS AND ACTIVITIES

The majority of illustrated trickster tales are well suited to independent reading by primary-aged students. The titles below are suggested for independent reading because they match the reading levels of many first and second graders, and have been available in paperback for multiple-copy use by reading groups. Teachers and library media specialists may model their own reading programs on these suggestions. Discussion questions are also suggested. They can be used for small-group discussions or for students to respond to through journal writing and drawing.

■ Hayward, Linda. *All Stuck Up*. Step Into Reading. A Step 1 Book. Illustrated by Normand Chartier. New York: Random House, 1990.

1. Why does Brer Rabbit want to "bop" Mr. Boy?

2. When Brer Rabbit gets stuck on Mr. Boy, how does he feel when he sees Brer Fox coming toward him? If you were stuck like that and saw a bigger animal coming toward you, how would you feel? What would you do? Draw a picture of yourself getting stuck and watching a big animal coming toward you. Draw a word balloon coming out of your head. What words would you be thinking?

3. When Brer Fox says he is going to boil or drown Brer Rabbit and Brer Rabbit doesn't object, what is Brer Rabbit trying to do? What does Brer Fox think when Brer Rabbit says boiling or drowning is fine?

4. How does Brer Rabbit feel after Brer Fox throws him into the briar patch? Draw a picture of Brer Rabbit in the briar patch, with a word balloon coming out of his head. What words is he thinking?

5. Think of a time when you were worried or afraid or in trouble. How did you feel after it was over? Draw a picture of yourself and write about how you felt after the trouble was over.

■ Hayward, Linda. *Hello, House!* Step Into Reading. A Step 1 Book. Illustrated by Lynn Munsinger. New York: Random House, 1988.

1. When Brer Rabbit and his family come back from their picnic, Brer Rabbit "feels funny" because the door to his house is open. Why is he worried? What would you do in his situation? Would you go inside? Where would you go?

2. Why does Brer Rabbit yell, "Hello, House!" into his house?

3. Do houses talk back? Does Brer Wolf know this? Why does Brer Wolf yell "hello" back?

4. Why does Brer Wolf get mad?

5. Draw a picture of Brer Rabbit at the end of the story. What is he thinking about Brer Wolf? Write what Brer Rabbit is thinking.

■ Bang, Molly. *Wiley and the Hairy Man: Adapted from an American Folk Tale.* Ready-to-Read. Illustrated by the author. New York: Aladdin Books, 1976 (reissued 1996).

1. When Wiley sees the Hairy Man for the first time, he is scared. Draw a picture of you meeting the Hairy Man, and make a list of all the things you would do if you met him.

2. Why does Wiley take his hound dogs with him to the swamp the first time? Why does Wiley tie his dogs up the second time? Is Wiley brave to leave his dogs at home? Why?

3. Wiley tells the Hairy Man that he bets the Hairy Man can't change himself into other animals. Why does he say this? What does Wiley want to do with the Hairy Man after he has changed himself into a small animal?

4. When the Hairy Man comes to Wiley's house, he tells Wiley's mother that he will do all kinds of mean things to her. Does Wiley's mother act scared? Where is Wiley during this time? Draw a picture of the whole house. Show Wiley, his mother, and the Hairy Man. Write what each person is thinking.

5. When the Hairy Man picks up the pig, he is angry. Why? Draw a picture of the Hairy Man with the pig, and write what he is thinking.

■ McKissack, Patricia. *Monkey-Monkey's Trick: Based on an African Folk Tale.* Step Into Reading, A Step 2 Book. Illustrated by Paul Meisel. New York: Random House, 1988.

1. Monkey-Monkey needs help building his house, but he does not let Hyena help him. Why?

2. While Monkey-Monkey is working, he is visited by Beautiful Creature and Ugly Monster. Who are these two really? Why doesn't Monkey-Monkey know this?

3. How does Monkey-Monkey discover that Hyena is fooling him?

4. Who is Skinny Zebra really? How can you tell?

5. Skinny Zebra tells Hyena that he used to be big, but Monkey-Monkey put a spell on him. How does this make Hyena feel? Why is this a trick? What does Hyena do now?

6. Count how many disguises are used in this trickster tale. Have you ever fooled anyone with a costume or disguise? Draw a picture of yourself in a disguise, and write or tell a short story about how you fool someone with your disguise.

Other titles with a primary reading level and paperback availability include:

• McDermott, Gerald. *Zomo the Rabbit: A Trickster Tale from West Africa.* Illustrated by the author. New York: Harcourt Brace Jovanovich, 1992.

• McDermott, Gerald. *Raven: A Trickster Tale from the Pacific Northwest.* Illustrated by the author. New York: Harcourt Brace Jovanovich, 1993.

• London, Jonathan, and Lanny Pinola. *Fire Race: A Karuk Coyote Tale About How Fire Came to the People.* Illustrated by Sylvia Long. San Francisco: Chronicle Books, 1993.

CULMINATING ACTIVITIES

Making Connections: A Final Story Web

By the time the trickster tales unit draws to a close, students will have read and listened to a variety of stories. Many stories have connections to one another, and several contain numerous references to motifs in other stories. Such is the case with *The Tale of Rabbit and Coyote* by Tony Johnston. Short, simply told, and humorous in text and illustrations, this story is almost a summary of classic tricks and motifs from other tales. While this is a story of the Zapotec Indians of Mexico, it contains elements of stories from African, African American, and Latin American cultures. It is a prime example of the folk process, illustrating how the great tradition of storytelling incorporates bits of tales from many cultures—and creates a new one.

Save this book until the end of the trickster tale unit. Then, as *The Tale of Rabbit and Coyote* unfolds, watch the lights go on as students' minds spark with the knowledge of these stories from other cultures. Again, here is an optimal time to formalize the children's comparison skills by using a graphic organizer such as the one on the following page (fig. 2.8) to organize and display story associations. This is a great way to summarize, review, compare, and contrast the rich variety found in trickster tales.

A Trickster Party

To celebrate the end of the trickster tales unit of study, have the children participate in a Trickster Character Dress-Up Day for which they can dress up as a character from any of the tales they have read. For students who can't bring a costume from home, have them create paper masks or dress up like Anansi the Spider by attaching eight black accordion-folded paper strips to their body (for Anansi's eight legs).

During the party, children can present projects they have worked on, such as stick-puppet tellings, shadow-puppet presentations, a reader's theater based on trickster stories, and plays (see "Other Curricular Tie-Ins and Creative Extensions" on pages 28–43 for more on these projects). They can also sing "Oh, John the Rabbit," found in *From Sea to Shining Sea* by Amy Cohn or other songs found in trickster tales.

Have children recall the various tales and tricksters they have come to know. The class can produce a bar graph (fig. 2.9) showing each child's favorite trickster character, working in a little bit of math in the process.

Top off the party with foods that are found in trickster stories. There are lots of food ideas in titles such as *Anansi and the Moss-Covered Rock, Anansi and the Talking Melon, The Dancing Granny, Ma'ii and Cousin Horned Toad,* and *Tops and Bottoms.* Students may be introduced to foods they have not tried before, such as yams, beets, and coconut. In recognition of Native American foods of the Southwest, include blue corn in such form as corn chips, popcorn, or cornmeal.

Web of Interconnecting Elements in
The Tale of Rabbit and Coyote
by Tony Johnston

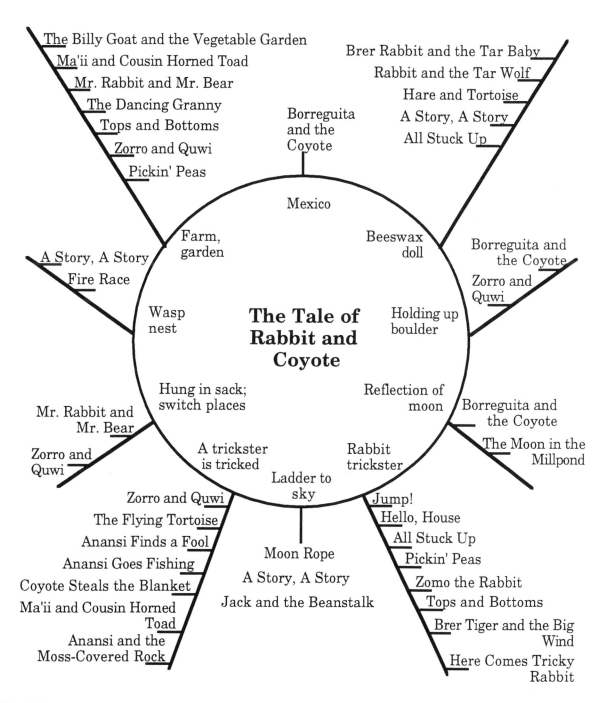

The Billy Goat and the Vegetable Garden
Ma'ii and Cousin Horned Toad
Mr. Rabbit and Mr. Bear
The Dancing Granny
Tops and Bottoms
Zorro and Quwi
Pickin' Peas

Brer Rabbit and the Tar Baby
Rabbit and the Tar Wolf
Hare and Tortoise
A Story, A Story
All Stuck Up

Borreguita
and the
Coyote

Mexico

A Story, A Story
Fire Race

Farm,
garden

Beeswax
doll

Borreguita and
the Coyote
Zorro and
Quwi

Wasp
nest

**The Tale of
Rabbit and
Coyote**

Holding up
boulder

Hung in sack;
switch places

Reflection of
moon

Mr. Rabbit and
Mr. Bear
Zorro and
Quwi

A trickster
is tricked

Rabbit
trickster

Borreguita and
the Coyote
The Moon in the
Millpond

Zorro and Quwi
The Flying Tortoise
Anansi Finds a Fool
Anansi Goes Fishing
Coyote Steals the Blanket
Ma'ii and Cousin Horned
Toad
Anansi and the
Moss-Covered Rock

Ladder to
sky

Moon Rope
A Story, A Story
Jack and the Beanstalk

Jump!
Hello, House
All Stuck Up
Pickin' Peas
Zomo the Rabbit
Tops and Bottoms
Brer Tiger and the Big
Wind
Here Comes Tricky
Rabbit

Fig. 2.8.

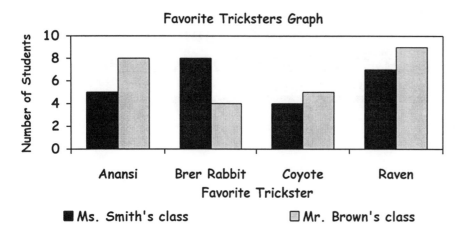

Fig. 2.9.

OTHER CURRICULAR TIE-INS AND CREATIVE EXTENSIONS

Creative Writing

A logical extension of this study is the writing of original trickster stories. Some students may model their stories after classic tricks seen in familiar folktales. Others may opt for totally original material. Both of these options are valid writing experiences. Encourage students first to do some basic planning before fleshing out their stories. Use the "Trickster Story Planning Page" (fig. 2.10) for this purpose. After drafting the story on the planning sheet, students can complete the story-writing process established within the classroom.

Graphs

A common math activity in primary classrooms involves students collecting and counting data, and then transferring this data to a bar graph. A "favorite trickster" graph is suggested above, as part of a trickster party. Another way to integrate math graphing into this literature experience involves the systematic tracking of tales studied during the trickster tales unit. Graph items can be tabulated (see fig. 2.11 on p. 30) for a variety of topical or thematic elements found in the stories, such as . . .

- When the trickster succeeds in his trick

- When the trickster loses or fails

- When the trickster is tricked in return by the victim

- When the trickster acts to help others

- When the trickster plays a trick just for himself or for selfish reasons

- When the trickster steals food

- When the trickster uses a song, tries to fly, escapes, transforms himself, etc.

Trickster Story Planning Page

The Trickster character in my story is

_____

The one being tricked is _____

How the story starts:

How the trick happens:

How the story ends:

Fig. 2.10.

From *Folktale Themes and Activities for Children, Vol. 2* . © 1999 Anne Marie Kraus. Libraries Unlimited. (800) 237-6124.

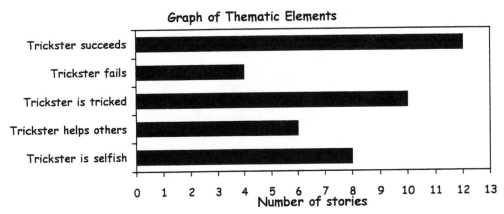

Fig. 2.11.

Stick Puppets and Storytelling Aids

A basic skill important to developing readers is the ability to retell a story. Recalling a story's basic content and its sequence of events is an important thinking skill. An enjoyable way to retell a story is through the use of stick puppets. Children can lay out the puppets in order of appearance, and then entertain others with their story. Have children draw their major characters and objects from a trickster tale. Then have them cut out and tape or glue each character or object onto a Popsicle stick. After practicing telling the story with the puppets, have them present their retelling to the rest of the class. (Some suggestions for creating stick puppets are found in *Crocodile! Crocodile! Stories Told Around the World* by Barbara Baumgartner.)

An alternate version of this activity is to make a "storytelling necklace" or "storytelling bracelet." Have children cut out small drawings of the characters and objects in a trickster tale. After they punch a hole in the top edge of each picture, have them assemble the pictures in order and string them onto a piece of yarn. They can then tie the ends of the yarn together and wear it as a necklace or bracelet. As the wearer points to each picture on the necklace, he or she can tell the story in proper event sequence, as each subsequent picture serves as a reminder of the next character or event.

Some stories lend themselves more readily to this sequencing activity than others. Stories with linear plots and repeated elements work the best. Titles well suited to stick puppets and storytelling necklaces include the following:

- *Ananse's Feast* by Tololwa M. Mollel
- *Anansi and the Moss-Covered Rock* by Eric Kimmel
- *Anansi and the Talking Melon* by Eric Kimmel
- *Borreguita and the Coyote: A Tale from Ayutla, Mexico* by Verna Aardema
- "Coyote and Woodpecker," in *Coyote Goes Walking* by Tom Pohrt
- *Lord of the Animals* by Fiona French
- *Quail Song: A Pueblo Indian Tale* by Valerie Scho Carey

For additional ideas on storytelling by children, including several story texts, consult *Stories in My Pocket* by Martha Hamilton and Mitch Weiss.

Shadow Puppet Theater

Shadow puppetry is an effective, creative, low-cost (in both time and money) activity for involving groups of children in a cooperative, arts-based experience. Directions are given below for simple construction of puppets and a shadow puppet stage. In addition, books are suggested for stories easy to adapt for shadow puppet plays. Finally, figs. 2.12–2.12g on pp. 32–38 show silhouette figures based on characters in Gavin Bishop's *Māui and the Sun*. For more information on shadow puppet theater construction and activities, consult *Worlds of Shadow: Teaching with Shadow Puppetry* by David and Donna Wisniewski. Englewood, CO: Teacher Ideas Press, 1997.

A Simple Shadow Screen Stage

Construct a simple stage using a large corrugated cardboard box. The library may have one from a computer or TV. Using a razor-knife, cut the box in half vertically (this produces two stages out of one box). Cut a rectangular hole (for the screen "stage") in the large side. The size of the hole will depend on the box, but it can range from 16 to 24 inches wide and 16 to 20 inches tall. Leave a margin on all sides and a 3- to 6-inch border along the bottom edge. This size allows three to six children to take turns moving into place to operate their puppets. Separate the top and bottom flaps from the box. Stand the stage on the bottom flaps, and adjust the sides in or out so that puppet operators can move into the space more easily. Have the top center flap rest on the two side flaps, and weight down the bottom flaps with a couple of heavy books for stability. The exterior of the stage (the part facing the audience) may be painted, depending on time and supplies.

Next, cover the hole with a screen. A large piece of white paper works well. More permanent shadow screens can be constructed of fabric stretched over a wooden frame, but white paper produces the desired effect quickly and inexpensively. Use masking tape to fasten the paper over the hole from the inside, making sure you stretch it as flat and taut as possible.

A Source of Light

The light source can be a simple lamp (minus the lampshade) with a 100-watt lightbulb. If the lamp is placed directly behind the puppeteers, the audience may detect dim shadows from the arms and sticks backstage, but this is not an extremely distracting feature. A light placed at the top or bottom of the screen, between the screen and the puppeteers, gives the best effect. Try to angle the light up or down toward the screen. If available, a light with a clamp and gooseneck offers more opportunities for experimenting with light placement. But if time and resources are short, a secondhand living room lamp, placed on a table behind the screen, does an adequate job. When putting on the play, darken the room to optimize the backlighting of the stage. Warn children not to touch the hot bulb.

Text continues on page 39.

Fig. 2.12. Shadow puppet silhouette characters for *Māui and the Sun*. Fig. 2.12a. Māui; Sun.

Shadow puppet illustrations drawn by Andrea McGann Keech based on *Māui and the Sun: A Maori Tale* retold and illustrated by Gavin Bishop. Text and illustrations © 1996 by Gavin Bishop. Used by permission of North-South Books, Inc., New York.

From *Folktale Themes and Activities for Children, Vol. 2*. © 1999 Anne Marie Kraus. Libraries Unlimited. (800) 237-6124.

Fig. 2.12b. Māui and his brothers fishing.

From *Folktale Themes and Activities for Children, Vol. 2.* © 1999 Anne Marie Kraus. Libraries Unlimited. (800) 237-6124.

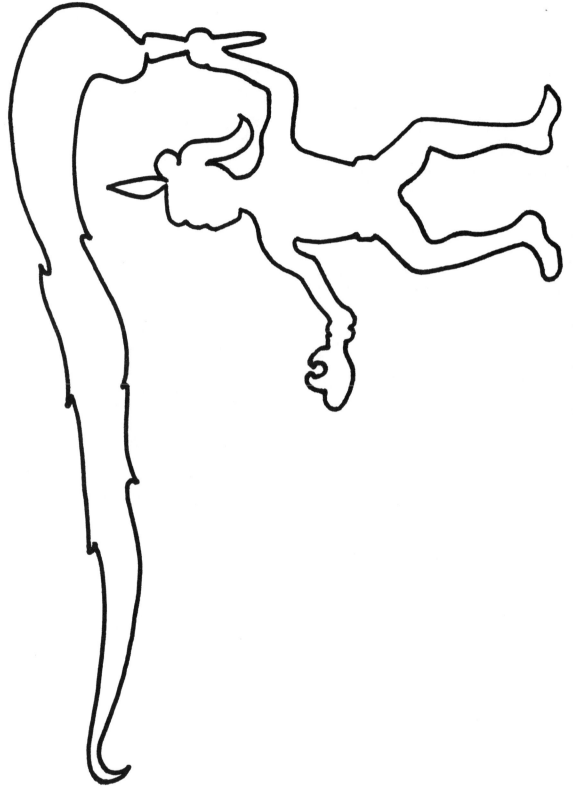

Fig. 2.12c. Māui leading his brothers east, holding a torch and his enchanted weapon.

From *Folktale Themes and Activities for Children, Vol. 2.* © 1999 Anne Marie Kraus. Libraries Unlimited. (800) 237-6124.

Fig. 2.12d. Villagers cutting flax to make ropes for Māui's plan.

From *Folktale Themes and Activities for Children, Vol. 2.* © 1999 Anne Marie Kraus. Libraries Unlimited. (800) 237-6124.

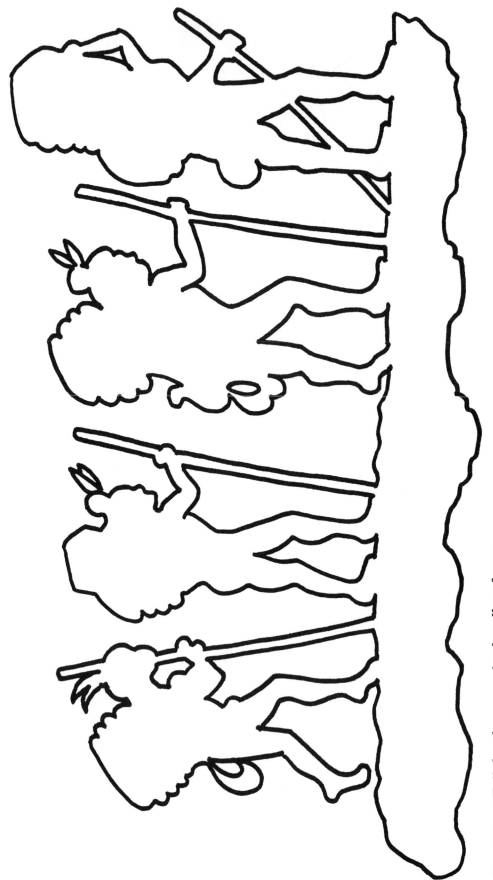

Fig. 2.12e. Māui's brothers carrying bundles of rope.

From *Folktale Themes and Activities for Children, Vol. 2.* © 1999 Anne Marie Kraus. Libraries Unlimited. (800) 237-6124.

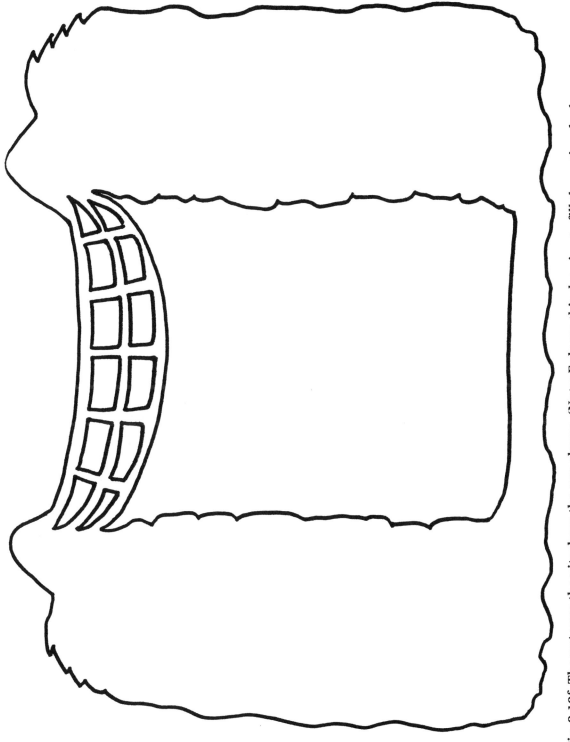

Fig. 2.12f. The net over the pit where the sun sleeps. (Note: Enlarge this drawing to fill the entire shadow screen area.

Fig. 2.12g. The sun and the moon, attached by Māui's rope, to keep day and night in balance.

From *Folktale Themes and Activities for Children, Vol. 2.* © 1999 Anne Marie Kraus. Libraries Unlimited. (800) 237-6124.

Create the Puppets

The easiest puppets are silhouette puppets. Children can draw and cut out their characters on construction paper. Slightly heavier paper or cardstock can also be used. Black is the most effective. Colored paper may show a hint of color, but it still conveys the silhouette look. More elaborate puppets can be created by cutting out parts of the puppet and covering the holes with colored tissue paper or plastic.

By using brass fasteners, students can create puppets with moving parts. In general, however, it is best to keep puppets simple and of one piece. And keep in mind that every moving part will need its own rod.

Each puppet needs a stick, or rod, attached to it that the puppeteer can hold onto from the rear. Try using bamboo skewers, found wherever Asian food supplies are sold. Thin doweling, cut to 8- to 10-inch lengths, also works well. The easiest fastening material is masking tape. Press one end of a piece of masking tape around the rod, and press the other end onto the paper puppet. Allow the puppet to flap and wiggle just a little. This hinged attachment allows the puppeteer to gently press the puppet to the paper screen from a variety of angles.

Special See-Through Color Effects

Special dramatic effects can be created with the use of colored acetate, available at art stores for a modest price. For example, in creating scenery for *How Snowshoe Hare Rescued the Sun,* tape a wide sheet of blue acetate across the screen to simulate the darkness that falls after the demons steal the sun. Continue the action of the animal puppets against the blue acetate, as they meet in the dark to plan to rescue the sun. For the scene in which Snowshoe Hare goes to find the sun, create scenery using black construction paper for the mountains and black paper to outline the cavern under the mountains. Tape blue acetate above the mountains (where it is still night), and tape red acetate over the cavern, where the demons are hiding the sun. Move the demons and rabbit against the red background. A yellow acetate puppet is effective as the sun.

Pick a Story and Adapt It

The story or play can be as elaborate as time and creativity allow, but a simple first effort is often best. Take an already published tale and analyze it for characters, movement, and plot. Choose a simple story that can be read aloud by one or more readers while the puppeteers (two to six children) move their puppets accordingly. The puppeteers can display their recall of the story as the readers sharpen their read-aloud skills. Students who might not otherwise be comfortable in a performance situation can experience confident storytelling or dramatic action by working with silhouette puppets. For stories that run long, shorten the narrative and keep the action going. Stories can also be rewritten into a play format, with dialogue in addition to narration.

Some easy-to-adapt stories are listed here, along with lists of characters and color suggestions.

■ *How Snowshoe Hare Rescued the Sun* by
Emery Bernhard
    Demons
    Sun—transparent yellow
    Harpoon
    Night—wide sheet of transparent blue
    Old Snowy Owl
    Raven
    Polar Bear
    Walrus
    Wolf
    Snowshoe Hare
    Other characters as desired (Lemming,
        Seal, Fox, Caribou, wolves in den)
    Scenery—mountains with transparent
        red cavern underneath and trans-
        parent blue sky above
    Moon—transparent yellow
    Stars—attach four or five to tooth-
        picks then tape toothpicks in a
        cluster to the rod. (Or try decora-
        tive toothpicks, the kind used for
        hors d'oeuvres, with tufts of colored
        cellophane at one end.)

■ *Imani in the Belly* by Deborah M. Newton
Chocolate
    Imani (woman)
    Her three children
    Mama Mzazi spirit—transparent
    Simba—large with transparent belly
    Jungle trees, brush—optional
    Other animals (monkey, elephant, giraffe,
        hyena)
    three objects used by Imani (sticks,
        two stones, meat)
    fire—transparent red

■ *Coyote in Love* by Mindy Dwyer
    Sky with stars—pale tissue paper with
        stars glued or drawn on

    Blue star—transparent blue
    Coyote (two—one howling, one running)
    Mountain
    Coyote tears—blue transparent
    Crater Lake—paper mountain with
        transparent blue in center for lake

■ *Māui Goes Fishing*, by Julie Stewart Williams
    Māui
    Three brothers (one set of brothers
        standing, one set sitting in boat)
    Fish
    Fishhook
    Sea—transparent blue
    Rope
    Islands—mountain peaks with trans-
        parent red tops and cracks to show
        volcanic activity

■ *The Hunterman and the Crocodile* by
Baba Wagué Diakité
    Hunterman
    Crocodile family
    Stacked crocodiles
    Crocodile head—large and open-mouthed
    Cow
    Horse
    Chicken
    Mango tree
    Rabbit
    Crocodile tears—transparent color

■ *Tiger Soup* by Frances Temple
    Tiger
    Anansi the Spider
    Pot of soup—transparent in center to
        show soup
    Blue swimming hole—transparent blue
    Group of monkeys
    Tree (or draw tree on the screen at the
        side)

Ready-to-Use Shadow Puppets

    Figures 2.12–2.12g on pages 32–38 are silhouette drawings for a ready-to-produce shadow puppet play. Using Gavin Bishop's book *Māui and the Sun* for the story narration, enjoy experimenting with these puppets to dramatize the story.

Singing

A number of trickster tales include songs as part of the plot. Because the actual tune is not usually included, have children create their own tunes to accompany any lyrics that they encounter during this unit of study. Consider collaborating with the music teacher to create melodies and rhythms. The titles below include songs:

- *Abiyoyo* by Pete Seeger (Note: The melody is written out in the book; also, the book/audiocassette edition includes singing.)

- *The Banza* by Diane Wolkstein (Note: The book/audiocassette edition includes singing.)

- *Bouki Dances the Kokioko* by Diane Wolkstein

- *The Dancing Granny* by Ashley Bryan (Note: Much of the text is rhythmic, and Ananse beats rhythms with sticks, so this could be a rhythm-and-chant activity, with or without the melodies.)

- *Jackal's Flying Lesson* by Verna Aardema

- *Ma'ii and Cousin Horned Toad* by Shonto Begay (Note: Shonto Begay sings the song himself on a tape no longer available from the publisher.)

- *Mollie Whuppie and the Giant* by Robin Muller

- "Oh, John the Rabbit" in *From Sea to Shining Sea: A Treasury of American Folklore and Folk Songs* by Amy L. Cohn (Note: The song is written out with accompaniment. The song "John the Rabbit" is also found in the Silver Burdett *Music* textbook series, 1976 edition, in the early childhood/kindergarten volume. The two versions differ slightly.)

- *Pickin' Peas* by Margaret Read MacDonald (Note: The short melody is written out, with suggestions for children's participation.)

- *Quail Song* by Valerie Scho Carey

- *Shadow Dance* by Tololwa M. Mollel (Note: The song is written out.)

- "Snow Bunting's Lullaby" in *Tuck-Me-In Tales* by Margaret Read MacDonald

- *Tiger Soup* by Frances Temple

- *Tukama Tootles the Flute* by Phillis Gershator

Drama

The dramatization of stories can range from simple, informal retellings with action to full-blown stage plays.

For an informal retelling in which children participate in the action, try "Why Anansi Has a Narrow Waist." (This story is found in *African-American Folktales for Young Readers* by Richard and Judy Dockrey Young. It is also found in *The Adventures of Spider* by Joyce Cooper Arkhurst.) Arrange the children in a large circle; these children will be the villagers in Anansi's village. Children can be in small groups of two or three, as families, or each child can represent one household. The storyteller can be either a narrator on the side or Anansi, who walks around inside the circle. Anansi should have several lengths of yarn or string, all tied onto a belt around his waist. The children/villagers should all be prepared to tell Anansi what food they are cooking for the evening's meal. Anansi walks about, sniffing the food smells in the air. He greets each villager and exchanges pleasantries. Each time, the neighbor abides by good manners and invites Anansi to share the meal. Each time, Anansi is anxious to eat at that dwelling, but he makes excuses and says he must go somewhere else first. Upon leaving, he gives the neighbor the free end of one of his strings. He asks the neighbor to give a tug on the line when the food is finished cooking. Then he will know that it is time to eat, and he will return. He does this at each of the households in the village, greedy to taste everyone's meals. At the narrator's signal, all villagers pull on their strings simultaneously. Greedy Anansi's waist is squeezed tight, and the villagers all laugh at his foolish gluttony.

Ready-to-use play scripts are available in the following books:

- "Jack Visits the Queen" in *Trickster Tales from Around the World: An Interdisciplinary Guide for Teachers* by Barbara G. Schutz-Gruber and Barbara Frates Buckley. (Ann Arbor, MI: Barbara G. Schutz-Gruber, 1991.)

- *Multicultural Plays for Children: Volume I: Grades K-3* and *Volume II: Grades 4-6* by Pamela Gerke. Young Actors Series. (Lyme, NH: Smith and Kraus, 1996.) Volume I comprises "The Adventures of Anansi," a set of four short trickster stories including "How Anansi Got a Thin Waist" and "How Anansi Helped a Fisherman." Volume II includes "La Culebra (The Snake)."

- "Wahoo!" by June Melser in *Tiddalik* by Joy Cowley. (San Diego, CA: The Wright Group, 1982.)

Additional Curricular Material and Activities

For more curricular tie-ins with trickster tales, including science, social studies, different graphic organizers, storytelling, paper folding, games, and additional puppet ideas, see the following resources:

- *Trickster Tales from Around the World: An Interdisciplinary Guide for Teachers* by Barbara G. Schutz-Gruber and Barbara Frates Buckley. (Ann Arbor, MI: Barbara G. Schutz-Gruber, 1991.) Schutz-Gruber and Buckley offer social studies, science, language arts, music, drama, and art activities to coordinate with specific stories. The stories are included in the book (transcripts of Schutz-Gruber's entertaining storytelling tape).

- *A Treasury of Trickster Tales* by Valerie Marsh. Illustrated by Patrick K. Luzadder. (Ft. Atkinson, WI: Alleyside Press, 1997.) Marsh, a storyteller, tells 20 trickster tales and gives detailed instructions on how to incorporate special techniques to accompany each story. Storytelling methods are given for paper-cutting, "mystery-folding," sign language, "storyknifing," and story puzzles; all 20 stories are fully illustrated.

- "From Anansi to Zomo: Trickster Tales in the Classroom" by Terrell A. Young and Phyllis M. Ferguson in *Reading Teacher* 48 (March 1995): 490–503. Young and Ferguson take an in-depth look at the literature and its benefits in the school reading program. They offer methods for engaging students in the stories, including graphic organizers, a readers theater, a game, "wanted" posters, puppets, and "riddle me" books. An extensive bibliography provides titles not listed in this book, and the text provides a nice discussion of cultures and titles.

REFERENCES

Cowley, Joy. 1982. *Tiddalik*. San Diego, CA: The Wright Group.

Del Negro, Janice M. 1996. "Trickster Tales." *Book Links* 5 (March): 43–47.

Gerke, Pamela. 1996. *Multicultural Plays for Children: Volume I: Grades K-3* and *Volume II: Grades 4-6*. Lyme, NH: Smith and Kraus.

Marsh, Valerie. 1997. *A Treasury of Trickster Tales*. Illustrated by Patrick K. Luzadder. Ft. Atkinson, WI: Alleyside Press.

Schutz-Gruber, Barbara G., and Barbara Frates Buckley. 1991. *Trickster Tales from Around the World: An Interdisciplinary Guide for Teachers*. Ann Arbor, MI: Barbara G. Schutz-Gruber (available by writing Barbara Schutz-Gruber, 2855 Kimberly, Ann Arbor, MI, 48104; or call 734-761-5118).

Wisniewski, David, and Donna Wisniewski. 1997. *Worlds of Shadow: Teaching with Shadow Puppetry*. Englewood, CO: Teacher Ideas Press.

Young, Terrell A., and Phyllis M. Ferguson. 1995. "From Anansi to Zomo: Trickster Tales in the Classroom." *The Reading Teacher* 48 (March): 490–503.

Chapter 3

story themes and topics

This chart groups stories by their topical and thematic elements. It is a useful tool for planning which tales to group for storytelling/storyhour programs, thematic units for reading classes, or compare-and-contrast activities. This chart is also useful for pointing out thematic and topical associations among tales and across cultures. To obtain full bibliographic information on the stories, consult the annotated bibliography in Chapter 4. Stories may also be accessed through the index at the end.

Topic/Characters	Trickster Elements	Title/Author/Culture
Stealing or taking food		
Ma'ii (Coyote) Horned Toad	Ma'ii swallows Toad to take over Toad's farm; Toad torments Ma'ii from inside	*Ma'ii and Cousin Horned Toad* (Begay) Native American/Navajo
Anansi Animals Bush Deer	Anansi uses magic rock to make animals faint; steals their food	*Anansi and the Moss-Covered Rock* (Kimmel) African
Ananse Granny	Ananse sings to make Granny dance away; steals her garden crops	*The Dancing Granny* (Bryan) Central American/Caribbean
Anansi Turtle	Anansi keeps making Turtle wash his hands; eats entire meal while Turtle is gone	"Anansi and Turtle" in *African-American Folktales* (Young) African
Brer Rabbit Brer Fox	Rabbit "helps" Fox shingle his roof; nails his tail down and eats Fox's dinner	"Brer Rabbit Gets Brer Fox's Dinner" in *More Tales of Uncle Remus* (Lester) African American
Brer Rabbit Brer Fox Mr. Man	Rabbit convinces Man his meat stinks, offers to "help"; steals it; then tricks Fox and keeps the meat for himself	"Brer Rabbit Gets the Meat" in *More Tales of Uncle Remus* (Lester) African American
Anansi Elephant King	Anansi hides inside melon; convinces others that the melon can talk	*Anansi and the Talking Melon* (Kimmel) African
Rabbit Wolf	Both are to share meat; Rabbit sends Wolf to get fire from sunset; hides meat while Wolf is gone	"Rabbit Sends Wolf to the Sunset" in *How Rabbit Tricked Otter* (Ross) Native American/Cherokee
Raven Crow	Raven replaces Mama Crow's meat with rock	*Supper for Crow* (Morgan) Native American/Pacific Northwest
Raven Her three friends	Raven eats the berries and fish while her friends work	*Raven Goes Berrypicking* (Cameron) Native American/Pacific Northwest
Tortoise Birds	Tortoise "advises" birds at Skyland feast; claims he eats first and eats all the food	*The Flying Tortoise* (Mollel) African/Nigerian (Igbo)
Rabbit Ostrich Others	Rabbit eats all the berries and lies about it; makes exchanges of food	*This for That* (Aardema) African/Tonga
Ananse Akye the Turtle	Ananse eats the feast while making Turtle wash his hands; Turtle pays him back	*Ananse's Feast* (Mollel) African/Ashanti
Hershele Travelers Innkeeper	Hershele sets up a feast at the inn for the travelers, promising the other party would pay for it	"Hershele's Feast" in *Trickster Tales* (Sherman) Jewish (in a collection of many cultures)

Topic/Characters	Trickster Elements	Title/Author/Culture
Stealing or taking food		
Molly Cottontail Mr. Fox Hungry Billy	Molly eats Billy's butter and then frames Mr. Fox for the theft	"Molly Cottontail" in *Cut from the Same Cloth* (San Souci) African American (in a collection of several cultures)
Brother Rabbit Woman	Rabbit plays dead so woman puts him in her basket; he eats the bananas inside	*Brother Rabbit* (Ho) Asian/Cambodian
Brer Anansi Brer Rabbit Brer Bear	Anansi gets a boat race going; convinces Rabbit and Bear to unload their supplies	*Brer Anansi and the Boat Race* (Makhanlall) Central American/Caribbean
Punia King of Sharks	Punia devises distractions for sharks so he can steal lobsters	*Punia and the King of Sharks* (Wardlaw) Hawaiian
Māui His Three Brothers	Māui takes the fish off his brothers' lines and claims they are his own	*Māui Goes Fishing* (Williams) Hawaiian
Making a fool of someone		
Rabbit Lion	Rabbit plays series of tricks to steal Lion's honey and torments him	*Rabbit Makes a Monkey of Lion* (Aardema) African
Tío Tigre Uncle Rabbit	Rabbit ties a knot in Tigre's tail and later makes fun of him for it	"How Uncle Rabbit Tricked Uncle Tiger" in *Señor Cat's Romance* (González) South American/Latin American (Puerto Rican)
Brother Rabbit Crocodile	Rabbit says if it is a log, it will float upstream; crocodile hears and floats upstream; Rabbit laughs and knows it is a crocodile	*Brother Rabbit* (Ho) Asian/Cambodian
Bruh Rabby Bruh Gator	Rabby gets Gator to dance, resulting in Gator's passing out and burning his tail	"Bruh Rabby and Bruh Gator" in *A Ring of Tricksters* (Hamilton) African American (in a collection of several cultures)
Mr. Turtle Mr. Leopard	Turtle claims he will ride Leopard like a horse; feigns illness and gets Leopard to give him a ride	"Old Mister Turtle Gets a Whipping" in *A Ring of Tricksters* (Hamilton) African (West)
Trickster's deed for the benefit of others		
Anansi Sky God	Anansi accomplishes three tasks to get stories for the world	*A Story, A Story* (Haley) African
Anansi Sky God	Anansi tricks python, fairy, and hornets for Sky God to get stories	*Anansi Does the Impossible* (Aardema) African/Ashanti

Topic/Characters	Trickster Elements	Title/Author/Culture
Trickster's deed for the benefit of others		
Anansi Villagers Anansi's Son	Anansi asks villagers to put wisdom in his gourd; he recognizes his son is wiser than he, so he gives away wisdom to the world	"Anansi Tries to Steal All the Wisdom in the World" in *African-American Folktales for Young Readers* (Young) African/Ashanti
Raven Sky Chief	Raven transforms into baby to get into Sky Chief's lodge; steals sun to bring to earth for all people	*Raven* (McDermott) Native American/Pacific Northwest
Glooskap Animals	Glooskap re-shapes animals from giant- to normal-sized, to prepare world for humans	"How Glooskap Made Human Beings" in *How Glooskap Outwits the Ice Giants* (Norman) Native American/Maritime Northeast
Coyote Yellow-Jacket Sisters	Coyote steals fire; animals have relay to steal and keep fire for all	*The Fire Race* (London) Native American/Karuk
Brer Rabbit Brer Tiger	Brer Rabbit stages a "wind" that frightens Tiger into wanting to be tied up	*Brer Tiger and the Big Wind* (Faulkner) African American
Coyote Three Evil Spirits	Coyote steals fire; animals have relay to steal and keep fire for all	*Coyote and the Fire Stick* (Goldin) Native American/Pacific Northwest
Cayman Animals	Animals make Cayman laugh to let out fire hidden in his mouth	*How Iwariwa the Cayman Learned to Share* (Crespo) South American/Yanomami
Manabozho Magician	Manabozho turns into a rabbit to gain access to a magician's wigwam to bring fire to the people	"How Manabozho Stole Fire" in *Manabozho's Gifts* (Greene) Native American/Chippewa
Little red ant Billy Goat	Little red ant makes goat think garden is infested with ants; goat leaves garden	"The Billy Goat and the Vegetable Garden" in *Señor Cat's Romance* (González) South American/Latin American (Puerto Rican)
Puss Puss's Master Ogre	Puss tricks Ogre into transforming himself into a mouse, so that Puss can eat him up; gets Ogre's estate for his master	*Puss in Boots* (Perrault and Marcellino) European/French
Monkey Giant Pedro	Monkey tricks giant into believing there is an ogre more terrible, so he runs off; gets giant's estate for his master, Pedro	*Pedro and the Monkey* (San Souci) Asian/Filipino
Coyote Five giant sisters	Coyote turns into baby to get to giants who are keeping salmon for themselves; Coyote turns into man to dig hole in giants' dam; Coyote turns giants into swallows	"Coyote and the Giant Sisters" in *Giants!* (Walker) Native American/Pacific Northwest (in a collection of several cultures)

Topic/Characters	Trickster Elements	Title/Author/Culture
Trickster's deed for the benefit of others		
Mollie Whuppie Giant	Mollie goes back three times to steal giant's possessions so he can't terrorize the kingdom anymore	*Mollie Whuppie and the Giant* (Muller) European/British
Revenge		
Fish Eagle Hyena	Hyena tricks Fish Eagle out of fish; Fish Eagle plans trick to humiliate the hyenas	*Hungry Hyena* (Hadithi) Original
Dragon/Snake Boy	Dragon/Snake tricks boy's brother, who was usurping boy's honor	"The Grateful Snake" in *Crocodile! Crocodile!* (Baumgartner) Asian/Chinese (in a collection of several cultures)
Manabozho Buzzard	Buzzard purposely drops Manabozho from the sky; Manabozho transforms into dead deer to catch and punish Buzzard	"The Tricker's Revenge" in *Trickster Tales* (Sherman) Native American/Menominee (in a collection of several cultures)
Story-spirits Prince Servant	Story-spirits transform themselves to harm prince for not sharing stories	"The Spirits in the Leather Bag" in *The Barefoot Book of Trickster Tales* (Walker) Kampuchean (in a collection of several cultures)
Escape is made possible by the trick		
Mollie Whuppie Giant	Mollie steals giant's ring; it makes her invisible so she can escape	*Mollie Whuppie and the Giant* (Muller) European/British
Monkey Crocodile	Monkey tells Crocodile he left his heart in a tree; then escapes	"Crocodile! Crocodile!" in *Crocodile! Crocodile!* (Baumgartner) Asian/Indian (in a collection of several cultures)
Shulo the hare King Lion Animals	Hare gets animals to dance, making dust, so they don't see him escape	"The Animals Share" in *A Ring of Tricksters* (Hamilton) African (in a collection of several cultures)
Turtle Children	Turtle plays song and dances to get let out of cage	*The Dancing Turtle* (DeSpain) South American/Brazilian
Girl Mr. Rabbit	Rabbit sings to get let out of the box and dances out the window	*Pickin' Peas* (MacDonald) African American
Monkey Crocodile	Monkey tells Crocodile he left his heart in a tree, so Chief can't eat it; then escapes	"The Monkey's Heart" in *The Dial Book of Animal Tales from Around the World* (Adler) African/Kenyan (in a collection of many cultures)

Topic/Characters	Trickster Elements	Title/Author/Culture
Escape is made possible by the trick		
Ma'ii (Coyote) Cousin Horned Toad	Toad gets swallowed; pokes and frightens Coyote from Coyote's insides; escapes	*Ma'ii and Cousin Horned Toad* (Begay) Native American/Navajo
Borreguita the lamb Coyote	Lamb pretends to hold up cliff; gets Coyote to hold it for her so she can escape	*Borreguita and the Coyote* (Aardema) Central American/Mexican
Quwi (Guinea pig) Zorro (Fox)	Quwi pretends to hold up boulder; gets Zorro to hold it for him so he can escape	*Zorro and Quwi* (Hickox) South American/Peruvian
Rabbit Coyote	Rabbit pretends to hold up boulder; gets Coyote to hold it for him so he can escape	*The Tale of Rabbit and Coyote* (Johnston) Central American/Mexican
Singam (Lion) Sparrow Lamb Deer	All three animals defer lion from devouring them, sending him for cooking supplies and messages	*The Very Hungry Lion* (Wolf) Asian/Indian
Obtaining the sun		
Raven Sky Chief	Raven transforms into baby to get into Sky Chief's lodge; steals sun to bring to earth	*Raven* (McDermott) Native American/Pacific Northwest
Raven Sky Chief	Raven transforms into baby to get into Sky Chief's lodge; steals sun to bring to earth	*Raven's Light* (Shetterly) Native American/Pacific Northwest
Snowshoe Hare Demons	Hare finds cavern where demons hid Sun; Hare kicks it out into sky	*How Snowshoe Hare Rescued the Sun* (Bernhard) Native American/Yuit Eskimo (Siberian)
Raven Loon Evil spirits	Spirits steal sun; Loon tries and fails to get it back; Raven hides it under his wing and steals it back	*How the Loon Lost Her Voice* (Cameron) Native American/Pacific Northwest
Bear Boy	Bear steals sun; boy disguises self as fish; shaves off Bear's fur; Bear gets cold and releases sun	*The Day Sun Was Stolen* (Oliviero) Native American/Haida (Pacific Northwest)
Māui Sun	Sun moves too fast; Māui traps and harnesses the sun and ties it to the moon to slow it down	*Māui and the Sun* (Bishop) New Zealand/Maori (Polynesian)
Obtaining Fire		
Coyote Yellow-Jacket Sisters	Coyote tells Sisters he will make them pretty; steals fire; animals have relay to keep fire	*The Fire Race* (London) Native American/Karuk

Topic/Characters	Trickster Elements	Title/Author/Culture
Obtaining Fire		
Cayman Animals	Animals make Cayman laugh to let out fire hidden in his mouth	*How Iwariwa the Cayman Learned to Share* (Crespo) South American/Yanomami
Coyote Three evil spirits	Coyote hides then steals fire; animals have relay to steal and keep fire	*Coyote and the Fire Stick* (Goldin) Native American/Pacific Northwest
Firekeeper Blue Jay Swallow	Blue Jay steals fire from Firekeeper; Swallow catches it, cools it, and gives it to warm boy	"Blue Jay and Swallow Take the Heat" in *When Birds Could Talk and Bats Could Sing* (Hamilton) African American
Trickster affects the placement of the stars		
Coyote First Woman	Coyote wants to help Woman place stars; gets impatient and flings blanketful of stars into sky	*How the Stars Fell into the Sky* (Oughton) Native American/Navajo
Coyote Animals	Coyote rearranges stars into shapes of animal friends	*Coyote Places the Stars* (Taylor) Native American/Wasco
Trickster affects the weather		
Glooskap Queen of Summer Giant of Winter	Glooskap kidnaps the Queen of Summer and brings her to the north	"The Capture of Summer" in *Little Folk* (Walker) Native American/Algonquin (in a collection of several cultures)
Trick is played to save someone's life		
Pelican Fish Crab	Pelican tells fish he must transport them to a new lake to save them; eats them instead; Crab suspects and defeats Pelican	"Never Trust a Pelican" in *The Dial Book of Animal Tales from Around the World* (Adler) Asian/Thai (in a collection of several cultures)
Imani (Woman) Simba	Imani keeps faith in herself; is swallowed by Simba; rescues children and others	*Imani in the Belly* (Chocolate) African/East African
Monkey Crocodile	Monkey tells Crocodile he left his heart in a tree; then escapes	"The Monkey's Heart" in *The Dial Book of Animal Tales from Around the World* (Adler) African/Kenyan (in a collection of several cultures)
Monkey Crocodile	Monkey tells Crocodile he left his heart in a tree; then escapes	"Crocodile! Crocodile!" in *Crocodile! Crocodile!* (Baumgartner) Asian/Indian (in a collection of several cultures)

Topic/Characters	Trickster Elements	Title/Author/Culture
Pursuit of wealth; economic venture		
Leprechaun Bridget Rooney	Leprechaun keeps Bridget from finding his gold	"The Red-Ribbon Leprechaun" in *Little Folk* (Walker) Irish (in a collection of several cultures)
Sir Whong Stranger	Stranger talks Sir Whong into a loan using "gold" pig as collateral; Whong tricks him back; gets money back	*Sir Whong and the Golden Pig* (Han) Asian/Korean
Tortoise Pig	Tortoise borrows money from Pig; then creates distraction to avoid repaying Pig	"Tortoise's Debt and Pig's Grunt" in *Trickster Tales* (Sherman) African/Cameroon (in a collection of several cultures)
Poor man Rich man	Rich man digs up treasure jar; tells poor man it isn't there	*The Bee and the Dream* (Long) Asian/Japanese
"Tar baby" motif		
Brer Fox Brer Rabbit	Fox makes "boy" from sticky stuff; Rabbit gets stuck on it	*All Stuck Up* (Hayward) African American
Brer Fox Brer Rabbit	Fox makes tar baby; Rabbit gets stuck on it	*Brer Rabbit and the Wonderful Tar Baby* videorecording, book and tape, CD (Metaxas) African American
Brer Fox Brer Rabbit	Fox makes tar baby; Rabbit gets stuck on it	"Brer Rabbit and the Tar Baby" in *Tales of Uncle Remus* (Lester) African American
Farmer Rabbit Coyote	Farmer makes beeswax doll to catch thief; Rabbit convinces Coyote to trade places in farmer's sack to escape	*The Tale of Rabbit and Coyote* (Johnston) Central American/Mexican
Anansi Fairy	Anansi makes gum baby to catch fairy	*A Story, A Story* (Haley) African
Rabbit Wolf Fox	Wolf and Fox make a tar wolf to catch Rabbit	"Rabbit and the Tar Wolf" in *How Rabbit Tricked Otter* (Ross) Native American/Cherokee
Hare Tortoise	To catch whoever muddied the pond, Tortoise covers shell with sap; catches Hare	"Hare and Tortoise" in *Crow & Fox* (Thornhill) West African (in a collection of several cultures)
Sister Fox Brother Coyote	Fox dupes Coyote four times; gets Coyote to take sticky wax doll from her in the henhouse	"Sister Fox and Brother Coyote" in *Cut from the Same Cloth* (San Souci) Mexican American (in a collection of several cultures)

Topic/Characters	Trickster Elements	Title/Author/Culture
"Briar patch" motif (Please don't throw me there!)		
Rabbit Fox	Caught by tar wolf, Rabbit laughs at Fox's death threats; Fox throws Rabbit into briar thicket	"Rabbit and the Tar Wolf" in *How Rabbit Tricked Otter* (Ross) Native American/Cherokee
Turtle Wolves	Turtle scoffs at threats of boiling or fire; gets himself thrown into the river	*How Turtle's Back Was Cracked* (Ross) Native American/Cherokee
Turtle Man	Turtle is grabbed by man, says he fears water most; gets himself thrown into river	"Turtle Makes War on Man" in *The Boy Who Lived with the Bears* (Bruchac) Native American/Abenaki
Brer Fox Brer Rabbit	Rabbit says he fears briar patch; Fox throws him into the briar patch	*All Stuck Up* (Hayward) African American
Brer Fox Brer Rabbit	Rabbit shows no fear of Fox's threats; gets Fox to throw him in briar patch	*Brer Rabbit and the Wonderful Tar Baby* videorecording, book and tape, CD (Metaxas) African American
Brer Fox Brer Rabbit	Rabbit shows no fear of Fox's threats; gets Fox to throw him in briar patch	"Brer Rabbit and the Tar Baby" in *Tales of Uncle Remus* (Lester) African American
Little Turtle Coyote	Turtle doesn't fear Coyote's threats to throw him in sand or snow; fears the lake; Coyote throws him in the lake	*Coyote and Little Turtle* (Talashoema) Native American/Hopi
Lion Hare	Hare states fear of his great enemy on other side of river; Lion throws him there	"The Lion and the Hare" in *South and North, East and West* (Rosen) African/Botswana (in a collection of several cultures)
Old Meshikee (Turtle) Shagizenz (Sand crabs)	Sand crabs tie up turtle; turtle "fears" water most and gets himself thrown into the lake	*Old Meshikee and the Little Crabs* (Spooner and Taylor) Native American/Ojibwe
Sungura the Rabbit Lion	Rabbit tells Lion, "Please don't throw me into the air"	"Water, Water Will Be Mine" in *Hyena and the Moon* (McNeil) African/Kenyan
Disguise involved in trick		
Rabbit Tío Tigre	Disguised as a bush, Rabbit escapes Tío Tigre	"How Uncle Rabbit Tricked Uncle Tiger" in *Señor Cat's Romance* (González) South American/Latin American (Puerto Rican)
Ananse King	Ananse disguises himself as a bird to overhear the king's motives	"Ananse and the Impossible Quest" in *The Barefoot Book of Trickster Tales* (Walker) African/Ghanian (in a collection of several cultures)

Topic/Characters	Trickster Elements	Title/Author/Culture
Disguise involved in trick		
Monkey-Monkey Hyena	Hyena in disguise steals Monkey's stew; Monkey in disguise frightens Hyena into building Monkey's house	*Monkey-Monkey's Trick* (McKissack) African
Bear Boy	Bear steals sun; boy disguises self as fish; shaves off Bear's fur; Bear gets cold and releases sun	*The Day Sun Was Stolen* (Oliviero) Native American/Haida (Pacific Northwest)
Race between two animals		
Toad Deer	Toad uses look-alike friends positioned along route to give appearance of winning race against Deer	*The Race of Toad and Deer* (Mora) Central American/Guatemalan
Deer Rabbit	Animals discover Rabbit cheating in preparation for race against Deer	"How Deer Won His Antlers" in *How Rabbit Tricked Otter* (Ross) Native American/Cherokee
Rabbit Turtle	Turtle uses look-alike relatives to win race against Rabbit	"Rabbit Races with Turtle" in *How Rabbit Tricked Otter* (Ross) Native American/Cherokee
Brer Rabbit Brer Turtle	Turtle challenges Rabbit to a race and wins by using look-alike relatives along the route	"Brer Rabbit Finally Gets Beaten" in *Tales of Uncle Remus* (Lester) African American
Coyote Rabbit	Rabbit wins race against Coyote by using look-alike relatives	"The Coyote and the Rabbit" in *Nursery Tales Around the World* (Sierra) Native American/Pueblo (in a collection of several cultures)
Fox Crab	Crab wins race by hanging on to Fox's tail	"The Fox and the Crab" in *Nursery Tales Around the World* (Sierra) Chinese (in a collection of several cultures)
"Hello, House" trick		
Rabbit Lion	Rabbit suspects someone is in his house, so he calls to the house and it calls back, exposing Lion	*Rabbit Makes a Monkey of Lion* (Aardema) African
Brer Rabbit Brer Wolf	Rabbit suspects Lion is in his house, so he calls to the house and it calls back, exposing Lion	*Hello, House!* (Hayward) African American
Spider Leopard	Spider suspects Leopard is in his house, so he calls to the house and it calls back, exposing Leopard	"Why Spider Lives in Ceilings" in *The Adventures of Spider* (Arkhurst) African
Crocodile Monkey	Crocodile pretends he is a rock; Monkey gets the "rock" to say hello	"Crocodile Hunts for the Monkey" in *Crocodile! Crocodile!* (Baumgartner) Asian/Indian (in a collection of several cultures)

Topic/Characters	Trickster Elements	Title/Author/Culture
Invitation to dinner trick		
Crow Fox	Fox gives Crow porridge on a rock, so Crow can't eat it; Crow invites Fox to eat dates; throws them into thornbush so Fox can't eat them	"Crow and Fox" in *Crow and Fox* (Thornhill) Middle East (in a collection of several cultures)
Crane Fox	Fox gives Crane dinner in shallow plate so he can't eat; Crane gives Fox soup in tall jar so he can't reach it	"Manners for True" in *Bo Rabbit Smart for True* (Jaquith) African American/Gullah
Anansi Turtle	Anansi eats the feast while making Turtle wash his hands; Turtle pays him back with an invitation to dinner under water; Anansi can't eat it	"Anansi and Turtle" in *African-American Folktales for Young Readers* (Young) African/Ashanti
Ananse Akye the Turtle	Ananse eats the feast while making Turtle wash his hands; Turtle pays him back with an invitation to dinner under water; Ananse can't eat it	*Ananse's Feast* (Mollel) African/Ashanti
"Tug-of-war" trick		
Chameleon Leopard Crocodile	Chameleon puts rope around Leopard and Crocodile, feigning tug-of-war with Chameleon; Crocodile and Leopard pull against each other unknowingly	*Crafty Chameleon* (Hadithi) Original
Turtle Hippo Elephant	Turtle challenges tug-of-war, but sets it up between Hippo and Elephant	"Tug-of-War" in *How Many Spots Does a Leopard Have?* (Lester) African/Fan (in a collection of several cultures)
Mother Hare Elephant Hippo	Mother Hare decides to teach Elephant and Hippo not to threaten her children; plays tug-of-war trick with them; gives one end of rope to each	"The Little Hares Play Hop, Skip, and Jump" in *Tortoise's Flying Lesson* (Mayo) African (in a collection of several cultures)
James the turtle Elephant Whale	Turtle ties vine to whale and elephant; they think they are pulling against turtle	*James the Vine Puller* (Stiles) South American/Brazilian (Arawak and African)
Bo Rabbit Elephant Whale	Rabbit ties rope to Whale and Elephant; they think they are pulling against Rabbit	"Bo Rabbit Smart for True" in *Bo Rabbit Smart for True* (Jaquith) African American/Gullah
Stealing another animal's children		
Jackal Dove Blue Crane	Jackal threatens mother dove; she throws down her children; Crane plays trick to get babies back	*Jackal's Flying Lesson* (Aardema) African/Khoikhoi

Topic/Characters	Trickster Elements	Title/Author/Culture
Stealing another animal's children		
Lioness Mother Ostrich and chicks Mongoose	Mongoose insults Lioness to distract her	*The Lonely Lioness and the Ostrich Chicks* (Aardema) African/Masai
Mama Simba (Lion) Baboon Ground Squirrel	Lion steals Baboon's children; Ground Squirrel faces Lion, gets her to return children	"Not So!" in *Hyena and the Moon* (McNeil) African/Kenyan
Use of reflection in water to trick someone		
Borreguita (Lamb) Coyote	Lamb tells Coyote there is a cheese in the water; he swims out, but is reflection of moon	*Borreguita and the Coyote* (Aardema) Central American/Mexican
Brer Terrapin Rabbit Brer Fox, Wolf, Bear	Rabbit and Terrapin get Fox, Wolf, and Bear to fetch the moon out of the water so they can get a pot of money	"The Moon in the Millpond" in *Jump! The Adventures of Brer Rabbit* (Harris) African American
Rabbit Coyote	Rabbit gets Coyote to drink up the lake in order to eat the "cheese" (moon's reflection)	*The Tale of Rabbit and Coyote* (Johnston) Central American/Mexican
Hare Elephant	Hare tells Elephant he had made moon god angry; when he dips trunk into water, the moon's reflection breaks apart	"Elephant and Hare" in *Crow and Fox* (Thornhill) Asian/Indian
Sister Fox Brother Coyote	Fox dupes Coyote four times, with "tar baby" trick and telling him the reflection of moon is cheese	"Sister Fox and Brother Coyote" in *Cut from the Same Cloth* (San Souci) Mexican American (in a collection of several cultures)
Trickster gets victim to switch places		
Mollie Whuppie Giant	Mollie sings song enticing giant's wife to take her place in the hanging sack	*Mollie Whuppie and the Giant* (Muller) European/British
Quwi (Guinea pig) Zorro (Fox)	Quwi gets Fox to take his place in farmer's trap, claiming he is marrying the farmer's daughter	*Zorro and Quwi* (Hickox) South American/Peruvian
Rabbit Coyote	Rabbit gets Coyote to take his place in the farmer's sack, claiming he is marrying the farmer's daughter	*The Tale of Rabbit and Coyote* (Johnston) Central American/Mexican
Mr. Rabbit Mr. Bear	Rabbit gets Bear tied by the leg to a tree limb in Rabbit's place because it's "a new way of thinking"	"Mr. Rabbit and Mr. Bear" in *The Knee-High Man and Other Tales* (Lester) African American

Topic/Characters	Trickster Elements	Title/Author/Culture
Mathematical trick		
Rani (Girl) Raja	Rani asks reward of one grain of rice, double each day for 30 days; cleans Raja out of rice and teaches him lesson about greed	*One Grain of Rice* (Demi) Asian/India
Old man King	Old man asks reward of one grain of rice, doubled for each square on chessboard—more rice than there is in the world	*The Token Gift* (McKibbon) Asian/Indian
Old Fox Cat and Rat	Fox helps Cat and Rat "divide" some cheese by doing some "adding" and "subtracting" to his own advantage	"The Cat and the Rat" in *A Ring of Tricksters* (Hamilton) African American/Gullah (in a collection of several cultures)
Monkey Dog and Cat	Monkey "helps" divide food in half, eating the overage	"Cat, Dog, and Monkey" in *Monkey Tales* (Gugler) Indonesian (in a collection of several cultures)
Business deal trick		
Brother Anansi Tiger	Anansi divides the cattle with Tiger, marking them so they are all his	*Brother Anansi and the Cattle Ranch* (Rohmer) Central American/Nicaraguan
Hare Bear	Hare divides the crops with Bear, changing the contract each year	*Tops and Bottoms* (Stevens) African American
Bruh Rabbit Bruh Wolf	Rabbit divides the crops with Wolf, giving him tops or bottoms	"Bruh Wolf and Bruh Rabbit Join Together" in *A Ring of Tricksters* (Hamilton) African American (in a collection of several cultures)
Trickster tricks victim from inside its body		
Brother Rabbit Crocodile	Rabbit is swallowed; torments crocodile from inside its belly to get out	*Brother Rabbit* (Ho) Asian/Cambodian
Old Sally Cato Giant	Old Sally lets Giant get close, then runs inside his mouth, tormenting and killing him	"Old Sally Cato" in *Cut from the Same Cloth* (San Souci) African American (in a collection of several cultures)
Ma'ii (Coyote) Cousin Horned Toad	Toad gets swallowed; pokes and frightens Coyote from his insides to escape	*Ma'ii and Cousin Horned Toad* (Begay) Native American/Navajo
Imani (Woman) Simba, the King of Beasts	Imani gets swallowed to rescue children and others; brings food and fire to feed them and gets coughed out	*Imani in the Belly* (Chocolate) East African

Topic/Characters	Trickster Elements	Title/Author/Culture
Trickster tricks victim from inside its body		
Sungura the Rabbit Elephant	Rabbit hides inside pumpkin; gets swallowed; inside, Rabbit drums to scare Elephant into running until tired and caught	"Rabbit's Drum" in *Hyena and the Moon* (McNeil) African/Kenyan
Trickster "holds up" a boulder or cliff		
Borreguita (Lamb) Coyote	Lamb pretends to hold up cliff; gets Coyote to hold it for her so she can escape	*Borreguita and the Coyote* (Aardema) Central American/Mexican
Quwi (Guinea pig) Zorro (Fox)	Quwi pretends to hold up boulder; gets Zorro to hold it for him so he can escape	*Zorro and Quwi* (Hickox) South American/Peruvian
Rabbit Coyote	Rabbit pretends to hold up boulder; gets Coyote to hold it for him so he can escape	*The Tale of Rabbit and Coyote* (Johnston) Central American/Mexican
Song is involved in the trick		
Coyote Quail	Coyote repeatedly demands song from Quail; Quail paints a rock to look like her so he stops bothering her	*Quail Song* (Carey) Native American/Pueblo
Anansi Tiger Monkeys	Anansi teaches monkeys to sing a song, foisting the blame on them	*Tiger Soup* (Temple) Central American/Caribbean (Jamaican)
Cabree (Goat) Tigers	Cabree sings a song of bravery, which scares the tigers off	*The Banza* (Wolkstein) Central American/Caribbean (Haitian)
Raven Snow Buntings	Raven steals the Bunting's song; Papa Bunting shoots arrows at Raven to get it back	"Snow Bunting's Lullaby" in *Tuck-Me-In Tales* (MacDonald) Siberian (in a collection of several cultures)
Spider Ananse Granny Anika	Spider Ananse sings and drums to get Granny dancing away from her garden	*The Dancing Granny* (Bryan) Central American/Caribbean (West Indies)
Mollie Whuppie Giant	Mollie sings song enticing giant's wife to take her place in the hanging sack	*Mollie Whuppie and the Giant* (Muller) European/British
Abiyoyo the giant Boy Father	Boy sings song to get giant to dance; giant falls down so father can make him disappear	*Abiyoyo* (Seeger) African/South African
Tukama Two-headed giant Giant's wife	Boy plays flute and sings to get released from captivity	*Tukama Tootles the Flute* (Gershator) Central American/Caribbean

Topic/Characters	Trickster Elements	Title/Author/Culture
Song is involved in the trick		
Malice (Man) Bouki (Man)	Malice sings a song to get Bouki to dance away from his money sack	*Bouki Dances the Kokioko* (Wolkstein) Central American/Caribbean (Haitian)
Turtle Children	Turtle plays song and dances to get let out of cage	*The Dancing Turtle* (DeSpain) South American/Brazilian
Girl Mr. Rabbit	Rabbit sings to get let out of the box and dances out the window	*Pickin' Peas* (MacDonald) African American
Transformation is part of the trick		
Great Rabbit Wildcat	Rabbit turns into human form to elude Wildcat	*Great Rabbit and the Long-Tailed Wildcat* (Gregg) Native American/Passamaquoddy
Muwin the bear Magic Hare	Magic Hare turns into human form to elude bear	*Muwin and the Magic Hare* (Shetterly) Native American/Passamaquoddy
Raven Sky Chief Chief's Daughter	Raven turns into pine needle, then baby boy, then raven, to steal the sun	*Raven* (McDermott) Native American/Pacific Northwest
Raven Woman and daughter	Raven transforms into a baby to steal moon	*How Raven Freed the Moon* (Cameron) Native American/Pacific Northwest
Puss Puss's Master Ogre	Puss tricks Ogre into transforming himself into a mouse so that Puss can eat him	*Puss in Boots* (Perrault and Marcellino) European/French
Jack Wizard	Jack tricks wizard into transforming himself into an ant so Jack can get away	"Jack and the Wizard" in *The Barefoot Book of Trickster Tales* (Walker) English (in a collection of several cultures)
Coyote Man named White Smoke	Coyote transforms into a man to take his place; Coyote changes the man's appearance so he won't be recognized	"The Coyote" in *Full Moon Stories* (Eagle Walking Turtle) Native American/Arapaho
Manabozho Buzzard	Buzzard drops Manabozho from the sky; Manabozho transforms into dead deer to catch and punish Buzzard	"The Tricker's Revenge" in *Trickster Tales* (Sherman) Native American/Menominee (in a collection of several cultures)
Manabozho Magician	Manabozho turns into a rabbit to gain access to a magician's wigwam to bring fire to the people	"How Manabozho Stole Fire" in *Manabozho's Gifts* (Greene) Native American/Chippewa
Coyote Five giant sisters	Coyote turns into baby to get to giants; turns into man to dig hole in giants' dam; turns giants into swallows	"Coyote and the Giant Sisters" in *Giants!* (Walker) Native American/Pacific Northwest (in a collection of several cultures)

Topic/Characters	Trickster Elements	Title/Author/Culture
Transformation is part of the trick		
Mollie Whuppie Giant	Mollie steals giant's ring; it makes her invisible so she can escape	*Mollie Whuppie and the Giant* (Muller) European/British
Glooskap Ice Giants	Glooskap turns into an Ice Giant to look like them; turns a stick into a hideous skull to frighten the Ice Giants away	*How Glooskap Outwits the Ice Giants* (Norman) Native American/Maritime Indians
Gilly Martin the Fox Giant, Witch Prince and Princess	Fox changes himself into a series of animals and objects to take the place of the real thing required by the Giant and the Witch	*Gilly Martin the Fox* (Hunter) European/Scottish
Trickster Tarantula Swift Runner Grandmother Spider	Animals turn back into sandstone to defeat trickster Tarantula, tricking the trickster back	"Swift Runner and Trickster Tarantula" in *Spider Spins a Story* (Max) Native American/Zuni
Anansi Tiger Goats	Anansi helps goats escape from Tiger by turning them into rocks and throwing them across the river	"Magic Anansi" in *A Ring of Tricksters* (Hamilton) West Indies/Gullah (in a collection of several cultures)
Trickster tries to fly		
Coyote Crows	Coyote gets crows to give him feathers to fly; becomes boastful, so crows sabotage his flight	*Coyote* (McDermott) Native American/Southwest
Jackal Dove Blue Crane	Crane offers Jackal flying lessons from her back; drops him	*Jackal's Flying Lesson* (Aardema) South African/Khoikhoi
Tortoise Birds	Birds give feathers to Tortoise; he flies to Skyland and eats all the food; birds take feathers back	*The Flying Tortoise* (Mollel) African/Nigerian (Igbo)
Weaker creature outwits bully or beast		
Tukama (Boy) Giant's wife	Boy plays flute and sings to get released from captivity	*Tukama Tootles the Flute* (Gershator) Central American/Caribbean
Imani (Woman) Beast	Imani keeps faith in herself; is swallowed; rescues children and others	*Imani in the Belly* (Chocolate) East African
Mother Hare Elephant Hippo	Mother Hare decides to teach Elephant and Hippo not to threaten her children; plays tug-of-war trick with them	"The Little Hares Play Hop, Skip, and Jump" in *Tortoise's Flying Lesson* (Mayo) African (in a collection of several cultures)
Elephant Bat	Elephant challenges all to wrestling match; Bat wins by flying into his ear	*The Elephant's Wrestling Match* (Sierra) African

Topic/Characters	Trickster Elements	Title/Author/Culture
Weaker creature outwits bully or beast		
Cabree (Goat) Tigers	Cabree sings a song of bravery, which scares the tigers off	*The Banza* (Wolkstein) Central American/Caribbean (Haitian)
Brer Rabbit Brer Coon Colonel Tiger	Rabbit buries watermelons; tells Tiger they are graves of victims	"The Watermillion Patch" in *With a Whoop and a Holler* (Van Laan) African American (in a collection of several cultures)
Squirrel Bear	Squirrel gets Bear to crawl out on small branch and jump	"Sody Saleratus" in *Crocodile! Crocodile!* (Baumgartner) American/Appalachian (in a collection of several cultures)
Giant Bird, crab, eel, bedbug, mosquito	Small creatures conspire to torment Giant in his house	"Odon the Giant" in *Nursery Tales Around the World* (Sierra) Filipino (in a collection of several cultures)
Ram Ant	Ant gets ram out of chile patch by stinging him	"The Ram in the Chile Patch" in *Nursery Tales Around the World* (Sierra) Mexican (in a collection of several cultures)
Beaver Face (Girl) Tsonoqua the Timber Giant	Offering to pierce the Giant's ears for earrings, girl pins Giant's ears to ground	"Beaver Face" in *Echoes of the Elders* (Smith) Native American/Kwakiutl
Trickster loses at his own game		
Desert Spirit Coyote Hummingbird	Coyote steals blanket; Desert Spirit sends rolling boulder after him; Hummingbird humbles Coyote	*Coyote Steals the Blanket* (Stevens) Native American/Ute
Ma'ii (Coyote) Cousin Horned Toad	Ma'ii tricks Toad into being swallowed so he gets Toad's farm; Toad makes Coyote miserable from inside Coyote	*Ma'ii and Cousin Horned Toad* (Begay) Native American/Navajo
Anansi Villagers	Anansi gets invitations to many homes for dinner, asks for a tug on his line; everyone tugs at once, squeezing him	"Why Anansi Has a Narrow Waist" in *African-American Folktales for Young Readers* (Young) African/Ashanti
Miz Partridge Brer Rabbit	Miz Partridge pretends to get sick on "snake eggs" so Brer Rabbit won't steal her eggs	"Miz Partridge Tricks Brer Rabbit" in *More Tales of Uncle Remus* (Lester) African American
Brer Rabbit Brer Turtle	Turtle challenges Rabbit to a race and wins by using look-alike relatives along the route	"Brer Rabbit Finally Gets Beaten" in *Tales of Uncle Remus* (Lester) African American
Anansi Friend	Anansi sets up fishing business with friend, but ends up doing all the work	*Anansi Finds a Fool* (Aardema) African

Topic/Characters	Trickster Elements	Title/Author/Culture
Trickster loses at his own game		
Anansi Animals Bush Deer	Bush Deer spies on Anansi's trick; uses same magic rock trick against Anansi	*Anansi and the Moss-Covered Rock* (Kimmel) African
Borreguita (Lamb) Coyote	Borreguita keeps escaping Coyote with tricks like telling Coyote to hold up the cliff	*Borreguita and the Coyote* (Aardema) Central American/Mexican
Tortoise Birds	Because Tortoise eats all the food, birds tear off his flying feathers and make a hard landing for him	*The Flying Tortoise* (Mollel) African/Nigerian (Igbo)
Poor Boy Zee Brother Chu	Brother steals magic wealth; dragon gives poor boy magic stick to stop brother	"The Grateful Snake" in *Crocodile! Crocodile!* (Baumgartner) Asian/Chinese (in a collection of several cultures)
Pelican Fish Crab	Pelican tells fish he must transport them to a new lake to save them; eats them instead; Crab suspects and defeats Pelican	"Never Trust a Pelican" in *The Dial Book of Animal Tales from Around the World* (Adler) Asian/Thai
Monkey Crocodile	Crocodile offers Monkey a ride on his back; goes underwater; Monkey tells Crocodile he left his heart in a tree and escapes	"Crocodile! Crocodile!" in *Crocodile! Crocodile!* (Baumgartner) Asian/Indian (in a collection of several cultures)
Ananse Akye the Turtle	Ananse eats the feast while making Turtle wash his hands; Turtle pays him back with a feast under the river that he cannot eat	*Ananse's Feast* (Mollel) African/Ashanti
Tortoise Hyena	Hyena strands Tortoise in a tree; Tortoise gives Hyena a coat of messy mats and blobs	*The Mean Hyena* (Sierra) African/Malawi
Trickster Tarantula Swift Runner Grandmother Spider	Tarantula steals clothes; animals turn into sandstone piled on top of Tarantula	"Swift Runner and Trickster Tarantula" in *Spider Spins a Story* (Max) Native American/Zuni
Coyote Mice	Coyote crashes mice's dance; mice chew the fur off Coyote's head	"Coyote and Mice" in *Coyote Goes Walking* (Pohrt) Native American
Fox Dog	Fox tells dog to get cure for fleas from pond, steals chickens while he's gone; dog tells fox juicy ducks are at pond; takes chickens back and gives fox fleas	*A Flea in the Ear* (Wyllie) Original
Coyote Crows	Coyote wants to fly; crows help, but he boasts, so they sabotage his feathers	*Coyote* (McDermott) Native American/Southwest

Topic/Characters	Trickster Elements	Title/Author/Culture
Three tasks assigned by the sky god, creator, or magician		
Zomo the Rabbit Sky God	Zomo uses trickery to get fish scales, milk of wild cow, tooth of leopard, to earn wisdom	*Zomo the Rabbit* (McDermott) African (West)
Anansi Sky God	Anansi tricks leopard, hornets, and fairy to obtain stories	*A Story, A Story* (Haley) African
Anansi Sky God	To get stories, Anansi uses tricks to get python, fairy, and hornets for Sky God	*Anansi Does the Impossible* (Aardema) African/Ashanti
Papá Dios Tío Conejo the Rabbit	Rabbit uses trickery to get eagle feather, snake egg, and lion's tooth to get Creator to make him bigger	*Rabbit Wishes* (Shute) Central American/Cuban
Compère Lapin Madame Tortue	Lapin obtains objects (alligator eggs, wildcat milk, grizzly tooth) by trickery for *gris-gris* woman	"Why Lapin's Ears Are Long" in *Why Lapin's Ears Are Long* (Doucet) American/Cajun (Creole)
Reward from the sky god		
Tortoise Leopard	Tortoise tricks Leopard into crawling inside his drum; Sky-God gives him a hard shell	*The Leopard's Drum* (Souhami) African (West)
Anansi Creatures	Anansi obtains three creatures by tricks; sky god gives him stories	*A Story, A Story* (Haley) African
Gardening or farming central to the trick		
Spider Ananse Granny Anika	Spider Ananse sings and drums to get Granny dancing away from her garden	*The Dancing Granny* (Bryan) Central American/Caribbean (West Indies)
Hare Bear	Hare strikes deal with Bear to divide crops; bear always loses	*Tops and Bottoms* (Stevens) African American
Billy Goat Red ant	Ant repeatedly stings Billy Goat to get him out of the garden	"The Billy Goat and the Vegetable Garden" in *Señor Cat's Romance* (González) South American/Latin American
Ma'ii (Coyote) Cousin Horned Toad	Ma'ii tricks Toad into being swallowed so he can get Toad's farm; Toad makes Coyote miserable from inside Coyote	*Ma'ii and Cousin Horned Toad* (Begay) Native American/Navajo
Nisse (Little man) Other nisses Hired farmhand	Nisse moves hay around, plays pranks	"My Friend, the Nisse" in *Little Folk* (Walker) Danish (in a collection of several cultures)

Topic/Characters	Trickster Elements	Title/Author/Culture
Poor versus rich		
Rani (Girl) Raja	Girl asks reward of one grain of rice, double each day for 30 days; cleans Raja out of rice and teaches him lesson about greed	*One Grain of Rice* (Demi) Asian/India
Poor couple Rich neighbor	Poor woman tells of friend who uses new spoon for every bite; rich man spends all his wealth on spoons to outdo this story	*Spoon for Every Bite* (Hayes) Original
Poor silversmith Rich neighbor	Poor silversmith makes greedy rich man believe that spoons and bowls can give birth	"The Silversmith and the Rich Man" in *Stories in My Pocket* (Hamilton and Weiss) Jewish (in a collection of several cultures)
Clever female trickster		
Mollie Whuppie Giant	Mollie goes back three times to steal giant's possessions; she gets the wife to switch places with her in the giant's sack to escape	*Mollie Whuppie and the Giant* (Muller) European/British
Molly Giant/Ogre	Molly proves her frugality during courtship so well it torments the Ogre; he buys her off just so he won't have to marry her	"Managing Molly" in *Diane Goode's Book of Giants and Little People* (Goode) British (in a collection of several cultures)
Rani (Girl) Raja	Girl asks reward of one grain of rice, double each day for 30 days; cleans Raja out of rice and teaches him lesson about greed	*One Grain of Rice* (Demi) Asian/India
Poor couple Rich neighbor	Poor woman tells of friend who uses new spoon for every bite; rich man spends all his wealth on spoons to outdo this story	*Spoon for Every Bite* (Hayes) Original
Imani (Woman) Beast	Imani keeps faith in herself; gets herself swallowed; rescues children and others	*Imani in the Belly* (Chocolate) East African
Fatima Giant	Fatima calls giant's bluff, tricks him back, releases the dreams he stole	*Fatima and the Dream Thief* (Schami) Original
Caterina King	Caterina matches wits with one-upmanship	*Caterina the Clever Farm Girl* (Peterson) European/Italian
Bláithín, wife of Fionn MacCumhail Giant	Bláithín bakes stone cakes and puts Fionn in a cradle to foil giant	"The Giant's Causeway" in *Irish Fairy Tales and Legends* (Leavy) European/British Isles (Irish)

Topic/Characters	Trickster Elements	Title/Author/Culture
Clever female trickster		
Molly Cottontail Mr. Fox Hungry Billy	Molly eats Billy's butter and then frames Mr. Fox for the theft	"Molly Cottontail" in *Cut from the Same Cloth* (San Souci) African American (in a collection of several cultures)
Old Sally Cato Giant	Old Sally lets giant get close, then runs inside his mouth, tormenting and killing him	"Old Sally Cato" in *Cut from the Same Cloth* (San Souci) African American (in a collection of several cultures)
Sister Fox Brother Coyote	Fox dupes Coyote four times with "tar baby" trick, reflection of moon in water, etc.	"Sister Fox and Brother Coyote" in *Cut from the Same Cloth* (San Souci) Mexican American (in a collection of several cultures)
Borreguita (Lamb) Coyote	Lamb pretends to hold up cliff; tells Coyote the moon's reflection is cheese	*Borreguita and the Coyote* (Aardema) Central American/Mexican
Aunt Nancy Old Man Trouble	Aunt Nancy doesn't let Old Man Trouble bother her	*Aunt Nancy and Old Man Trouble* (Root) Original
Beaver Face (Girl) Tsonoqua the Timber Giant	Offering to "help," girl pins Giant's ear to ground; helps other children escape	"Beaver Face" in *Echoes of the Elders* (Smith) Native American/Kwakiutl
Pourquoi, origin, creation elements		
Coyote Animals	Coyote waits for animals to fall asleep to design the model for Lord of the Animals	*Lord of the Animals* (French) Native American/Miwok
Tortoise Birds	Tortoise comes to birds' feast and makes up a name so he gets all the food first; birds trick Tortoise back	*The Flying Tortoise* (Mollel) African/Igbo
Dog M'su Cocodrie (Mr. Alligator)	Dog promises Alligator food; barks and brings man with a broom to chase off Alligator	*Why Alligator Hates Dog* (Reneaux) American/Cajun
Rabbit Turtle	Rabbit escapes, saying he has not brought his liver with him; gives ginseng to Turtle	*The Rabbit's Escape* (Han) Asian/Korean
Rabbit Papá Dios	Rabbit gets three objects by trickery; gets long ears	*Rabbit Wishes* (Shute) Central American/Cuban
Anansi Tiger Monkeys	Anansi steals food and foists blame on monkeys, who stay in trees to this day	*Tiger Soup* (Temple) Central American/Caribbean
Coyote Woman	Coyote gets impatient and flings the stars into the sky	*How the Stars Fell into the Sky* (Oughton) Native American/Navajo

Topic/Characters	Trickster Elements	Title/Author/Culture
Pourquoi, origin, creation elements		
Coyote Butterflies	Butterflies carry Coyote off while he sleeps; butterflies flutter in laughter	*Coyote and the Laughing Butterflies* (Taylor) Native American/Tewa
Fox Mole	Fox tricks Mole into climbing to moon; Fox's face is in the moon; Mole hides in disgrace	*Moon Rope* (Ehlert) South American/Peruvian
Compère Lapin Madame Tortue	Lapin obtains objects by trickery for magic spells; Tortue can't do magic but pulls his ears longer	"Why Lapin's Ears Are Long" in *Why Lapin's Ears Are Long* (Doucet) American/Cajun (Creole)
Compère Lapin Compère Alligator	Lapin gets alligators to line up for a free bridge across the bayou, but gets his tail snapped off	"Why Lapin's Tail Is Short" in *Why Lapin's Ears Are Long* (Doucet) American/Cajun (Creole)
Coyote Blue Star	Coyote insists on loving Blue Star; she drops him, and his tears become Crater Lake	*Coyote in Love* (Dwyer) Native American/Pacific Northwest
Beaver Face (Girl) Tsonoqua the Timber Giant	Offering to "help," girl pins Giant's ears to ground; Giant's ashes become stinging insects	"Beaver Face" in *Echoes of the Elders* (Smith) Native American/Kwakiutl
Raven Sea Gull	Raven puts spiny shells out for Gull to step on; Gulls walk like their feet hurt, to this day	"Raven and Sea Gull" in *Echoes of the Elders* (Smith) Native American/Kwakiutl
Tortoise Hyena	Hyena strands Tortoise in a tree; Tortoise gives Hyena a coat of messy mats and blobs	*The Mean Hyena* (Sierra) African/Malawi
Māui His Three Brothers	Māui fishes land out of the ocean—the islands of Hawaii	*Māui Goes Fishing* (Williams) Hawaiian
Raven Loon Evil spirits	Spirits steal sun; animals try to steal it back, resulting in animal traits	*How the Loon Lost Her Voice* (Cameron) Native American/Pacific Northwest
Anancy King Nature Spirits	Anancy enlists help of Spirits to create palm trees, but schemes to claim full credit	*First Palm Trees* (Berry) Original
Series of trades		
Anancy Animals and people	Anancy trades one thing for another, but ends up with nothing	*Don't Leave an Elephant to Go and Chase a Bird* (Berry) Central American/Caribbean
Rabbit Animals	Rabbit trades one kind of food for another; everyone gets mad at him	*This for That* (Aardema) African/Tonga
Gilly Martin the Fox Giant, Witch Prince and Princess	Fox changes himself into a series of animals and objects to trade for the real thing required by the Giant and the Witch	*Gilly Martin the Fox* (Hunter) European/Scottish

Topic/Characters	Trickster Elements	Title/Author/Culture
Drought		
Brer Rabbit Brer Tiger	Brer Rabbit stages a "wind" that frightens Tiger into wanting to be tied up	*Brer Tiger and the Big Wind* (Faulkner) African American
Shulo the hare King Lion Animals	Shulo won't help dig the well, but tricks his way past guards to use it; animals trap him, but he escapes	"The Animals Share" in *A Ring of Tricksters* (Hamilton) African (in a collection of several cultures)
Trickster as judge		
Judge Rabbit Tree Spirit	Rabbit judges that true husband fits into bottle, exposing Tree Spirit as imposter	*Judge Rabbit and the Tree Spirit* (Spagnoli) Asian/Cambodian
Rabbit Man Tiger	Rabbit tells the disputers to return to original positions; now Tiger is in the pit so he can't eat the man	*The Rabbit's Judgment* (Han) Asian/Korean
Rabbit Crocodile Hunterman	Rabbit expresses disbelief at carrying crocodiles; they re-create scene so crocs can't eat hunterman	*The Hunterman and the Crocodile* (Diakité) African (West)
Bo Rabbit Rattlesnake Bear	Rabbit expresses disbelief at the scene; they put snake back under log to show how it started; they get away from snake	"Rattlesnake's Word" in *Bo Rabbit Smart for True* (Jaquith) African American/Gullah
Salome (Girl) Crocodile Pigeon	Pigeon gets Crocodile to return to trapped position	*Shadow Dance* (Mollel) African/Tanzanian
Trickster is tricked back by the trickee		
Ananse Akye the Turtle	Ananse eats up the feast while making Turtle wash his hands; Turtle pays him back with a feast under the river that he cannot eat	*Ananse's Feast* (Mollel) African/Ashanti
Anansi Animals Bush Deer	Bush Deer spies on Anansi's trick; uses same magic rock trick against Anansi	*Anansi and the Moss-Covered Rock* (Kimmel) African
Monkey Crocodile	Crocodile offers Monkey a ride on his back; goes underwater; Monkey tells Crocodile he left his heart in a tree, then escapes	"Crocodile! Crocodile!" in *Crocodile! Crocodile!* (Baumgartner) Asian/Indian (in a collection of several cultures)
Fox Dog	Fox tells dog to get cure for fleas from pond, steals chickens while he's gone; dog tells fox juicy ducks are at pond; takes chickens back and gives fox fleas	*A Flea in the Ear* (Wyllie) Original

Topic/Characters	Trickster Elements	Title/Author/Culture
Trickster is tricked back by the trickee		
Tortoise Birds	Because Tortoise tricks birds out of the food, birds tear off his flying feathers and make a hard landing for him	*The Flying Tortoise* (Mollel) African/Nigerian (Igbo)
Ma'ii (Coyote) Cousin Horned Toad	Ma'ii tricks Toad into being swallowed so he will get Toad's farm; Toad makes Coyote miserable from inside Coyote	*Ma'ii and Cousin Horned Toad* (Begay) Native American/Navajo
Tortoise Hyena	Hyena strands Tortoise in a tree; Tortoise gives Hyena a coat of messy mats and blobs	*The Mean Hyena* (Sierra) African/Malawi
Monkey-Monkey Hyena	Hyena in disguise steals Monkey's stew; Monkey in disguise frightens Hyena into building Monkey's house	*Monkey-Monkey's Trick* (McKissack) African
Sir Whong Stranger	Stranger borrows money from Sir Whong; the golden pig proves worthless, so Whong tricks stranger into returning the money	*Sir Whong and the Golden Pig* (Han) Asian/Korean

Chapter 4

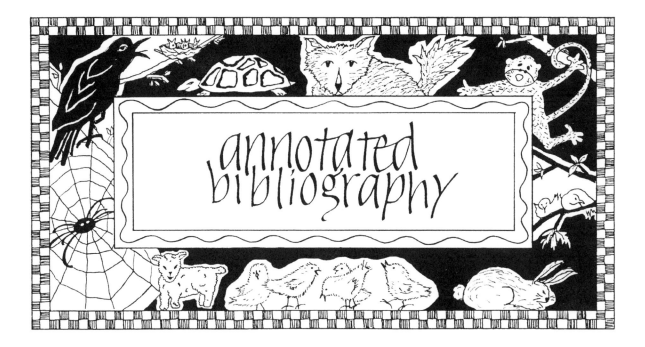

This annotated bibliography is arranged first by continent. Within each continent, tales are listed by cultural groups. Following the continent/cultural group sections, there is a listing of story collections that encompass tales from many cultures. Finally, there is a section of original stories featuring trickster elements. To aid in planning story experiences, consult the "Story Themes and Topics" section; its chart points out common thematic and topical elements that prevail across cultural groups. Titles may also be accessed using the index at the back of the book.

AFRICAN

Aardema, Verna. *Anansi Does the Impossible: An Ashanti Tale.* Illustrated by Lisa Desimini. New York: Atheneum Books for Young Readers, 1997.

Anansi goes to the Sky God to buy his stories, so that stories can belong to the earth people. The Sky God's price is three tasks: to bring him a live python, a fairy, and 47 hornets. Anansi's wife, Aso, devises a plan. When the python comes along, Anansi and his wife stage an argument about whether the snake is longer than the log they are sitting on. Wanting to prove his superior size, the python stretches himself along the log, and Anansi ties him up. To catch the fairy, Aso tells Anansi to carve a wooden fairy-doll and cover it with sticky sap; he then lures her with a dish of fu-fu to eat. To catch the hornets, Anansi pours water on their nest and offers them a dry shelter in his calabash. Anansi brings his captives to the Sky God, and the Sky God gives him the stories as promised. Compare with *A Story, A Story*, by Gail E. Haley. This tale is for primary grade reading and read-alouds.

———. *Anansi Finds a Fool: An Ashanti Tale.* Illustrated by Bryna Waldman. New York: Dial Books for Young Readers, 1992.

Anansi devises a plan to go into the fishing business with a friend, intending to fool his friend into doing all the work. His friend turns the tables on him by giving him the choice either to work or get tired. Anansi's choice is to avoid getting tired, so he ends up doing all the work and the joke is on him. Compare with Kimmel's *Anansi Goes Fishing*.

———. *Jackal's Flying Lesson: A Khoikhoi Tale.* Illustrated by Dale Gottlieb. New York: Apple Soup Books, 1995.

In this tale from southwest Africa, Jackal tricks a mother dove and swallows her babies. A blue crane, seeing that it is the birds' turn to trick Jackal, offers to teach Jackal to fly. Looking and feeling foolish, Jackal falls from the sky, and the baby doves pop out of his mouth unharmed. A song and moral complete this tale written in large print and accessible text. Compare with *Coyote* by Gerald McDermott.

———. *The Lonely Lioness and the Ostrich Chicks: A Masai Tale.* Illustrated by Yumi Heo. New York: Alfred A. Knopf, 1996.

A mother ostrich and her four chicks walk under a tree, not realizing a lioness is asleep on one of its branches. The lioness, wanting the chicks as her own children, takes them from the mother ostrich. The lioness treats the chicks kindly, so they follow her. The mother ostrich seeks the help of many different animals to recover her chicks. Finally, the little mongoose agrees to help her. He insults the lioness, who springs at him. The mongoose escapes into his hole, and the lioness waits for him to emerge. While the lioness focuses on the mongoose's hole, the mother ostrich gathers her chicks and takes them home. The simple text is appropriate for primary grades.

———. *Misoso: Once upon a Time Tales from Africa.* Illustrated by Reynold Ruffins. New York: Apple Soup Books, 1994.

This collection of 12 tales represents a wide variety in types of tales and tribal cultures. The second tale, "Anansi and the Phantom Food," is a notable Anansi story. In this tale, the whole village is starving, so Anansi goes to find food. He heads toward the smoke of a village, and finds an entire village of cassava, just waiting to be eaten! But then he sees another village, and finding that it is a village of plantains, he gives up the cassava for plantains. He encounters more villages of food-beings, finally ending up at his own village, having eaten nothing at all. Use this collection as a read-aloud or storytelling source.

———. *Rabbit Makes a Monkey of Lion: A Swahili Tale.* Illustrated by Jerry Pinkney. New
York: Dial Books for Young Readers, 1989.

In this tale, Rabbit fools Lion repeatedly. The honey guide bird leads Rabbit to a
honey tree. Rabbit brings her small friends, one by one, to the tree to eat honey. Each
time, Lion threatens the stealers of his honey, but the fast-thinking creatures keep
devising tricks to escape. The final escape uses the "hello, house" trick (see *Hello,
House!* by Linda Hayward). Students enjoy joining in the refrain "That rabbit made a
monkey of me!"

———. *This for That: A Tonga Tale.* Illustrated by Victoria Chess. New York: Dial Books
for Young Readers, 1997.

This tale begins with Lion and Elephant digging a well. Rabbit wants to drink from
the well even though she won't help with the work. Lion and Elephant won't let Rabbit
drink, so she complains to Ostrich. Ostrich offers solace to Rabbit by helping her collect
berries instead. They hide the berries under a bush for later. Rabbit returns and eats
up all the berries, saving none for Ostrich. When Ostrich comes back to the bush,
Rabbit not only does not admit to having eaten the berries but she also accuses Ostrich
of having eaten them. Rabbit has Ostrich pay her with a feather, which she then
exchanges for some meat. More exchanges occur with a near-mayhem effect: the meat
for a bowl of sour milk, the milk for a bowl of winged ants, and the ants for a drink at
the well. The near-slapstick comedy culminates with the animal's complete frustration
with Rabbit, whose tricks have gotten out of hand. This piece has a reading level of
second grade.

Arkhurst, Joyce Cooper. *The Adventures of Spider: West African Folktales.* Illustrated by
Jerry Pinkney. Boston: Little, Brown, 1964.

This collection of six humorous pourquoi/trickster tales is in easy-reader format
for independent reading by second- and third-graders. Four of the stories are versions
of tales also found in picture-book format, allowing for comparison opportunities.
These four stories are "How Spider Helped a Fisherman" (compare with *Anansi Goes
Fishing* by Kimmel), "How Spider Got a Bald Head" (compare with *Anansi* by Gleeson),
"Why Spiders Live in Ceilings" (compare with *Hello, House!* by Hayward), and "Why
Spiders Live in Dark Corners" (compare with "tar baby" motif picture books).

Bennett, Martin. *West African Trickster Tales.* New York: Oxford University Press, 1994.

This is an extensive collection for storytellers and other adults, for source material or reading aloud.

Berry, James. *Don't Leave an Elephant to Go and Chase a Bird.* Illustrated by Ann
Grifalconi. New York: Simon & Schuster Books for Young Readers, 1996.

This tale of Anancy Spiderman originates in Ghana, West Africa, and is retold
here in Caribbean speech rhythms by its Jamaican-raised author. Anancy makes a
series of trades: a corn cob for a gourd of water, the water for a yam, and so on. In his
attempt to trade a sack of corn flour for an elephant, he becomes distracted by a bird
and ends up with nothing. Hence, the tale explains the saying, "Don't leave an
elephant . . ." In one of the trades, a woman gives Anancy one of her children. As the
author explains in his author's note, the sharing of a child is common is the culture;
this arrangement may need to be explained to children.

Chocolate, Deborah M. Newton. *Imani in the Belly.* Illustrated by Alex Boies. Mahwah,
NJ: BridgeWater Books, 1994.

Imani, an East African woman, must travel a long distance to sell her crops at
market. In her absence, Simba, the King of Beasts, thunders into Imani's house and
swallows her children. Imani is advised in a dream to get meat, sticks, and stones and
to act on her faith. She herself is then swallowed by Simba. In his belly she finds other
villagers and her children. She uses her supplies to feed the people and help them

escape. While there is no overt trick here, Imani is using her wits against a more powerful, bullying creature. The African flavor of the text and illustrations is very appealing to primary grades.

Diakité, Baba Wagué. *The Hunterman and the Crocodile: A West African Tale.* Illustrated by the author. New York: Scholastic, 1997.

This simply told tale illustrates the interdependence between humans and animals and teaches the lesson that humans belong with, not in power over, animals. A hunterman comes upon a family of crocodiles far from the river. They were on a pilgrimage, but their food has run out, and they beg the man to carry them back to the river. They promise not to bite him, so he ties them up and carries them on his head. At the river, they beg him to take them deep into the river's current. Now one crocodile takes the man's hand in his mouth, reminding him he needs a meal. The man argues with the hungry crocodile and asks the other animals to side with him. One by one, the animals state that since humans have treated them badly, they will not stand up for him. At last the man asks clever Rabbit, who expresses disbelief that any man could carry a stack of crocodiles on his head. The crocodile insists it is true, and he reassembles the crocodiles to prove it. Once they are again stacked and tied, Rabbit laughs and tells the hunterman to take them home for a meal. However, when he gets home, he discovers that his wife is ill and can recover only with a dose of crocodile tears. The man and the crocodiles all cry and make peace, the crocodiles give their tears for the wife's cure, and hunterman learns a lesson about living in harmony with nature.

Haley, Gail E. *A Story, A Story: An African Tale.* Illustrated by the author. New York: Atheneum, 1970.

In this well-known Caldecott winner, Anansi wants all the stories of the world, but they are kept in a box by Nyame, the sky god. Nyame agrees to give Anansi the box if he performs three seemingly impossible tasks. Anansi accomplishes all three tasks through his tricky plotting. He is awarded the box of stories, which he opens, allowing the stories to float up and out to the whole world. Compare the "gum baby" scene to the "tar baby" scene in the Brer Rabbit story in *The Tales of Uncle Remus* by Julius Lester.

How Anansi Obtained the Sky God's Stories: An African Folktale from the Ashanti Tribe. Illustrated by Janice Skivington. Told by Donna Washington. Chicago: Children's Press, 1991. Audiocassette and book kit.

This wordless picture book, accompanied by an audiotape of the story, is similar to Haley's *A Story, A Story.* Anansi the spider wants all the world's stories, so he asks Nyame, the sky god, for them. Nyame assigns three difficult tasks to Anansi, which he accomplishes through trickery. Nyane then gives Anansi the stories. This book/tape kit works well for students with special needs in speech or reading or for ESL students.

Kimmel, Eric. *Anansi and the Moss-Covered Rock.* Illustrated by Janet Stevens. New York: Holiday House, 1988.

Anansi discovers a rock that can cause individuals to become unconscious for an hour. Anansi uses the rock to trick his jungle friends out of their food. However, a clever Little Bush Deer spies on these events and later turns the trick on Anansi. Students enjoy finding the bush deer hiding on each page.

———. *Anansi and the Talking Melon.* Illustrated by Janet Stevens. New York: Holiday House, 1994.

Anansi bores a hole into a melon in Elephant's garden and eats until he is too bloated to crawl out. From inside the melon, Anansi speaks through the hole, tricking the other animals into believing the melon can speak. When the animals take the melon to the king, the humor reaches its peak. The melon does not speak for the king, who repeatedly talks to the melon until the melon ridicules the king for talking to melons. This final insult establishes Anansi once again as a masterful mischief-maker.

———. *Anansi and the Talking Melon.* Pine Plains, NY: Live Oak Media, 1994. Videocassette.
This 11-minute reading of the book above uses Janet Stevens's illustrations. The animals' voices and sound effects add to the humor of the story.

———. *Anansi Goes Fishing.* Illustrated by Janet Stevens. New York: Holiday House, 1992.
Anansi goes fishing with Turtle. Turtle explains that fishing is hard work and that Anansi can either work or get tired. Anansi is irritated to find that he is doing all the work in order to avoid the other option, getting tired. His skill at weaving fishnets is still evident today in all spiders' webs. Compare with *Anansi Finds a Fool* by Verna Aardema.

———. *Anansi Goes Fishing.* Pine Plains, NY: Live Oak Media, 1993. Audiocassette.
This well-done reading of the Kimmel book above is complete with different character voices for Turtle and Anansi. The reading is slow enough for most primary students to have an easy time following along in the book. This is a good choice for classroom learning centers.

Knutson, Barbara. *Sungura and Leopard: A Swahili Trickster Tale.* Illustrated by the author. Boston: Little, Brown, 1993.
Sungura, a hare, is featured in this retelling from Tanzania. Both Leopard and Sungura unwittingly build the same house on the same site, each working independently. Unaware of the other's activity, they credit their ancestors for helping them. Once they realize that both claim ownership, they try cohabiting, which tries Leopard's nerves. Sungura and his wife conspire to intimidate Leopard by talking of their fierce hunger for Leopard meat. The aggravation proves too much for Leopard, who flees, leaving Sungura with the house.

McDermott, Gerald. *Anansi the Spider: A Tale from the Ashanti.* Illustrated by the author. New York: Henry Holt, 1972.
Anansi gets into trouble, and his six sons use their clever and unique powers to rescue him. At home that night, Anansi finds a glowing orb, and he wants to give it to the son who helped him most. He asks the god Nyame to help him decide. Nyame and Anansi see that each son helped an equal amount. Nyame places the ball of light into the sky; it becomes the moon. This book features simple writing and large text for primary grades.

———. *Zomo the Rabbit: A Trickster Tale from West Africa.* Illustrated by the author. New York: Harcourt Brace Jovanovich, 1992.
Zomo, as the refrain in the story states, is not big or strong, but he is clever. He wants wisdom from the Sky God. The Sky God tells Zomo he must do three difficult tasks, which he accomplishes through his cleverness. Many primary students will be able to read this attractively illustrated book independently. Compare with *A Story, A Story* by Gail Haley.

McKissack, Patricia. *Monkey-Monkey's Trick: Based on an African Folk Tale.* Step Into Reading, A Step 2 Book. Illustrated by Paul Meisel. New York: Random House, 1988.
Monkey-Monkey discovers that Hyena has been tricking him out of his stew, so Monkey-Monkey devises his own tricks to get Hyena to help him build his house. The tricks involve animal disguises, and children with sharp eyes can detect clues hiding in the illustrations of this tale of double trickery. This easy-reader book is suitable for independent reading by primary students.

McNeil, Heather. *Hyena and the Moon: Stories to Listen to from Kenya.* World Folklore Series. Performed by the author. Englewood, CO: Libraries Unlimited, 1995. Audiocassette.

Expertly performed by storyteller Heather McNeil, these tales have a dramatic effect. Three are trickster tales. In "Not So!" Mama Simba brags about her children so much that Mama Baboon is annoyed. She tells Simba off, and Simba doesn't forget. Simba steals Baboon's children and won't give them back unless another animal looks her in the eyes and tells her she is in the wrong. The only animal brave enough to do so is clever Ground Squirrel. He organizes the baboons to help him deliver the message "Not So!" and still escape with his life. In "Rabbit's Drum," Elephant is eating the farmer's crops, and he calls a meeting to get help. Rabbit hides inside a pumpkin, which is then swallowed by Elephant. Rabbit then drums with a stick inside Elephant. Elephant runs until he is so tired he is caught. In "Water, Water Will Be Mine," Sungura the lazy rabbit uses the "briar patch" motif to escape punishment from Lion. All of the stories are very entertaining; McNeil's use of an African accent and different voices for her characters contribute to a delightful storytelling experience for all ages. (Note: These stories are also available in book form: *Hyena and the Moon: Stories to Tell from Kenya.* Englewood, CO: Libraries Unlimited, 1994.)

Mollel, Tololwa M. *Ananse's Feast: An Ashanti Tale.* Illustrated by Andrew Glass. New York: Clarion Books, 1997.

The familiar motivation of food is central to this tale readable by primary-grade children. Ananse is cooking himself a feast. Akye the turtle smells the food and pays Ananse a visit. Ananse is reluctant to share his food, so when Akye begins to eat, Ananse stops him. He says that Akye's hands are dirty, and he must wash them, as the rules of manners dictate in Ananse's house. Akye plods to the river to wash while Ananse gobbles up a large portion of the food. By the time Akye returns, the rice and beans are gone, and his hands are dirty again. Ananse makes him go wash a second time, and he consumes more of the food while the turtle is gone. This happens a third time, and Ananse polishes off the remaining food. Akye remains polite. Later, Akye invites Ananse to his own home at the bottom of the river for a meal. Eager Ananse finds he cannot sink to the bottom until he puts rocks into the pockets of his robe. This time, the tables are turned on Ananse. When Ananse is about to eat, Akye tells him that the manners of his home require that he remove his robe. When he does, Ananse's light body floats up, and he cannot partake of the feast.

———. *The Flying Tortoise: An Igbo Tale.* Illustrated by Barbara Spurll. New York: Clarion Books, 1994.

Both a trickster and a pourquoi tale, this story features a trick played back on the trickster. Like many tricksters, Mbeku the tortoise is always scheming ways to get food. When he hears that the birds have been invited to a feast in Skyland, he convinces the birds that he should go, too. He gets the birds and his friend, Lizard, to make him some wings to fly to Skyland. He tells the birds that Skylanders like special names and that his special name is "Aaaaalllll-of-You." At the Skylanders' feast, the king says that the feast is for "Aaaaalllll of you." Tortoise explains to the birds that he is to eat first. Tortoise eats all the food, and the infuriated birds tear off his feathers so he can't fly back to Earth. He cries piteously, and the birds agree to help him get home by constructing a pile of soft things for Tortoise to land on. However, one bird overhears Tortoise calling all the birds fools, so in counter-trickster fashion, the birds construct a pile of hard things instead. When Tortoise falls to Earth and lands on the pile, his shell cracks. His embarrassment is the reason tortoises pull their heads inside their shells. Text and illustrations are very appealing to primary and middle grades.

——. *The King and the Tortoise.* Illustrated by Kathy Blankley. New York: Clarion, 1993.

In this tale from Cameroon, a king believes himself to be the most clever person in the world. He challenges all the creatures: Anyone who can make him a robe of smoke will be named the most clever of all. Many creatures try and fail, and then Tortoise steps up. Tortoise tells the king that to make a robe of smoke, he needs a thread of fire. Everyone is speechless. Then the king smiles with appreciation for Tortoise's match of wits.

——. *Shadow Dance.* Illustrated by Donna Perrone. New York: Clarion Books, 1998.

Set in Tanzania, this tale features a rescue, followed by an attempt to victimize the girl who rescues the creature. A little girl, Salome, hears a cry for help. She finds a crocodile trapped in a gully. After she pulls him out with vine ropes, he appeals piteously for further assistance to guide him back into the river. There he grabs her, threatening to eat her. The girl pleads for mercy. Crocodile says he will release her if she can give a good reason for him to do so. She asks a nearby tree to support her, but the tree declares that girls just ignore her, so why should she care for the girl? Then Salome asks a cow, who says that she, too, has been abandoned by the girl who used to care for her. Then a pigeon wants to help. The pigeon challenges the situation and gets Crocodile to reposition himself in the gully to prove the story. Now Salome is free. Compare with *The Hunterman and the Crocodile* by Baba Wagué Diakité. Story and text are for first grade and up.

Seeger, Pete. *Abiyoyo: Based on a South African Lullaby and Folk Story.* Illustrated by Michael Hays. New York: Macmillan, 1986.

This is a short retelling of the beloved story about the boy who sings a song to get the fearsome giant to dance. The faster the boy sings, the more the giant dances. Finally, the giant falls to the ground. Once the giant is on the ground, the boy's father uses his magic wand to make the giant disappear. This story is suitable for all ages.

Sierra, Judy. *The Elephant's Wrestling Match.* Illustrated by Brian Pinkney. New York: Lodestar Books, 1992.

An elephant boastfully challenges all animals to a wrestling match. One by one, the animals try: the leopard, the crocodile, even the rhinoceros. Finally, a little bat challenges the elephant. Bat can quickly evade the elephant, and then she flies into his ear. The pain brings the elephant down.

——. *The Mean Hyena: A Folktale from Malawi.* Illustrated by Michael Bryant. New York: Lodestar Books, 1997.

Mean Hyena plays a trick on Tortoise: He picks him up, sticks him in the branches of a tree, and leaves him. The next day, Tortoise decides to make something of his predicament, so from his place in the tree, he offers to give the animals new coats. He paints stripes on the plain white zebra and spots on the plain leopard. Hyena now wants a new coat, too, so Tortoise takes the opportunity to play a trick back on him. He dabs blobs of sticky tree gum all over Hyena's fur, which attracts sticks and burrs and mats of fur. When others laugh at him, Hyena laughs back, as though he meant to make everyone laugh. The story ends with a lesson to think before playing tricks because they could backfire on you. This is a simple story for primary grades, with pourquoi explanations for the traits of several animals.

Souhami, Jessica. *The Leopard's Drum: An Asante Tale from West Africa.* Illustrated by the author. Boston: Little, Brown, 1995.

The lowly tortoise tricks the leopard and wins his hard shell in this tale. Proud Osebo, the leopard, has a large drum, which is coveted by all the animals. Nyame the Sky-God wants the drum so much that he promises a reward to the animal who can get it from Osebo. Many animals try, but they back off from Osebo's fearful presence. The little soft-shelled tortoise tricks Osebo into proving he can fit inside his drum. Once Osebo is inside, the tortoise seals up the bottom of the drum with a pot and takes it to the Sky-God. When Nyame offers a reward, the tortoise asks for a tough, hard shell as protection from the larger animals. Short, simply told, and brightly colored, this book is appropriate for primary-grade readers. Compare with *A Story, A Story* by Gail Haley, in which Anansi plays tricks and collects a reward from the sky-god.

AFRICAN AMERICAN

Bang, Molly. *Wiley and the Hairy Man: Adapted from an American Folk Tale.* Ready-to-Read. Illustrated by the author. New York: Aladdin Books, 1976 (reissued 1996).

The big, ugly, mean Hairy Man lives in the swamp, and he intends to get Wiley with his magical powers and brutish ways. Both a trickster and transformation tale, this story features frequent shifts of power as Wiley and Hairy Man match wits. Wiley and his mother outwit the Hairy Man three times so that he'll never bother them again. The large typeface and easy reader format make this a candidate for independent reading by primary students. An audiocassette version of this folktale is dramatically told by Diane Ferlatte.

Faulkner, William J. *Brer Tiger and the Big Wind.* Illustrated by Roberta Wilson. New York: Morrow Junior Books, 1995.

There is a drought, and the only food and drink are guarded by selfish Brer Tiger. Brer Rabbit hatches a plan in which all the animals cooperate, tricking Brer Tiger into believing that a big wind could carry him away. Tiger begs Brer Rabbit to tie him to a tree so that he won't get blown off the face of the earth. The tale ends with the animals getting the food they need, and Brer Rabbit gives a gentle reminder about sharing food with those in need.

Ferlatte, Diane. *Diane Ferlatte: Favorite Stories.* Performed by the author. Oakland, CA: Diane Ferlatte, 1991. Audiocassette.

Ferlatte's telling of five African American stories is animated, authentic, and enjoyable. The tape includes "Wiley and the Hairy Man," in which Wiley and his mother outwit the frightening Hairy Man. Ferlatte's voice modulations make this telling quite dramatic.

Hamilton, Virginia. *Her Stories: African American Folktales, Fairy Tales, and True Tales.* Illustrated by Leo and Diane Dillon. New York: Blue Sky Press, 1995.

This highly acclaimed collection of stories features a wide range of African American stories "of the female kind," including a trickster tale and several transformation tales, as well as pourquoi tales, tales of the supernatural, and biographical stories. In the first story, "Little Girl and Buh Rabby," the rabbit Buh Rabby tricks the farmer's daughter into letting him into the garden. The girl's father captures the rabbit in a gunnysack, but Buh Rabby later tricks his way out by convincing Wolf to change places with him. Compare this telling with "Mr. Rabbit and Mr. Bear" in *The Knee-High Man and Other Tales* by Julius Lester.

———. *When Birds Could Talk & Bats Could Sing: The Adventures of Bruh Sparrow, Sis Wren, and Their Friends.* Illustrated by Barry Moser. New York: Blue Sky Press, 1996.

These eight tales, all featuring birds, are filled with numerous pourquoi explanations, and each states a sassy moral at the end. One story features the trickster element of stealing fire from the powerful Firekeeper. In "Blue Jay and Swallow Take the Heat," Bruh Blue Jay steals a fire chunk to help out a cold, sick child. Firekeeper sees him and chases him, and Jay drops the fire chunk. Miss Swallow then picks up the fire chunk, unbeknownst to Firekeeper. She holds on to the hot coal despite a harrowing chase and delivers it to the boy's door. Although young children could enjoy some of these stories, the subtle and sophisticated humor is better suited to middle and older grades.

Harris, Joel Chandler. *Jump! The Adventures of Brer Rabbit.* Adapted by Van Dyke Parks and Malcolm Jones. Illustrated by Barry Moser. New York: Harcourt Brace Jovanovich, 1986.

This is a collection of five Brer Rabbit tales. Superb illustrations by Barry Moser capture the characters well. A notable tale is "The Moon in the Millpond," which features the trick of using the moon's reflection on water to make fools of the animals. Dialect and dense text make these volumes best suited to read aloud. Additional books by the authors: *Jump Again! More Adventures of Brer Rabbit* (1987) and *Jump on Over! The Adventures of Brer Rabbit and His Family* (1989).

Hayward, Linda. *All Stuck Up.* Step Into Reading. A Step 1 Book. Illustrated by Normand Chartier. New York: Random House, 1990.

This is an easy-reader version of "Brer Rabbit and the Tar Baby," perfect for independent reading by primary students.

———. *Hello, House!* Step Into Reading. A Step 1 Book. Illustrated by Lynn Munsinger. New York: Random House, 1988.

This is an easy-reader version of "Heyo House," in which Brer Rabbit exposes Brer Wolf, who is hiding in Brer Rabbit's house. Brer Rabbit dupes Brer Wolf into thinking the house can talk.

Jaquith, Priscilla. *Bo Rabbit Smart for True: Tall Tales from the Gullah.* Illustrated by Ed Young. New York: Philomel Books, 1995.

Six tales told in modified Gullah dialect are accompanied by an informative essay on Gullah, source notes, and a bibliography. From the Sea Islands off Georgia and South Carolina, these tales make entertaining read-alouds, although the format of the book (it must be held 90° from the usual) and its tiny drawings may be problematic in large-group settings. The dialect gives a full flavor of the unique storytelling style without interfering with understanding. Some stories are more akin to fables, while some are true tricksters. "Bo Rabbit Smart for True" describes the same tug-of-war trick found in the Brazilian tale *James the Vine Puller* by Martha Stiles. In "Manners for True," Fox invites Crane to dinner, but he serves it in a shallow saucer so that Crane can't use his long beak. Crane returns the trick by serving soup in a tall jar that Fox can't get into. "Rattlesnake's Word" is the story of Snake getting stuck under a big fallen branch and his attempts to get the other animals to help him escape.

Lester, Julius. *The Knee-High Man and Other Tales.* Illustrated by Ralph Pinto. New York: Dial Press, 1972.

In this collection of six tales, "Mr. Rabbit and Mr. Bear" makes a particularly humorous read-aloud. Mr. Rabbit gets the farmer's daughter to let him into the garden. When the farmer strings up Mr. Rabbit to teach him a lesson, Mr. Rabbit tricks Mr. Bear into switching places with him. This tale can provide a springboard to a creative writing activity. Read to students the descriptive words preceding the word "lettuce." Count them together. Challenge students to write a short story in which they use many varied descriptive words. Compare with Lester's "Brer Rabbit in Mr. Man's Garden" in *From Sea to Shining Sea.*

———. *The Tales of Uncle Remus: The Adventures of Brer Rabbit* (1987); *More Tales of Uncle Remus: Further Adventures of Brer Rabbit, His Friends, Enemies, and Others* (1988); *Further Tales of Uncle Remus: The Misadventures of Brer Rabbit, Brer Fox, Brer Wolf, the Doodang, and Other Creatures* (1990); *The Last Tales of Uncle Remus* (1994). Illustrated by Jerry Pinkney. New York: Dial Books.

These are definitive collections of the Brer Rabbit tales. The tales are fairly short and use dialect. Pre-read for age appropriateness. These are good sources for storytelling, reading aloud, and for research. Humor abounds in the text and the illustrations.

MacDonald, Margaret Read. *Pickin' Peas.* Illustrated by Pat Cummings. New York: HarperCollins, 1998.

Lively narrative, punctuated by short bursts of song and vibrant illustrations, provides a playful mood for this tale of mischief. A girl plants and picks her own garden of peas, but she discovers and captures a rabbit munching her crop. She puts him in a box, but soon his singing and dancing are so intriguing that she lets him out of the box to perform. Rabbit tricks the girl into letting him dance closer and closer to the window, until he hops out and away. Text and story are for primary grade reading or reading aloud. Compare with *The Dancing Turtle* by Pleasant DeSpain.

Metaxas, Eric, adapter. *Brer Rabbit and the Wonderful Tar Baby.* Performed by Danny Glover. Story by Joel Chandler Harris; music by Taj Mahal. Compact disc, Windam Hill WD-0716. Also available as audiocassette and book: Simon & Schuster Children's Books, 1993. Also available as a videocassette: Rabbit Ears Productions, 1990.

Using music by Taj Mahal and narration by Danny Glover, the tale is told of Brer Fox's catching Brer Rabbit with a tar baby and how Brer Rabbit finagles his way out of trouble. The telling is 22 minutes long; the rest of the selections on the CD feature the background music only.

Sanfield, Steve. *The Adventures of High John the Conqueror.* Illustrated by John Ward. New York: Orchard, 1989.

This collection of 16 tales is for older children. John, or High John, is a Black slave who uses his wits to get out of scrapes with his White so-called master. He always ends up looking like a "good" slave to the so-called master, but the joke is really on the master. These stories are good read-alouds for middle and upper grades. Be sure to explain that "John" stories were told among slaves as a way to cope with their oppression.

Sierra, Judy. *Wiley and the Hairy Man.* Illustrated by Brian Pinkney. New York: Lodestar Books, 1996.

This is essentially the same story line as the version by Molly Bang. However, Pinkney's illustrations are more vivid and dramatic, and the Hairy Man is more vicious-looking. Bang's telling is an established favorite and is easier for primary-aged readers. Use this version for comparison.

Stevens, Janet. *Tops & Bottoms.* Illustrated by the author. New York: Harcourt Brace, 1995.

In this Caldecott honor book, clever Hare is in debt and has a family to feed, so he makes a business deal with Bear. Hare and family plant vegetables on Bear's land, promising to pay him either tops or bottoms. Three seasons in a row, Hare gets all the crops, no matter how Bear changes the contract.

Young, Richard Alan, and Judy Dockrey Young. *African-American Folktales for Young Readers: Including Favorite Stories from African and African-American Storytellers.* Little Rock, AR: August House, 1993.

Both African and African American, these 31 short tales can be told or read aloud. A section of eight trickster tales is included. Especially successful are "Why Anansi has a Narrow Waist" and "Anansi and Turtle." This is a good resource for teachers and librarians.

AMERICAN

Doucet, Sharon Arms. *Why Lapin's Ears Are Long: And Other Tales from the Louisiana Bayou*. Illustrated by David Catrow. New York: Orchard, 1997.

Compère Lapin (Brother Rabbit) is the cunning trickster in these Cajun and Creole tales with pourquoi elements. In "Why Lapin's Ears Are Long," Compère Lapin wants to be bigger so he can get some respect. He asks Madame Tortue to work a spell on him. She first requires three impossible tasks, which Lapin accomplishes by trickery. Being only an amateur, Madame Tortue cannot pull off a magic spell, so she pulls Lapin's ears instead. As Lapin's ears lengthen, Tortue stumbles backward into her own conjure pot. In "Why Lapin's Tail Is Short," Lapin offers to teach Alligator what trouble is. He pours syrup between Alligator's toes to attract the wasps and bees to Alligator's softest flesh. Later, Lapin starts a bragging contest with Alligator about who has more relatives, and he gets the alligators to line up across the bayou under the pretense of counting them. In reality, he just wants an easy bridge to the other side of the water, but at last, Alligator snaps at Rabbit's fine long tail, leaving it a mere puff of fur to this day. In the final tale, Lapin figures a way to win a contest for the hand of his beloved in marriage. Cajun dialect and humorous illustrations make this a read-aloud delight for all ages.

Hayes, Joe. *Watch Out for Clever Women! Hispanic Folktales*. Illustrated by Vicki Trego Hill. El Paso, TX: Cinco Puntos Press, 1994.

This collection of five tales from the Hispanic Southwest features poor women or couples locked in a money struggle with powerful, wealthy, unscrupulous characters. In each case, the humble woman quietly turns the scoundrel's trick back on himself. Tellings are straightforward, with a few black-and-white drawings. Use as effective read-alouds and discussion-starters for middle or upper grades.

Reneaux, J. J. *Why Alligator Hates Dog: A Cajun Folktale*. Illustrated by Donnie Lee Green. Little Rock, AR: August House LittleFolk, 1995.

M'su Cocodrie (Mr. Alligator) has the respect of everyone except that taunting Dog. One day, Dog, in the frenzy of chasing a rabbit, finds himself face-to-face with M'su Cocodrie. Dog slyly diverts M'su Cocodrie by promising to give him the "juicy scraps" fed to him by Man. Once Alligator gets up on Man's porch, Dog barks for Man, who beats M'su Cocodrie with a broom. M'su Cocodrie gets away and lies in wait for Dog to this very day. Told simply and with Cajun flair, this is a humorous trickster/pourquoi tale for primary grades and up.

Sloat, Teri. *Sody Sallyratus*. Illustrated by the author. New York: Dutton Children's Books, 1997.

Told in mountain dialect, this traditional Appalachian tale recounts the story of a family and their clever pet squirrel. The old woman is about to start a batch of baking soda biscuits, but she's out of sody salyratus. She sends the boy to the store, but on his way back he stops to pick berries and is eaten by a big black bear. Back home, they wonder what happened to the boy, so the old woman sends the little girl to find him. The same thing happens to the girl, then to the old man, and finally to the old woman. When the pet squirrel decides to check on the family, he meets the bear. The squirrel leads the bear on a chase up a tree. The bear boasts that he can climb and jump just like the squirrel. So the squirrel leaps to another tree, and when the bear attempts the feat, he falls. Out pop the boy, the girl, the man, and the woman. This is a good read-aloud for primary grades.

ASIAN

Cambodian

Ho, Minfong, and Saphan Ros. *Brother Rabbit: A Cambodian Tale.* Illustrated by Jennifer Hewitson. New York: Lothrop, Lee & Shepard, 1997.

Brother Rabbit sails through a series of five tricks in this tale for primary and middle grades. First, by making promises, he persuades a crocodile to give him a ride across the river. Next, he plays dead so that a woman puts him in her basket for dinner. While in the basket, Rabbit eats her bananas. Then the crocodile, vowing to pay Rabbit back for his last trick, pretends to be a log floating on the water. Rabbit, seeing this, says loudly that if it is a log, it will float upstream, and if it is a crocodile, it will float downstream. The crocodile, hearing this, "floats" upstream, falling for the trick. Then Rabbit insults some elephants to get their help in yanking him free from some tree resin. Finally, Rabbit gets careless, and walks into the crocodile's mouth, thinking it is dead. When the crocodile snaps his jaws shut, Rabbit wastes no time tormenting the beast from its insides, until he begs Rabbit to get out.

Spagnoli, Cathy. *Judge Rabbit and the Tree Spirit: A Folktale from Cambodia.* Told by Lina Mao Wall. Illustrated by Nancy Hom. San Francisco: Children's Book Press, 1991.

A young couple's happiness is disrupted when the husband is called away to war. A tree spirit, seeing the husband's regret at leaving, assumes the shape of the husband and goes to live with the wife. When the real husband returns, no one can prove who the true husband is. Judge Rabbit settles it by declaring that the true husband can fit inside a bottle. The tree spirit moves into the bottle, and Judge Rabbit seals it up, proving even spirits can be fooled.

Chinese

Yep, Laurence. *The Man Who Tricked a Ghost.* Illustrated by Isadore Seltzer. Mahwah, NJ: BridgeWater Books, 1993.

Sung is not afraid of ghosts. While on the road alone at night, he meets a fearsome and powerful ghost who is out to get a man named Sung who says he is not afraid of ghosts. Sung tricks the ghost into telling him what ghosts fear most. Armed with this knowledge, Sung is able to put the ghost out of its scary business forever. The illustrations are effective.

Filipino

San Souci, Robert D. *Pedro and the Monkey.* Illustrated by Michael Hays. New York: Morrow Junior Books, 1996.

A poor young Filipino farmer traps a pesky monkey who is stealing his corn. The monkey begs to be let go. Pedro agrees, and the monkey promises to arrange Pedro's marriage to Maria, the daughter of a rich landowner, Don Francisco. The monkey first asks Don Francisco to borrow his ganta-measure, a box usually used to measure rice, to measure his master's money. The monkey impresses Don Francisco, who wonders who could be so wealthy that he needs a ganta-measure to count his coins. The monkey next arranges for Pedro to have a fine set of clothes and a dinner with Maria, and the two fall in love. Next, the monkey goes to the mansion of a giant. He tells the giant that an ogre is coming. The giant flees, and the monkey takes over the mansion as Pedro's. Now that he has a fine home, Pedro can marry Maria. This Filipino variant of *Puss in Boots* makes a delightful read-aloud for first through fourth grades.

Indian

Demi. *One Grain of Rice: A Mathematical Folktale*. New York: Scholastic, 1997.

The added benefit of a dramatic lesson in mathematics enhances this tale. A greedy raja requires all the people of his province to give him most of their rice crop for safekeeping, year after year. During a famine, he reneges on his promise to share the stores. When a girl named Rani sees rice trickling from the basket of a royal elephant, she catches it in her skirt. With a clever plan in mind, she returns the spilled rice to the raja, who offers her a reward. Rani asks only for one grain of rice. When the raja insists on more, Rani asks for double the rice each day for 30 days, hence, two grains of rice on the second day, four on the third day, and so on. On the 30th day, the raja must give Rani over a billion grains of rice, and all his stores have been depleted. Rani gives her rice to the people and offers one basket to the raja if he promises to take only what he needs from now on. The story is appealing for all ages, from primary grades through adult. The math concept is something to ponder for older children and adults; all children would benefit from using concrete materials, such as real grains of rice, to begin to understand the doubling concept. Compare with *The Token Gift* by Hugh McKibbon.

McKibbon, Hugh William. *The Token Gift*. Illustrated by Scott Cameron. New York: Annick Press, 1996.

This tale of trickery recounts the origins of the game of chess and dramatizes a mathematical principle as well. An old man is given the title Rajrishi, the "wise one." He laments that he has not been a king and made a true improvement in the world. His wife reminds him that he has indeed made a difference. She reminds him that as a young man, he devised a game of strategy called Chaturanga. It became popular all over the country, and its production made him wealthy. Now, the king summons the Rajrishi to the palace. The king commends the Rajrishi for his invention of the game and asks him to name a suitable reward. At first, the Rajrishi tells the king he has no wants, but the king commands the Rajrishi to name a reward. The Rajrishi tells the king he would like one grain of rice for the first square of the game board, two grains for the second, four for the third, eight for the fourth, and so on. As the request is fulfilled, it becomes evident that doubling the rice for each of the board's 64 squares totals more rice than there is in the world. The king, distressed that he cannot fulfill the promise, steps down and installs the Rajrishi as king. As king, the Rajrishi makes one decree: to reinstate the original king. Why? Because the Rajrishi tricked the king with cleverness, but he believes that honor is more important than cleverness. Compare with *One Grain of Rice* by Demi.

Wolf, Gita. *The Very Hungry Lion: A Folktale*. Illustrated by Indrapramit Roy. New York: Annick Press, 1996.

This book is an exceptional work of art; bright stylized silk-screened images stand out on textured paper. Singam the lion thinks he's going to get several meals of fresh meat this day at the market, but all three of his prey elude him with humorous results. First, Kuruvi the sparrow sends Singam to the market for ingredients to make the feast more complete. Singam takes the train, which results in disaster. Next, Singam finds Adu the lamb tethered at the market. Adu convinces Singam he needs seasoning and roasting equipment from the village. At the village, the people throw things at him to get rid of him. Finally, Singam plans to eat Maan the deer. Maan tells Singam he has a message for him from another lion written on his hind foot. When Singam looks at the foot, Maan gives him a kick. Defeated, Singam decides that hunting, not the market-place, is the best way to get a meal after all. This book is suitable for primary and middle grades.

Japanese

Long, Jan Freeman. *The Bee and the Dream: A Japanese Tale*. Illustrated by Kaoru Ono. New York: Dutton Children's Books, 1996.

Shin and his friend, out gathering firewood to sell, take a short nap. Shin sees a bee fly out of his sleeping friend's nose. Upon awakening, the friend remarks that he had a dream about golden treasure buried in a jar under a bush in a rich man's garden. Shin insists it is a sign to be acted upon and, finding the rich man, explains about the location of the gold. The rich man digs up the jar to keep for himself, but he finds inside it a swarm of bees rather than gold. He buries it back in the ground and lets Shin dig it up. Much to his shame, Shin finds just an empty jar, and he returns home with a heavy heart. His wife greets him, excitedly showing him the riches in their house, which appeared after a swarm of bees flew through. This story is suitable for all ages.

Korean

Han, Oki S., and Stephanie Haboush Plunkett. *Sir Whong and the Golden Pig*. Illustrated by Oki S. Han. New York: Dial Books for Young Readers, 1993.

A stranger approaches wealthy Sir Whong and asks to borrow one thousand nyung. He gives Sir Whong a golden pig as collateral, promising to pay him back in a year. The stranger squanders the money, while the pig corrodes, proving it was not a valuable gold object after all. Sir Whong then cleverly tricks the man into returning the money.

Han, Suzanne Crowder. *The Rabbit's Escape*. Illustrated by Yumi Heo. New York: Henry Holt, 1995.

The Dragon King of the Sea is ill and can be cured only with the fresh raw liver of a rabbit. The sea creatures have never seen a rabbit, and travel to land is dangerous. Turtle is selected for the mission, and when he brings Rabbit to the sea kingdom, Rabbit states he has not brought his liver with him. He tricks his way back to land, where a god gives Turtle some ginseng roots to cure the King. This is also a pourquoi tale explaining the origin of the use of ginseng as a medicine. Written bilingually, in Korean and English. Illustrations are fanciful and surreal.

————. *The Rabbit's Judgment*. Illustrated by Yumi Heo. New York: Henry Holt, 1994.

A man helps a tiger get out of a deep pit. In return, the tiger announces he is going to eat the man. The man protests, begging to get the opinion of others in this case. They ask a tree and then an ox; both say the tiger should eat the man. The man asks for one more opinion, from a rabbit. The rabbit tells the two to return to their original positions at the pit. He then judges that the tiger should remain in the pit.

Malaysian

Day, Noreha Yussof. *Kancil and the Crocodiles: A Tale from Malaysia*. Illustrated by Britta Teckentrup. New York: Simon & Schuster Books for Young Readers, 1996.

Kancil, the mouse deer, and a tortoise trick 27 crocodiles into making a bridge across the river, so that they can get to the other side, where the juicy fruit tree is. Kancil tells the crocodiles that they need to line up and be counted because the king is having a party for them. They comply, and once Kancil and his friend are safely across the river, they tell the crocodiles there is no party. Kancil and the tortoise are safe, but now they have no way back. This tale is suitable for primary grades. Compare with "The Monkey's Heart" in *The Dial Book of Animal Tales from Around the World* by Naomi Adler and with "Crocodile! Crocodile!" in *Crocodile! Crocodile!* by Barbara Baumgartner.

AUSTRALIAN/NEW ZEALAND/POLYNESIAN/HAWAIIAN

Bishop, Gavin. *Māui and the Sun: A Maori Tale.* Illustrated by the author. New York: North-South Books, 1996.

In this New Zealand telling of a Polynesian tale, Māui the trickster gets the sun to move across the sky more slowly. Māui and his brothers don't have enough time to go fishing because the sun races across the sky so fast that the day ends too soon. Māui talks his brothers into helping him catch the sun. They gather flax and make ropes. Then they travel for weeks until they get to the pit where the sun sleeps. They stretch a net of rope over the pit and hold tight as the sun rises. Māui beats on the sun with his enchanted weapon (the jawbone of his grandmother). The sun cries and reveals his secret name. The knowledge of this secret gives Māui power over the sun, so he makes the sun move slowly. However, now the sun goes so slowly that it stays out for months, scorching everything. Māui then ties one end of a rope around the sun and the other end around the moon, obtaining a balance of night and day. This humorous tale is suitable for middle grades.

Wardlaw, Lee. *Punia and the King of Sharks: A Hawaiian Folktale.* Illustrated by Felipe Davalos. New York: Dial Books for Young Readers, 1997.

Punia and his mother are hungry. Punia's father used to fish for them, but once while diving in a lobster cave, he was eaten by sharks. Yearning for lobster meat, Punia devises a plan to distract the sharks so that he can dive into the cave. The plan works, and the sharks are angry. The next time, Punia's trick is to offer the sharks gourds full of sticky *poi* to eat; the sharks get their teeth stuck long enough for Punia to steal more lobsters. A third trick works as well. In a final show-down with the King of Sharks, Punia stages a fake volcano eruption, but ends up narrowly escaping the King of Sharks' teeth. He tricks the King of Sharks into swimming into shallow waters, where he becomes beached in the sand. The King of Sharks begs for help in getting dislodged. Punia and the villagers aid him only after he agrees to live far away from the lobster cave. This humorous narrative is appealing to primary grades and readable by second grade and up.

Williams, Julie Stewart. *Māui Goes Fishing.* Illustrated by Robin Yoko Burningham. Honolulu: University of Hawaii Press, 1991.

Māui, a trickster, fishes daily with his three brothers but never catches anything. After much teasing by his brothers, Māui starts catching fish by slipping the hooks out of his brothers' catches and claiming them as his own. His brothers tire of this trick and refuse to take him fishing with them anymore. So to persuade them, Māui makes a magic fishhook for them. He instructs his brothers that when the line begins to pull, they must all paddle home, and they must not look back to see what is on the line. Finally, they feel a powerful pull, and the sea gets rough. Māui yells to keep paddling, but then the brothers look back to see what's going on. At that moment the line breaks. What they see is land where before there was only sea! They have fished up from the bottom of the sea the islands of Hawaii. This trickster/pourquoi tale is for primary and middle grades.

CENTRAL AMERICAN

Caribbean

Bryan, Ashley. *The Dancing Granny.* Illustrated by the author. New York: Aladdin Books, 1977.

Spider Anansi is too lazy to grow his own food, but he has plenty of energy to tempt Granny Anika away from her garden so he can haul home the goods. Lots of rhythmic chanting provides the motivation for Granny to dance for miles away from the garden. Students love to chime in on "Shake it to the east. . . ."

———. *The Dancing Granny: And Other African Stories.* Performed by the author. Caedmon CPN 1765, 1989. Audiocassette.

On this audiocassette, Ashley Bryan tells the folktales from his books. His powerful and distinctive voice modulations add richness to his stories. Stories included are "Frog and Two Wives," "The Dancing Granny," "Elephant and Frog Go Courting," and "Hen and Frog."

Gershator, Phillis. *Tukama Tootles the Flute: A Tale from the Antilles.* Illustrated by Synthia Saint James. New York: Orchard, 1994.

Tukama runs off playing his flute, not heeding his grandmother's warnings about the two-headed giant. Sure enough, the giant hears Tukama's tune and catches him. He turns the boy over to his wife, to fatten up for eating. Tukama uses his flute music to distract the giant's wife, and he escapes. From then on, he stays close to home and does the chores.

Gleeson, Brian. *Anansi.* Illustrated by Steven Guarnaccia. Rowayton, CT: Rabbit Ears Books, 1992.

An easy Jamaican style punctuated by "Yah, mahn" makes this an entertaining read-aloud. Two Anansi stories are preceded by background information on the origin of the tales. In the first tale, Tiger has all the world's stories, and Anansi wants the stories from him. Tiger agrees to give them to him if he performs a dangerous task: bring him the big, big snake. Anansi appeals to Snake's pride to trick him into capture. Compare with *A Story, A Story* by Gail Haley. In the second tale, Anansi hides the beans he stole in his hat, burning his head bald.

———. *Anansi.* Performed by Denzel Washington. Rabbit Ears Productions, 1991. Videocassette.

This is an animated version of Gleeson's book told against a background of rhythmic Caribbean music, played by UB40. The narrator's Caribbean-style telling and dialect give it an authentic feel and accentuate the humor. The CD has 25 minutes of storytelling and eight tracks of background music.

Makhanlall, David P. *Brer Anansi and the Boat Race: A Caribbean Folk Tale.* Illustrated by Amelia Rosato. New York: Bedrick/Blackie, 1988.

The rains have caused a flood, and Brer Rabbit and Brer Bear have moved out of their homes and into a boat. To steal their provisions, Brer Anansi goads them into a boat race. Anansi convinces them that their boat will go faster if they unload their supplies. While Bear and Rabbit are busy winning the race, Anansi makes off with their provisions.

Shute, Linda. *Rabbit Wishes.* Illustrated by the author. New York: Lothrop, Lee & Shepard, 1995.

In this Cuban tale, *Tío Conejo* (Uncle Rabbit) complains to *Papá Dios* (the Creator) that he wishes he were bigger. *Papá Dios* considers the request, but first he assigns three difficult tasks to the rabbit. He accomplishes the three tasks using trickery and is rewarded only with longer ears. Both a trickster tale and a pourquoi tale, the book includes a Spanish glossary and background information. Compare with *A Story, A Story* by Gail Haley and *Zomo the Rabbit* by Gerald McDermott.

Temple, Frances. *Tiger Soup: An Anansi Story from Jamaica.* Illustrated by the author. New York: Orchard, 1994.

This delightful trickster/pourquoi tale reveals a double trick: one to steal food and another to place the blame elsewhere. Anansi lures Tiger away from the soup he is making, ostensibly to teach Tiger to swim. Once he gets Tiger to jump into the water, Anansi slurps down Tiger's soup. Anansi then goes on to teach the little monkeys a fun song: "We ate the Tiger soup!" Tiger angrily chases the monkeys into the trees, where they stay to this day. This book makes an entertaining read-aloud, especially for primary students.

Wolkstein, Diane. *The Banza: A Haitian Story*. Illustrated by Marc Brown. New York: Dial Books for Young Readers, 1981.

When faced by 10 intimidating tigers who threaten to eat her, Cabree, the little goat, finds the courage to play her banza (a banjo) and sing what is in her heart. It is a song about how she eats 10 tigers raw, and the tigers run away in fear. This tale is readable by second graders and up.

———. *The Banza: A Haitian Story*. Performed by the author and Shirley Keller. Old Greenwich, CT: Listening Library FTR 122, 1991. Audiocassette.

The author/storyteller reads the story of Cabree and the banza, accompanied by banjo music. Children can sing along.

———. *Bouki Dances the Kokioko: A Comical Tale from Haiti*. Illustrated by Jesse Sweetwater. New York: Gulliver Books, 1997.

The king loves dancing so much, he thinks up a way to get a crowd of dancers to join him every night. He makes up a dance known only to him—the Kokioko—and then announces that he will pay a large sum to anyone who can figure out the dance. Night after night, people come and try, but no one wins the money. One evening the king's gardener, Malice, hears the king singing the Kokioko song and spies him doing the dance. Malice learns every step by heart, but he knows he cannot give himself away and win the prize. Malice lures his friend Bouki into a plan: He will teach Bouki the dance, and the two will split the prize money. Bouki does the dance for the king and wins the money. As Bouki and Malice walk home, Bouki with his big sack of money, Malice offers to teach Bouki an easy dance. Bouki falls for the trick, dancing away and leaving the sack of money for Malice. Brightly and humorously illustrated, for primary and middle grades.

Guatemalan

Mora, Pat. *The Race of Toad and Deer*. Illustrated by Maya Itzna Brooks. Orchard, 1995.

Deer proclaims he is the fastest, and he challenges Toad to a race. Toad gets all his look-alike toad friends to position themselves along the race route. Every time Deer thinks he's ahead, he hears Toad's voice out in front. Toad's cleverness wins over Deer's speed.

Mexican

Aardema, Verna. *Borreguita and the Coyote: A Tale from Ayutla, Mexico*. Illustrated by Petra Mathers. New York: Alfred A. Knopf, 1991.

In this tale, a female lamb, Borreguita, presents a series of clever diversions to keep Coyote from eating her, until he decides never to bother her again. Her tricks include convincing Coyote to hold up a cliff so it doesn't fall and convincing Coyote that the moon's reflection in the pond is really a big round cheese. This is a favorite for primary grades.

Johnston, Tony. *The Tale of Rabbit and Coyote*. Illustrated by Tomie dePaola. New York: G. P. Putnam's Sons, 1994.

This delightful Mexican folktale incorporates motifs from the African American Brer Rabbit stories, as well as ones from Native American and Mexican trickster stories. It includes the trickster deceits of the tar baby (beeswax doll), holding up a huge boulder, hitting a wasps' nest, the reflection in the water, and a ladder to the moon. A new illustration style from Tomie dePaola provides the perfect humorous accompaniment to this humorous tale. See Chapter 2 for a special activity to do with this tale.

Nicaraguan

Rohmer, Harriet. *Brother Anansi and the Cattle Ranch*. Illustrated by Stephen Von Mason. San Francisco: Children's Book Press, 1989.

    This tale traveled from Africa to the Caribbean to Central America, changing at each location to reflect the spirit of the local oral tradition. In this Nicaraguan version, Brother Anansi persuades Brother Tiger to share his lottery winnings by buying cattle, which they can raise on Anansi's land. The ranch is a booming success, and when Anansi is ready to cash it in, he devises a plan to dupe Tiger out of his share of the profits.

EUROPEAN

British Isles

Forest, Heather. *The Woman Who Flummoxed the Fairies: An Old Tale from Scotland*. Illustrated by Susan Gaber. New York: Harcourt Brace Jovanovich, 1990.

    The fairy folk want to taste the cakes made by the bakerwoman. Blowing fern dust in her face, they put her to sleep and transport her to the King of the Fairies. The King commands her to bake. She agrees, but she has a plan for escaping. She sends the fairy folk to her home for ingredients. Then she tells the King she cannot bake without her husband, her wee babe, and her pets about her. She sets them all to making noise, which the bakerwoman knows will befuddle the fairies. The King lets her go, and the bakerwoman offers to bring them cakes if they leave her alone, and they leave her fairies' gold. The final message of the value of sharing is a satisfying conclusion to this delightful read-aloud.

Hunter, Mollie. *Gilly Martin the Fox*. Illustrated by Dennis McDermott. New York: Hyperion Books for Children, 1994.

    In this tale from the Scottish Highlands, the Prince of Alban is under the spell of a witch who requires him to bring her the magical Blue Falcon. Gilly Martin the fox instructs the Prince to be brave and face a five-headed giant who has the falcon. The plot moves on through several fantastic adventures with Gilly Martin giving advice and using his powers as a shape-shifter to help the prince. The prince is ordered to go on a series of quests, first for a sword known as the White Glave of Light, then the Bay Filly of the King of Erin, then the daughter of the King of Lochlan. On each voyage, Gilly Martin changes himself into a sailing vessel to take the Prince of Alban to his next adventure. In the end, Gilly Martin transforms himself into the sword and the filly to fool and foil the giants who want these prizes for themselves. Gilly's tricks of transformation rescue the Prince and secure the princess for the Prince of Alban. This book is suitable for middle grades.

Leavy, Una. *Irish Fairy Tales and Legends*. Illustrated by Susan Field. Boulder, CO: Robert Rinehart, 1996.

    This collection includes 10 Irish trickster tales, transformation tales, and legends. "The Giant's Causeway" is the story of how Fionn Mac Cumhail (Finn MacCoul) is saved from the giant's wrath by his quick-thinking wife's trickery. "The Bodach of the Grey Coat" tells of the Bodach, a scruffy, rumpled man, who agrees to run a race against the Prince of Greece to determine whose kingdom will be subservient to the other. The unlikely winner is the Bodach, who is then transformed into Mannán Mac Lir, the sea-god. "The Pot of Gold" is the story of a leprechaun who puts 10,000 red ties on the weeds to disguise which one marks the place where the gold is buried. "Tír na n-Óg" tells of a king who misuses the chief druid's magic stick to change his daughter's head into a pig's head to keep her from marrying. The spell is broken when Oisín, a son of Fionn Mac Cumhail, marries her. They live happily in the land of Tír na n-Óg, where

Oisín is unaware of the passing of time in his former land. When he makes a visit to his old world, 300 years have elapsed, and Oisín turns into a withered old man. Authentically told by an Irish author, these stories are good read-alouds for second graders and up.

McDermott, Gerald. *Tim O'Toole and the Wee Folk: An Irish Tale*. Illustrated by the author. New York: Viking, 1990.

When dirt-poor Tim goes out to find work, he spies a gathering of the wee folk. Knowing that he now has a right to their treasure, Tim demands gold. The little people give him a goose that lays golden eggs. On his way home, Tim stops and brags of his good fortune to the McGoons, who steal his goose, replacing it with a plain one. The next day, the same thing happens with a magic tablecloth. Tim complains to the little people, who give him a magic hat. When the McGoons try to steal it, 10 little men run out of the hat and club the McGoons about the ankles. These mischievous little people come in handy later, when the neighbors take undue advantage of Tim's newfound wealth. This tale is suitable for first grade and up.

Muller, Robin. *Mollie Whuppie and the Giant*. Illustrated by the author. Buffalo, NY: Firefly Books, 1995.

Echoes of "Hansel and Gretel," strong parallels to "Jack and the Beanstalk," and trickster and transformational elements are all evident in this English tale. Mollie Whuppie, a trickster of British folklore, is the youngest of three daughters abandoned in the forest by their poor parents. The bravest and most cheerful, Mollie leads her sisters to a house, the home of a cruel giant and his wife. A series of harrowing events follow. Mollie leads her sisters in an escape over a high bridge the width of a human hair. The bridge is magic, and they find refuge in a palace. But there, Mollie is asked by the king to go back to the giant three times, once to steal his magic sword, once to take back the purse of gold stolen from the people, and once to snatch his ring that makes him invisible. On the third mission, the giant catches Mollie, but she engineers a clever trick. She gets the giant to hang her in a sack, and while the giant goes off to find a stick to beat the sack, she tricks the giant's wife into switching places with her. To escape Mollie uses the ring to make her invisible, but she goes back to rescue the giant's wife. The giant falls into the river gorge and turns into stone. Mollie and her sisters all get husbands at the palace. Small typeface and long narrative make this better as a read-aloud selection.

Shute, Linda. *Clever Tom and the Leprechaun*. Illustrated by the author. Lothrop Lee & Shepard, 1988.

Tom discovers a leprechaun and does his best to force him to reveal where his pot of gold is hidden. Finally, the leprechaun takes Tom to a field of boliauns (ragweed). Tom marks a plant with his red garter to remember the exact spot to dig. However, when he returns with his shovel, every plant is marked with a red garter.

French

Perrault, Charles. *Puss in Boots*. Translated by Malcolm Arthur. Illustrated by Fred Marcellino. New York: Farrar, Straus & Giroux, 1990.

This is the classic fairy tale of the cat who uses his wits to win riches, prestige, and a princess for his impoverished master. The final in a series of tricks occurs when Puss enters the castle of a wealthy Ogre. Puss inquires about the Ogre's powers to transform himself into any animal. The Ogre shows off by turning into a lion. Then Puss muses that it must be impossible for the Ogre to turn himself into something small, like a mouse. That done, Puss eats the mouse and presents the castle as his master's. This tale is readable by middle grades and suitable listening for all ages. Compare with the Filipino variant, *Pedro and the Monkey* by Robert San Souci.

Italian

Peterson, Julienne. *Caterina the Clever Farm Girl: A Tale from Italy.* Illustrated by Enzo Giannini. New York: Dial Books for Young Readers, 1996.

In this Tuscan folktale, a young woman matches wits with a willful king. A poor farmer finds a golden mortar and presents it to the king. The king scoffs because it has no pestle. The farmer states that this is exactly what his daughter predicted that he would say. The king, interested in the farmer's daughter, sends her some challenging tasks via the farmer. Caterina responds to each with clever one-upsmanship, and the king marries her. Once she is queen, she sits with the king as he makes decisions on the disputes of his subjects. She often disagrees with the king's decisions, and finally, the king is so exasperated with her that he tells her she must return to her father's house. However, he says she may take the item that is most precious to her. She has her sleeping husband transported to her father's little house because he is the most precious thing to her. When the king awakens the next morning and realizes how cleverly she has stated her love and loyalty to him, he learns to value her and keep her expertise with him in court.

NATIVE AMERICAN

Begay, Shonto. *Ma'ii and Cousin Horned Toad: A Traditional Navajo Story.* Illustrated by the author. New York: Scholastic, 1992.

Lazy Coyote plans to move onto Cousin Horned Toad's farm and eat his harvest. When Coyote swallows Toad, Toad makes Coyote realize his mistake by tormenting him from the inside. This time, Coyote loses at his own game.

Bernhard, Emery. *How Snowshoe Hare Rescued the Sun: A Tale from the Arctic.* Illustrated by Durga Bernhard. New York: Holiday House, 1993.

This Yuit Eskimo legend is derived from a Siberian Eskimo legend. Selfish demons steal the sun and keep it under the earth. In response, the animals, organized by Owl, have a council meeting. They send animals, one by one, to try to rescue the sun, but no one is successful until fast-running Snowshoe Hare goes. This tale is suitable for primary grades and up.

Bruchac, Joseph. *The Boy Who Lived with the Bears: And Other Iroquois Stories.* Illustrated by Murv Jacob. New York: HarperCollins, 1995.

This collection, written and illustrated by people of Native American descent, is suitable for independent reading by middle grades or for reading aloud to younger children. All the stories teach lessons in the gentle way that is characteristic of good, humorous storytelling. In "Turtle Makes War on Man," Turtle takes animals out to wage war against man. When a man picks him up, Turtle bites, so the man threatens him. Turtle expresses his fear of the water (the old "briar patch" trick), so the man throws him in the river—right where he wants to be.

Caduto, Michael J., and Joseph Bruchac. *Keepers of the Earth: Native American Stories and Environmental Activities for Children.* Illustrated by John Kahionhes Fadden and Carol Wood. Golden, CO: Fulcrum, 1989.

This large collection of well-told stories is matched with nature activities and discussions. The 24 tales, told by Bruchac, work well as read-alouds for middle and upper grades; some work well with younger grades as well. One tale introduces the trickster character Kokopelli, known in this tale as "Kokopilau, the Hump-Backed Flute Player." It tells how the Hopi people found the land they would settle on. Kokopilau accompanies them. He is part insect, part human, with wings and a hump on his back in which he carries seeds for the people to plant. The people arrive at the Fourth World, which is guarded by Eagle. Eagle requires that a test be passed before the people can settle there. Kokopilau steps forward, ready to take the test. Eagle demonstrates the test by piercing himself with an arrow and pulling it out the other side without injury. Kokopilau takes the arrow and passes it beneath his wings so that it looks like he has pierced himself. Eagle recognizes Kokopilau's power, allows the people to stay, and offers his feathers to adorn their prayer sticks.

Cameron, Anne. *How Raven Freed the Moon.* Illustrated by Tara Miller. Madeira Park, British Columbia, Canada: Harbour, 1985.

Raven is introduced as a trickster, sometimes good and sometimes bad, and this time as a female. This simple tale, delightfully told, shows Raven acting for everyone's benefit, and yet as mischievous as ever. Raven loves shiny bright objects and has heard that an old fisherwoman and her daughter who live on a northern island keep a bright thing called Moon in a carved box. Raven transforms herself into a baby and lays down at the old fisherwoman's door, crying. The old woman and girl awaken to find the baby. The woman lets the girl keep the baby, with instructions to care for it and keep it quiet so she can sleep. The baby's fits of crying and the reactions it brings are told with gentle humor. The baby cries more and more insistently, reaching for the carved wooden box. The woman and girl try to keep the baby from their secret, but in exasperation they let the baby look at the box and then fall asleep. The baby opens the box, and the bright light awakens the woman and daughter. They realize now the baby is Raven! The trickster flies off with Moon through the smoke hole. She flies far, but Moon is heavy, and Raven almost drops it in the ocean. She tosses it into the sky, where, the old woman agrees, it looks better than it did in the box. This book can be used as a read-aloud for all ages or for independent reading by middle grades.

———. *How the Loon Lost Her Voice.* Illustrated by Tara Miller. Madeira Park, British Columbia, Canada: Harbour, 1987.

The author learned this story from a native storyteller on Vancouver Island. It recounts how Raven rescues the sun from evil spirits and how gentle Loon sacrifices her lovely voice in the rescue effort. Loon's song helps make the world a happy place, until the day the evil spirits steal the sun. The animals have a meeting, at which Raven reports that the light is locked in a box with a wall of ice surrounding it. One by one, the animals try to break through the wall of ice. Loon and Mole make a plan to tunnel in, but the evil spirits catch Loon and swing her around by the neck, ruining her voice. Raven becomes angry, finds the sun, hides the light under his wing, and escapes with it. This story explains why the loon has a mournful voice. It also explains some other animals' traits.

———. *Raven Goes Berrypicking.* Illustrated by Tara Miller. British Columbia, Canada: Harbour, 1991.

Raven is unusually rude in this tale from the Pacific Northwest Native Americans. Raven, female in this story, goes out in her boat with her friends Gull, Cormorant, and Puffin. Raven lets her friends do the paddling and suggests they dive for oysters. However, Raven doesn't swim, so she offers to open the oysters while the others do the diving. The three water birds tire themselves with the work, while Raven eats the oysters. Then Raven sees sardines swimming and suggests they catch them while Raven stays with the boat. Again, Raven eats the fish while the others work. By the time they land to go berrypicking, the three friends are irritated, and Raven is so full she cannot help pick berries. To add insult to injury, Raven sends her friends for a drink of water and eats the berries from the baskets while they are gone. On the return trip, the three friends tie Raven up in a blanket and call her a glutton. Raven is sorry and spends four days fishing and berrypicking to make it up to her friends. This book works as a read-aloud to primary and middle grades, and as independent reading for middle grades.

Carey, Valerie Scho. *Quail Song: A Pueblo Indian Tale*. Illustrated by Ivan Barnett. New York: G. P. Putnam's Sons, 1990.

In this tale, small industrious Quail tricks irritating Coyote. Quail is harvesting seeds and cuts herself. She cries out. Coyote hears the cry and demands that Quail teach him that song. Quail tries to tell him it is a cry, not a song. But he insists, or else he will eat her. She teaches him, and he leaves, but a distraction causes him to forget the song. He comes back to Quail again and again, having forgotten the song each time. The interruptions are too much for Quail, so she fashions a trick. She paints a rock to look like herself, and she leaves. The next time Coyote comes back, the "quail" does not respond, so he eats it, breaking off his teeth. Lizard admires Coyote's song, which angers Coyote, for it is a cry of pain. This tale is successful with primary grades.

Dominic, Gloria. *Brave Bear and the Ghosts: A Sioux Legend*. Illustrated by Charles Reasoner. Vero Beach, FL: Rourke, 1996.

Four ghosts talk about a man, Brave Bear, who is reputed not to fear anything. They wager horses to see who can scare him. One by one, the ghosts appear to Brave Bear as frightening skeletons. Each time, Brave Bear outwits them, snatching and breaking their bones. There are no source notes for the story, but the book ends with several pages of information on the Sioux people. Suitable for middle and upper grades.

Dwyer, Mindy. *Coyote in Love*. Illustrated by the author. Seattle, WA: Alaska Northwest Books, 1997.

In this short, sweet, vibrantly illustrated story, Coyote is seen not so much as a trickster but as the character who always insists on getting what he wants, whether it is accessible or not. Coyote falls in love with a beautiful blue star, and he goes to the top of a high mountain to get close enough to touch her. She only makes fun of him, pulling him into the sky and then dropping him. He falls into the top of the mountain, making a huge hole. There he lies, crying blue tears, which become Crater Lake in Oregon. This tale is suitable for primary grades and up.

Eagle Walking Turtle. *Full Moon Stories: Thirteen Native American Legends*. Illustrated by the author. New York: Hyperion Books for Children, 1997.

In this collection are 13 stories, one for each moon of the year, as told by the author's Arapaho grandfather. A strong sense of a close family setting pervades each tale. One tale about a notable trickster incorporates transformations. "The Coyote" presents Coyote at his malicious worst, transforming himself into a man called White Smoke. He takes White Smoke's place as husband and father of a family and plays destructive tricks on White Smoke to keep him away. One of these tricks is to transform White Smoke's appearance so that his family does not recognize him, although his youngest son intuitively knows it is his father. At the end of this story, the author comments that kids often trick each other, but sometimes it is not a good idea because it can hurt people's feelings or worse. This collection is most effective as a read-aloud to primary and middle grades.

Ehlert, Lois. *Mole's Hill: A Woodland Tale*. Illustrated by the author. New York: Harcourt Brace, 1994.

Fox tells Mole that he is constructing a path to the pond and that Mole must move her hill by autumn. Instead, Mole makes her hill higher and higher and plants seeds in it. By fall, Fox sees that Mole's hill is teeming with plant life, so he asks her to dig a tunnel through it instead, an option that is much more agreeable to Mole. Primary-aged children enjoy this story, its bright illustrations, and Mole's victory over Fox.

French, Fiona. *Lord of the Animals: A Miwok Indian Creation Myth*. Illustrated by the author. Brookfield, CT: Millbrook Press, 1997.

This is a simple, short tale, featuring pourquoi, trickster, and transformation elements. Coyote is a creator in this story, having just created the world and its creatures. He calls a meeting to decide how they will make the Lord of the Animals. The animals each speak up in turn, stating that one of their own traits is the most important attribute for the Lord of the Animals. Finally, Coyote tells them to each shape a model of the Lord of the Animals from a lump of mud from the river, and then choose one of them to be their ruler. The animals start the project, but nighttime comes, and they all fall asleep. This is part of Coyote's plan. He stays awake and finishes his model, allowing the others to melt away in the river. Coyote incorporates many of the characteristics suggested by the other animals, but he assembles them in a new way: He shapes a man and gives him life as Lord of the Animals. This tale is suitable for primary and middle grades.

Goble, Paul. *Iktomi and the Berries* (1989), *Iktomi and the Boulder* (1988), *Iktomi and the Ducks* (1990), *Iktomi and the Buffalo Skull* (1991), *Iktomi and the Buzzard* (1994), *Iktomi and the Coyote* (1998). Illustrated by the author. New York: Orchard.

For each tale, Goble also provides information about and sources of these Plains Indian stories about Iktomi. Iktomi is something of a noodlehead, who acts in silly and sometimes dishonorable ways. One of the purposes of these tales is to teach children through Iktomi's example how *not* to behave. In addition to the story line, Goble adds interactive comments and questions in gray typeface. The humor is slapstick, and children delight in "knowing better" than silly Iktomi.

Goldin, Barbara Diamond. *Coyote and the Fire Stick: A Pacific Northwest Indian Tale.* Illustrated by Will Hillenbrand. New York: Gulliver Books, 1996.

The people have no fire, so they ask Coyote to get it for them from three evil spirits. Coyote climbs the mountain to the evil spirits' dwelling and hides to watch the fire. When the coast is clear, Coyote grabs a burning stick and flees, with the spirits chasing him. Just as the spirits grab his tail, Coyote throws the stick to Mountain Lion. A relay ensues among the animals, ending with Frog in the river. Frog spits the fire onto a tree. The spirits are unable to get fire away from the tree, and they leave. Once they are gone, Coyote shows the people how to rub two sticks together to make fire. Compare with *Fire Race* by Jonathan London.

Greene, Jacqueline Dembar. *Manabozho's Gifts: Three Chippewa Tales.* Illustrated by Jennifer Hewitson. Boston: Houghton Mifflin, 1994.

Manabozho, great-grandson of the moon, has special powers beyond humans, yet he is not a god. All three of these tales present him as one who causes many things to be, often for the greater benefit of the people. The first tale describes how Manabozho turns into a rabbit to gain access to a magician's wigwam and bring fire from there to the people. The stories can be read by fourth graders and up.

Gregg, Andy. *Great Rabbit and the Long-Tailed Wildcat.* Illustrated by Gat Bowman Smith. Morton Grove, IL: Albert Whitman, 1993.

Wildcat wants to eat Rabbit, not just any rabbit, but Great Rabbit. Wildcat pursues him and is repeatedly tormented by Great Rabbit's tricks of transformation. Following Great Rabbit's tracks, Wildcat comes upon the dwelling of a medicine man, who offers him some roast rabbit and a night's sleep. The next morning, Wildcat wakes to find that he is out in the snow and has eaten squash, not rabbit! The same deception happens two more nights, first at the lodge of an old woman and then at the home of a warrior. Each time, Wildcat comments that the host looks as though she or he has rabbit ears. Wildcat howls with aggravation when he realizes that he has been eluded and made a fool of. Great Rabbit also cuts off Wildcat's tail, and that is why wildcats have short tails today. This Passamaquoddy/Algonquian legend works with second grade and up. Compare with *Muwin and the Magic Hare* by Susan Shetterly.

Hausman, Gerald. *Coyote Walks on Two Legs: A Book of Navajo Myths and Legends*.
    Illustrated by Floyd Cooper. New York: Philomel Books, 1995.
    These five tales are told in sparing text arranged like free verse. Three of the
stories find Coyote the victim of the trick. In "The Day Magpie Tricked Coyote," Magpie
is showing off, playing the game "Throw away Eyes." Coyote also wants to toss his head,
making his eyeballs fly out and come back. However, Coyote loses his eyes, and Bluejay
helps by making him new ones of pine sap. In "Coyote's New Coat," Coyote is jealous
of the spotted coat on Mother Deer's children. She tells him he can have a spotted coat
too if he builds a fire and lets the wind blow sparks on him. In the end, all the animals
laugh at him for getting burned and having a ragged coat. In "The Guardian of the
Corn," Coyote swallows his cousin Horned Toad so he can take Toad's corn. Horned
Toad makes Coyote miserable by poking his insides until Coyote spits him out.

Hilbert, Vi. *Coyote and Rock: And Other Lushootseed Stories*. Performed by Vi Hilbert.
    Harper Audio CPN 1895, 1992. Audiocassette.
    These are 10 authentic tellings by an elder of the Upper Skagit tribe of Washing-
ton state. She relates the stories as they were told to her as a child. She tells them in a
quiet voice, interspersing words from her native language.

London, Jonathan, and Lanny Pinola. *Fire Race: A Karuk Coyote Tale About How Fire Came
    to the People*. Illustrated by Sylvia Long. San Francisco: Chronicle Books, 1993.
    The animals have no fire because it is kept by the Yellow Jacket Sisters at the top
of the mountain. Coyote persuades them to let him into their home by promising to
make them pretty. He will do so by drawing black stripes around their bodies with a
charred piece of wood from their fire. However, once he has the piece of burning wood
in his mouth, he makes a run for it. What ensues is much like a relay race, with all the
animals doing their part to bring back the fire. In the end, the fire is swallowed by the
willow tree, and Coyote shows the animals how to get fire from the tree by rubbing two
sticks together. Compare with *Coyote and the Fire Stick* by Barbara Goldin.

Max, Jill, ed. *Spider Spins a Story: Fourteen Legends from Native America*. Illustrated by
    six Native American artists. Flagstaff, AZ: Rising Moon, 1997.
    This collection of 14 tales from various tribal traditions all feature the spider. In
the different tales, Spider acts variously as helper, magical agent, trickster, and Grandmother of the Earth. The Zuni legend "Swift Runner and Trickster Tarantula" features
both helper Spider Woman and malicious trickster Tarantula. Huge Tarantula tricks
Swift Runner, the son of a Zuni priest, out of his ceremonial clothing. Attempts by the
people to retrieve the regalia fail, until the elders instruct the people to seek the help
of the two war gods and their grandmother, Spider Woman. They create shapes of
animals out of flour and ground sandstone. These shapes come alive, and they are
placed where Tarantula will want to hunt them. Once Tarantula kills them and starts
to haul them home, the animals transform back to piles of flour and sandstone, and
Tarantula is defeated by the Zuni warriors. The story ends with the people roasting
Tarantula, but he has one trick left: He explodes into millions of little tarantulas. These
tellings are sophisticated, and the typeface is small, so this collection is best suited as
a read-aloud source for middle and upper grades.

Mayo, Gretchen Will. "Native American Trickster Tales" series. Illustrated by the
    author. New York: Walker. Titles include *Meet Tricky Coyote!* (1993); *That Tricky
    Coyote!* (1993); *Here Comes Tricky Rabbit!* (1994); and *Big Trouble for Tricky
    Rabbit!* (1994).
    Each book in this series is a collection of approximately seven trickster stories,
each four or five pages long with plenty of illustrations. Stories are humorous and
appealing. They are suitable for independent reading by second through fourth grade
readers.

McDermott, Gerald. *Coyote: A Trickster Tale from the American Southwest.* Illustrated by the author. New York: Harcourt Brace, 1994.

Coyote wants to fly like the crows, so the crows decide to toy with him. They poke their feathers into Coyote's forelegs, but his attempt to fly fails. They rearrange the feathers to balance him, and he becomes boastful. The crows, angered now, take Coyote out for another test flight, and he ends up falling to the ground in a crumpled, dusty, humiliated heap. Compare with *Jackal's Flying Lesson* by Verna Aardema.

———. *Raven: A Trickster Tale from the Pacific Northwest.* Illustrated by the author. New York: Harcourt Brace Jovanovich, 1993.

In this classic tale of the Native Americans of the Pacific Northwest, Raven decides to bring the gift of light to the creatures of earth. He uses his powers of transformation to become a pine needle and later a human baby in the lodge of the Sky Chief. Behaving like any child who insists on his own way, Raven grabs the Sky Chief's light and brings it to earth. After introducing students to this simpler telling, compare it with *Raven's Light* by Susan Shetterly. This tale is best suited to primary grades.

Morgan, Pierr. *Supper for Crow: A Northwest Coast Indian Tale.* Illustrated by the author. New York: Crown, 1995.

Raven is malicious rather than helpful in this Makah Indian tale. Mama Crow is gathering food for her hungry babies, while Raven watches. When Mama Crow finds seal meat, Raven offers to place it in the basket on her back. Raven substitutes a rock for the meat. Back at home, Mama Crow proudly empties her basket on a plate, and crash! The huge rock smashes the plate! Mama sends her children to Raven's house to get the meat back. Raven tells the baby crows to dance while he finishes cooking the seal meat, creating a diversion for the crows while Raven devours the meat. After a long dance, the babies look in the pot, but there is nothing left but bones. Large print, simple text, and humor make this a fine choice for independent reading by primary-grade students.

Norman, Howard. *How Glooskap Outwits the Ice Giants: And Other Tales of the Maritime Indians.* Boston: Joy Street Books, 1989.

This is a collection of six stories from Native Americans on the coast of New England and Canada. Glooskap is a giant who creates human beings, and he performs amazing feats of strength and endurance to protect the humans. In the second story, "How Glooskap Outwits the Ice Giants," the humans are afraid of the Ice Giants, who take another human every day. Glooskap sets out to deal with the Ice Giants, using his powers of transformation several times, first to look like them, then to trick them and scare them away. These tales are best suited to middle and upper grades.

Oliviero, Jamie. *The Day Sun Was Stolen.* Illustrated by Sharon Hitchcock. New York: Hyperion Books for Children, 1995.

This Haida (Pacific Northwest) legend contains elements of the pourquoi, trickster, and transformation tale. Illustrated with Haida totem symbols by a Haida artist, this simply told tale recounts how Bear hides Sun and how a boy disguises himself as a fish to get Sun back. Bear, deciding he is too hot, hides Sun in a hole. The boy gets himself caught by Bear, waits for Bear to sleep, then shaves off some of Bear's fur so he, too, will know what it's like to be cold. The boy leaves Bear's cave with the fur in a sack, but the sack has a hole through which some fur scatters. Bear becomes cold and releases Sun for warmth. Some of the other animals use the scattered fur for their own warmth, which is why some animals grow extra fur in the winter. This tale is a very successful, easy to read, easy to understand example of Haida folklore. It is suitable for second grade and up.

Oughton, Jerrie. *How the Stars Fell into the Sky: A Navajo Legend.* Illustrated by Lisa Desimini. Boston: Houghton Mifflin, 1992.

When First Woman is carefully placing the stars in the sky, Coyote wants to help, but he soon tires of the tedious task, so he picks up the blanket of stars and flings it, scattering stars all over the sky. This Navajo tale is also a pourquoi tale explaining why there is confusion in the world today: First Woman was writing the laws with stars in the sky, and thanks to Coyote, the job was not completed correctly. Compare with *Coyote Places the Stars* by Harriet Taylor.

Pohrt, Tom. *Coyote Goes Walking.* Illustrated by the author. New York: Farrar, Straus & Giroux, 1995.

This is a collection of four short Coyote stories. In "Coyote and Mice," Coyote's trick is paid back on him. Following the sound of music, he finds a group of mice having a dance inside an elk skull. He wants to join them, and despite their protests, he magically makes the skull larger so he can stick his head inside. Then he gets the skull stuck on his head and wanders about bumping into things until he finally breaks it off. Meanwhile, the mice have chewed the fur off Coyote's head, leaving him bald. In "Coyote and Woodpecker," Coyote is invited to Woodpecker's home for a delicious dinner; he watches in fascination as Woodpecker drives his beak into trees to get worms. A few days later, Coyote invites Woodpecker's family over. He carves a beak out of wood, ties it over his nose, and tries to peck the trees. He becomes dizzy and falls out of the tree. The Woodpeckers come to his aid and peck the worms for dinner. This is a very enjoyable volume for second through fourth graders, but source notes are sketchy and nonspecific.

Ross, Gayle. *How Rabbit Tricked Otter: And Other Cherokee Trickster Stories.* Illustrated by Murv Jacob. New York: HarperCollins, 1994.

This collection of 15 stories features the Cherokee trickster, Rabbit. Told and illustrated by people of Cherokee descent, these humorous stories have many parallels with the Brer Rabbit stories of African Americans. Among these, the most striking resemblances in this book are "Rabbit Races with Turtle," "Rabbit and the Tar Wolf," and "Rabbit Steals from Fox." Five tales double as pourquoi stories. The stories are accessible for independent reading by middle grades and listening by younger grades.

———. *How Rabbit Tricked Otter: And Other Cherokee Trickster Stories.* Performed by the author. Caedmon CPN 1898. Audiocassette.

Experienced storyteller Gayle Ross tells nine tales from the Cherokee tradition. Her style is smooth and even, and flute music provides pleasant interludes between stories. Six of the stories are trickster tales, some doubling as pourquoi stories. Six of the stories on the tape are found in her book by the same title (see above entry). "How Turtle's Back Was Cracked" has also been published separately as a picture book (see entry below). Her tellings follow the books fairly closely, but are not a word-for-word reading.

———. *How Turtle's Back Was Cracked: A Traditional Cherokee Tale.* Illustrated by Murv Jacob. New York: Dial Books for Young Readers, 1995.

Possum picks persimmons for his friend Turtle, and when Wolf steals some, Possum throws a persimmon hard and chokes Wolf to death. Turtle takes the credit for Wolf's demise and boasts about it in the village. The other wolves find out about Turtle's insulting actions and capture him. They threaten him with death by fire, then death by boiling. Using the same trickery as Brer Rabbit when he says, "Please don't throw me in the briar patch," Turtle gets himself thrown in the river, exactly where he wants to go, but not before he hits a rock and cracks his shell.

Shetterly, Susan Hand. *Muwin and the Magic Hare.* Illustrated by Robert Shetterly. New York: Atheneum, 1993.

In this tale from the Passamaquoddy Indians, a bear (Muwin) is in pursuit of a snowshoe hare. He comes upon a hunter, then an old woman, and finally a chief. At each of these stops in his journey, the host feeds the bear and tells him a story. There are verbal and visual clues that these three hosts, plus the boy at the end, are really the magic hare, who transforms himself. Because there are several stories within the story, students may need help mapping it as they go, so they don't lose the main story framework. Compare with *Great Rabbit and the Long-Tailed Wildcat* by Andy Gregg.

———. *Raven's Light: A Myth from the People of the Northwest Coast.* Illustrated by Robert Shetterly. New York: Atheneum, 1991.

Using the sources of the Tlingit, Kwakiutl, Haida, and Tsimshian peoples of the Pacific Northwest, Shetterly tells an extended version of how Raven brings light to the earth. Raven transforms himself to steal light from the lodge of the Great Chief of the Sky World. This is a more extensive telling than *Raven* by Gerald McDermott; it includes the concept of parallel worlds in the sky and the earth, and it begins with Raven creating earth and the creatures in it.

Smith, Don Lelooska. *Echoes of the Elders: The Stories and Paintings of Chief Lelooska.* Illustrated by the author. Edited by Christine Normandin. New York: DK Ink, 1997. Book and compact disc recording.

Of the five tales in this multimedia collection of Kwakiutl stories from the Pacific Northwest, two feature trickster elements. The humorous "Raven and Sea Gull" is the story of how Raven gets the sun back after Sea Gull steals it. He leaves spiny shells out for Sea Gull to step on. When Sea Gull cries and whines for help, Raven says he needs light to pull the spines out of the gull's feet. (This also explains why the gull still walks around as though his feet are sore.) "Beaver Face" is the name given by taunting peers to a girl who was born with a cleft lip. One day while playing near the forest's edge, the children are all snatched up by Tsonoqua the Timber Giant. The giant plans to devour the children, but Beaver Face helps them all escape, and then bravely faces Tsonoqua. She "helps" the giant, who wants to become beautiful with pierced ears so she can wear Beaver Face's earrings. Beaver Face pins the giant's ears to the ground with stakes and kills her. This collection is a work of art and a tribute to Chief Lelooska for all ages to treasure.

Spooner, Michael, and Lolita Taylor. *Old Meshikee and the Little Crabs: An Ojibwe Story.* Illustrated by John Hart. New York: Henry Holt, 1996.

Old Meshikee, a turtle, and a throng of little Shagizenz (sand crabs) star in this humorous tale. The busy and industrious Shagizenz are irritated that when they want to celebrate, they can't hear their own drumming because Old Meshikee's drumming drowns them out. So they capture the turtle, tie him up, and decide to throw him in the fire. Meshikee seems unconcerned, but he points out that he'll kick, and some coals might fall on the Shagizenz's children. The Shagizenz revise their plan over and over, and finally, they decide to throw Meshikee into the lake, which is right where he wants to be. The telling offers opportunities for children to join in the chorus of the Shagizenz: "Can't do that, can't do that."

Stevens, Janet. *Coyote Steals the Blanket: A Ute Tale.* Illustrated by the author. New York: Holiday House, 1993.

When Coyote steals a blanket, the spirit of the desert is angry and sends a big boulder rolling after him. Other animals try to help Coyote, but no one can until Hummingbird makes Coyote give the blanket back. The tiny hummingbird single-handedly stops the rock and fixes Coyote's tail.

J 398.2
STR

———. *Old Bag of Bones: A Coyote Tale.* Illustrated by the author. New York: Holiday House, 1996.

Coyote is complaining that he is nothing but an old, hungry bag of bones. When he sees the magical Young Buffalo, he persuades him to give him youth, strength, and power. Young Buffalo agrees to transform Coyote into a buffalo, but warns him that only a real buffalo has true power. Now a "Buffote," Coyote brags about his powers, but he ends up back where he was—a decrepit bag of bones. But he hasn't learned his lesson yet! By the last page, he is on the make for another creature to mooch from.

Strauss, Susan. *Coyote Stories for Children: Tales from Native America.* Illustrated by Gary Lund. Hillsboro, OR: Beyond Words, 1991.

This collection of four Coyote tales is told in a humorous, conversational story-teller's style and is accompanied by black ink drawings. The writing includes frequent asides, comments, pauses, and sound-effect words. These stories work best for better middle-grade readers, or as read-alouds.

Talashoema, Hershel. *Coyote and Little Turtle: A Traditional Hopi Tale.* Translated and edited by Emory Sekaquaptewa and Barbara Pepper. Illustrated by Hopi children. Santa Fe, NM: Clear Light, 1994.

A product of the Hopi Tribe Cultural Preservation Office and other agencies, this is more than an easy-read trickster tale for primary grades. The book provides a bilingual telling in Hopi and English, simple instruction on Hopi grammar, and a glossary for Hopi-English and English-Hopi expressions. Little Turtle gets lost and is caught by Coyote. Coyote threatens to throw him into sand, then into snow. Turtle, using the "briar patch" trick, gets himself thrown into the lake, where he lives. Coyote jumps in after him and drowns.

Taylor, Harriet Peck. *Brother Wolf: A Seneca Tale.* Illustrated by the author. New York: Farrar, Straus & Giroux, 1996.

In this tale for primary-grade children, Raccoon taunts and teases Wolf, and later, while Wolf is sleeping, Racoon covers Wolf's eyes with sticky tar and clay. When he wakes, Wolf howls in dismay, and the birds come. Wolf tells the birds that if they peck off the tar and clay, he will reward them. The birds do so and ask to be painted with the colors of the flowers. After he gives the birds their colors, Wolf paints the black circles around Raccoon's eyes.

———. *Coyote and the Laughing Butterflies.* Illustrated by the author. New York: Macmillan Books for Young Readers, 1995.

Both a trickster and pourquoi tale, this is a legend of the Tewa Indians. Coyote's wife asks him to make the day-long journey to the salty lake to collect salt crystals for cooking. When Coyote stops to take a nap, butterflies see him and decide to play a trick on him. The butterflies grab bits of his fur, lifting him and carrying him back home. He awakes at home, empty-handed and in ill favor with his wife. The same thing happens again, and on his third attempt, Coyote makes it to the lake and fills his sack before taking a nap. This time, the butterflies take pity on him and bring him home with his full sack. To this day, butterflies flutter about, rather than fly straight, because they are laughing as they remember the trick they played. This tale is suitable for independent reading by second and third grade students.

———. *Coyote Places the Stars.* Illustrated by the author. New York: Bradbury Press, 1993.

Coyote decides to use his bow and arrows first to make a ladder to the moon, then to move the stars around in the sky. He rearranges the stars to create pictures of his animal friends. Pleased with his work, he howls in the night and shows the other animals. The animals declare Coyote the most clever of them all. This Wasco Indian tale is suitable for independent reading by second- or third-grade students. Compare with *How the Stars Fell into the Sky* by Jerrie Oughton.

Ude, Wayne. *Maybe I Will Do Something*. Illustrated by Abigail Rorer. Boston: Houghton Mifflin, 1993.

This is a collection of seven Coyote tales. They are longer stories with few illustrations, suitable for additional material or for older readers. The tellings are humorous and sophisticated.

SOUTH AMERICAN/LATIN AMERICAN

Brusca, María Cristina, and Tona Wilson. *Pedro Fools the Gringo: And Other Tales of a Latin American Trickster*. A Redfeather Book. Illustrated by María Cristina Brusca. New York: Henry Holt, 1995.

In the format of a beginning chapter book, this collection presents 11 episodes in the life of Pedro Urdemales, a trickster character who came to Central and South America as the result of Spanish influence. He is a poor man who bests wealthy men, priests, and even the Devil with his cleverness. Most of the two- or three-page stories feature Pedro taking advantage of a situation to get bags of gold or horses from rich, self-serving men in exchange for an animal, a pot, or a tree thought to have exceptional value. Two stories deal with human or animal feces, presented as tastefully as possible. Compare "Pedro and the Devil" with the gardening/business ventures in *Tops and Bottoms* by Janet Stevens. Suitable for independent reading by third graders, these tales are told in a lively and entertaining style.

Crespo, George. *How Iwariwa the Cayman Learned to Share*. Illustrated by the author. New York: Clarion Books, 1995.

This Yanomami myth explains how the animals obtained fire, and also why animals' shining eyes can be seen from a distance watching fire at night. The animals eat their food raw, not knowing about fire. But they find out that the cayman (alligator-like reptile) and his wife have flames and smoke and delicious-smelling food. The cayman keeps the fire hidden in a basket in his mouth. The animals devise a trick to make the cayman laugh and lose the basket. A relay-race ensues, and the animals win the right to use fire. This trickster/pourquoi tale is accessible to middle-grade readers, although the long Yanomami names could deter some students. Compare with *Fire Race* by Jonathan London.

DeSpain, Pleasant. *The Dancing Turtle: A Folktale from Brazil*. Illustrated by David Boston. Little Rock, AR: August House LittleFolk, 1998.

This tale is set in the rain forest of Brazil. A man comes upon Turtle dancing and resting, and he captures her for dinner. He brings her home and puts her in a cage, telling his children to watch her until dinnertime. Turtle beguiles the children with her flute music, and they ask for more. Turtle tells the children she can also dance and tricks the children into letting her out of the cage to show them. When the children realize Turtle has gotten away, they try to fool their father by painting a large rock to look like Turtle and placing it in the cage. Story and illustrations are appealing to primary-grade students and readable by second grade and up. Compare with *Pickin' Peas* by Margaret Read MacDonald.

Ehlert, Lois. *Moon Rope: A Peruvian Folktale*. Illustrated by the author. New York: Harcourt Brace Jovanovich, 1992.

In this bilingual trickster/pourquoi tale, Fox tricks Mole into going to the moon with him by convincing him that there are lots of worms to eat there. Mole's disgraceful fall back to Earth is the reason he hides under the ground to this day. Large, easy text and prominent stylized illustrations make this tale suitable for primary-grade students.

González, Lucía M. *Señor Cat's Romance*. Illustrated by Lulu Delacre. New York: Scholastic, 1997.

This collection includes six tales commonly told to children in Latin American countries. Two of the six stories are trickster tales. "How Uncle Rabbit Tricked Uncle Tiger" shows Rabbit fooling Tío Tigre into believing that Rabbit is eating his own tail. He interests Tío Tigre in doing the same, with humorous results. Thinking he'll get Rabbit back for this joke, Tío Tigre waits by the pond for Rabbit, but Rabbit fools him again, disguised as a leafy creature. In "The Billy Goat and the Vegetable Garden," a goat is ruining the garden of an old couple. A little red ant offers to help the couple. He crawls onto the goat and stings him repeatedly, fooling him into thinking the garden is infested with stinging ants. The goat flees, and the elderly couple express their gratitude. This collection works well as a read-aloud for primary grades.

Hickox, Rebecca. *Zorro and Quwi: Tales of a Trickster Guinea Pig*. Illustrated by Kim Howard. New York: Doubleday Books for Young Readers, 1997.

In this Peruvian tale, Zorro the fox is always trying to catch Quwi the guinea pig. Knowing that Quwi eats the farmer's flowers at night, Zorro sets a trap. When Zorro finds Quwi in the trap, Quwi convinces him to switch places because he claims that the farmer will force him to marry his daughter and live a rich life. Zorro suffers blows from the farmer and realizes he's been tricked. When Zorro catches up to Quwi, Quwi is holding up a boulder, which could crush the village. He convinces Zorro to take a turn at holding up the rock because it would bring hero status. His muscles tired, Zorro finally realizes this is another trick. The next time, Quwi warns Zorro of an approaching rain of fire and helps Zorro hide in a hole. For dramatic effect, Quwi pokes thorns into the hole to simulate fire. Finally, Quwi lures Zorro into a man's house to steal cornmeal, where Zorro gets his head stuck in the jar. This is an entertaining read-aloud for primary grades and readable by second graders and up. Compare with *The Tale of Rabbit and Coyote* by Tony Johnston and *Borreguita and the Coyote* by Verna Aardema.

Stiles, Martha Bennett. *James the Vine Puller: A Brazilian Folktale*. Illustrated by Larry Thomas. Minneapolis, MN: Carolrhoda Books, 1992.

As the author's note explains, this tale shows a combination of traditions from the Arawak people (native peoples in Brazil who were forced to work as slaves on Portuguese plantations) and Africans who were brought over as slaves. James the turtle is told by an elephant who claims to be king of the jungle that the coconuts are his alone. So James tries eating out of the ocean, where a whale tells him that he is the king of the ocean and he may not eat there either. James then challenges both the elephant and the whale to a vine-pulling contest for rights to the jungle and the ocean. He ties one end of the vine to the whale and the other to the elephant. The two beasts struggle all day, never seeing each other but believing James is at the other end. When they have given up, James goes back to each, proposing that since no one won, they must live together and share. This tale is also an Arawak pourquoi tale explaining the reason for the ocean tides. It is suitable for primary-grade readers.

Weiss, Jacqueline Shachter. *Young Brer Rabbit and Other Trickster Tales from the Americas*. Illustrated by Clinton Arrowood. Owings Mills, MD: Stemmer House, 1985.

This collection of 15 stories features the African American influence on storytelling in South and Central America. These stories could be used as additional material. Because the text is small and dense, this collection is suitable for upper grades.

MANY CULTURES IN A COLLECTION

Adler, Naomi. *The Dial Book of Animal Tales from Around the World*. Illustrated by Amanda Hall. New York: Dial Books for Young Readers, 1996.

This is a useful collection of nine stories (four trickster, one transformation, and four pourquoi tales). "The Greedy Frog" (Australian) relates how the animals cooperate to get Tiddalick the frog to laugh and release all the world's water, which he has drunk. In "Never Trust a Pelican" (Thai), a greedy pelican tells the fish that the lake is drying up, and he offers to transport the fish to another lake. In so doing, he devours the fish, until a wise old crab suspects foul play. The crab asks the pelican for a ride and defeats him. In "The Monkey's Heart" (African), a good friendship develops between Monkey and Crocodile, until Monkey discovers he is about to become dinner for the Chief of the Crocodiles. Monkey's last-minute, quick-witted trick shames Crocodile and saves his life. In "Magic in the Rain Forest" (Brazilian Native American), Snake plays a trick on Jaguar, stealing Jaguar's eyes. Harpy Eagle tricks Snake back on Jaguar's behalf, and ever since that time, Jaguar leaves a portion of his kill for Harpy Eagle. This collection is suitable as a read-aloud or for independent reading by middle-grade students.

Baumgartner, Barbara. *Crocodile! Crocodile! Stories Told Around the World*. Illustrated by Judith Moffatt. New York: Dorling Kindersley, 1994.

This is a collection of six tales, with suggestions for stick puppet activities at the end. In the first story, "Crocodile! Crocodile!" (India), Monkey accepts a ride on Crocodile's back to the island of fruit trees. It is really a trick, for Crocodile then swims under water to try to drown Monkey. Monkey tells Crocodile he left his heart, the tastiest part of him, back in a tree, and they should go back for it. Then Monkey escapes. In "Crocodile Hunts for the Monkey" (India), Crocodile is trying to make Monkey believe he is just a rock, but Monkey dupes him into speaking. In "The Grateful Snake" (China), a poor boy is sent away and may not return unless he brings home something of value. He feeds a snake, who turns out to be a dragon who gives him magical help on successive occasions. The Dragon helps devise a trick to right the wrong done by the boy's greedy brother. In "Sody Saleratus," a squirrel tricks a bear and saves his family. Large typeface and bright illustrations make this appealing to primary-grade children.

Cohn, Amy L., compiler. *From Sea to Shining Sea: A Treasury of American Folklore and Folk Songs*. Illustrated by 15 Caldecott-winning artists. New York: Scholastic, 1993.

This large collection of folk literature is arranged by genre and historical era. Two chapters contain trickster tales; see also the index on page 398 under "Myths" and "Trickster Tales." A notable song is "Oh, John the Rabbit," for use with Brer Rabbit stories. Compare Julius Lester's "Brer Rabbit in Mr. Man's Garden" with his telling of the same tale ("Mr. Rabbit and Mr. Bear") in *The Knee-High Man and Other Tales*. In the one-page-long "Connecticut Peddler," the innkeeper's wife is duped into buying her own coverlet. In "Brer Possum's Dilemma," expertly told by Jackie Torrence, Brer Snake repeatedly asks Brer Possum for help. Possum keeps voicing his fear of being bitten, and each time, Snake appeals to Possum's kindhearted nature. True to his nature, Snake bites, leaving the listener with the lesson not to "trouble trouble." In "Juan Bobo and the Buñuelos," Juan's wife outwits her simpleminded husband to protect themselves from the thieves she knew would return to claim the gold Juan has found. This book is a rich resource with numerous curriculum connections.

Gerke, Pamela. *Multicultural Plays for Children: Volume 1: Grades K-3*, and *Volume 2: Grades 4-6*. Young Actors Series. Lyme, NH: Smith and Kraus, 1996.

These two volumes contain both general and specific instructions for producing plays derived from folktales. The 10 plays in each volume are introduced with cultural and literary information. The scripts include a sprinkling of words in other languages. The most easily accessible play is volume 1's "The Adventures of Anansi," a set of four short trickster stories, including "How Anansi Got a Thin Waist" and "How Anansi Helped a Fisherman." Also in volume 1 is "Ma Lien and the Magic Paintbrush," both a trickster and transformation tale, in which a girl is given a magic paintbrush. Everything she paints is transformed into a real object. When a greedy ruler commands her powers for his own use, she cleverly paints a scene in which he willingly participates in his own demise. Volume 2 contains "La Culebra (The Snake)," in which Coyote settles a dispute over a proverb, with humorous results.

Goode, Diane. *Diane Goode's Book of Giants and Little People.* Illustrated by the author. New York: Dutton Children's Books, 1997.

This collection of 17 tales and poems includes a telling of "Wiley and the Hairy Man" and "Anansi and the Plantains." "How Big-Mouth Wrestled the Giant" tells how a braggart keeps thinking up retorts for the giant who has caught him until his words send the giant running away. "Managing Molly" is the story of a poor young woman whom an ogre is courting to marry. During their courtship, the ogre is so tormented by Molly's tricks that he buys her off so that he doesn't have to marry her.

Gugler, Laurel Dee. *Monkey Tales.* Illustrated by Vlasta van Kampen. New York: Annick, 1998.

This collection of three tales features monkeys. In "Big Monkey's Banana Trouble" (Brazil), a monkey steals the bananas out of an old woman's garden. The woman makes a wax model of a banana peddler to catch the thief (the "tar baby" motif), and the monkey gets stuck to the wax. However, unlike Brer Rabbit's fate with the tar baby, the monkey calls for help, the sun melts the wax, and all the monkeys have a banana party. In "Cat, Dog and Monkey" (Indonesia), Cat and Dog quarrel over dividing their food, and the monkey helps them. But every time he divides the food, one side is bigger than the other, so he nibbles off the surplus. Text is readable by second graders and up.

Hamilton, Martha, and Mitch Weiss. *Stories in My Pocket: Tales Kids Can Tell.* Illustrated by Annie Campbell. Golden, CO: Fulcrum, 1996.

This collection of tales is organized by difficulty level for telling by children. Text appears in a column on the left-hand side of each page, and presentation tips (gestures, voice inflections, etc.) are found in a right-hand column. Trickster stories include "The Beautiful Dream" featuring Coyote, "How Coyote Was the Moon," "Why Crocodile Does Not Eat Hen," "Skunnee Wundee and the Stone Giant," and "The Silversmith and the Rich Man."

Hamilton, Virginia. *A Ring of Tricksters: Animal Tales from North America, the West Indies, and Africa.* Illustrated by Barry Moser. New York: Blue Sky Press, 1997.

This is an outstanding collaboration by a master storyteller and an illustrator of supreme style. The 11 tales are told in regional dialects, making them best suited to prepared read-alouds. In "The Cat and the Rat," the two animals call upon Old Fox to help them decide how to divide and share a piece of cheese. Fox uses this opportunity to divide, add, and subtract to his own advantage. In "The Animals Share," Shulo the hare won't help the animals dig a well, but he tricks his way past the guards to use it when it is completed. In "Bruh Rabby and Bruh Gator," Rabbit returns an insult with relentless, painful pranks. In "Bruh Wolf and Bruh Rabbit Join Together," Wolf and Rabbit enter a joint farming venture in which the division of the crops is similar to that in *Tops and Bottoms* by Janet Stevens. In "Magic Anansi," Anansi helps a goat and her kids escape from Tiger by turning them into rocks and throwing them cross the river. In "Old Mister Turtle Gets a Whipping," Turtle claims that he can ride Mr. Leopard like a horse. This insults Leopard, but Turtle feigns illness and gets the ride anyway. These tales are great read-alouds for all ages.

Lester, Julius. *How Many Spots Does a Leopard Have? And Other Tales.* Illustrated by David Shannon. New York: Scholastic, 1989.

This collection of 12 stories contains one trickster tale. "Tug-of-War" is a classic trick found in other trickster tales. Turtle boasts that he is as powerful as Elephant and Hippopotamus, and he challenges both beasts to a tug-of-war contest. He works it so that the two ends of the long vine are pulled by the two large animals, each thinking that Turtle is at the other end. Turtle lets them pull for hours then cuts them loose. The two beasts have a new respect for Turtle's strength! Use as a read-aloud for second grade and up.

MacDonald, Margaret Read. *Tuck-Me-In Tales: Bedtime Stories from Around the World.* Illustrated by Yvonne Davis. Little Rock, AR: August House LittleFolk, 1996.

In this collection of five stories, "Snow Bunting's Lullaby" (Siberian) features Raven, who steals the lullaby song from the snow bunting bird family. Papa Snow Bunting takes his bow and arrows to find Raven. Each time Raven taunts Papa Bunting with a line of the song, Papa Bunting shoots with his little arrows, until Raven drops the song. These stories are suitable for reading aloud or telling to young children.

Mayo, Margaret. *Tortoise's Flying Lesson.* Illustrated by Emily Bolam. New York: Harcourt Brace, 1994.

These eight animal tales feature large text and bright illustrations. Three are trickster tales. In "How to Count Crocodiles," Monkey tricks the crocodiles into forming a bridge across a river so she can get to the mango trees. In "Grandmother Rabbit and the Bossy Lion," Rabbit keeps Lion from eating her by using his reflection in a well to threaten Lion's ego. "The Little Hares Play Hop, Skip, and Jump" uses the classic "tug-of-war" trick, played by Mother Rabbit on the bullying Elephant and Hippo. The collection is appealing to primary-grade classes.

McCarthy, Tara. *Multicultural Fables and Fairy Tales: Stories and Activities to Promote Literacy and Cultural Awareness.* New York: Scholastic Professional Books, 1993.

In the format of a professional teacher resource book, this collection contains short tellings of different folktale genres for reading aloud. Each tale has a page of preparatory suggestions for the teacher and one page of student activities. Included are seven pourquoi tales, five trickster tales, and six fairy tales.

Mills, Lauren. *The Book of Little Folk: Faery Stories and Poems from Around the World.* Illustrated by the author. New York: Dial Press, 1997.

This is a collection of 29 folktales, original stories, and poems about faeries and little people. "Laka and the Menehunes" (Hawaiian) tells of mischievous little people called Menehunes. A boy named Laka works all day to cut down a tree for a canoe, but the next day the felled tree is gone. This happens three days in a row. The fourth day, he fells the tree and then hides to watch. That night, a giggling group of Menehunes comes along, planning to put the tree back into its place. Laka grabs two of the little people and threatens them. They beg for their lives, promising to make him a canoe. They do so, and never bother Laka again. Another story in the collection is the British "Tom Thumb." Although he does not intentionally play pranks in this retelling, he gets into plenty of scrapes just because of his size. Stories in this collection are long and are set in small typeface, making them most useful as read-alouds. Children in the first through sixth grades will enjoy listening to these tales.

Rosen, Michael, ed. *South and North, East and West: The Oxfam Book of Children's Stories.* Illustrated by numerous artists. Cambridge, MA: Candlewick Press, 1992.

This collection of 25 tales, including trickster, pourquoi, ghost story, and other genres, is useful as a read-aloud resource, or for additional material for comparison studies. "Fox, Alligator, and Rabbit" features a double trick, a slow-thinking alligator, and some hot porridge. In "Dog, Cat, and Monkey," Monkey makes a show of doing

Dog and Cat a favor but eats all their meat instead. In "The Lion and the Hare," Hare gets caught by Lion five times. Each time, Hare executes another wily escape trick, including the "briar patch" and the "hold up a heavy rock" tricks. "Hare, Hippo, and Elephant" features the "tug-of-war" trick.

San Souci, Robert D. *Cut from the Same Cloth: American Women of Myth, Legend, and Tall Tale.* Introduction by Jane Yolen. Illustrated by Brian Pinkney. New York: Philomel Books, 1993.

This collection of 15 tales spotlights the power and cleverness of women. The African American tale "Molly Cottontail" features the female counterpart of Brer Rabbit. Molly eats Hungry Billy's butter and then frames Mistah Fox for the crime. In "Old Sally Cato," a mean giant is chasing Sally's two sons, intending to eat them. When with his mouth open he approaches Sally on her porch, she waits until he gets close, and then she runs into his mouth. Armed with her knitting needles, feather duster, and knife, she torments and kills the giant from the inside. Written in dialect, these tales are most entertaining as read-alouds. The Mexican American "Sister Fox and Brother Coyote" strings together four mischievous tricks played by Sister Fox. In the first, Sister Fox is stuck to a sticky wax doll in the henhouse. She tricks Coyote into taking the wax doll. Later, she tricks Coyote into going into a courtyard guarded by dogs by convincing him that it is full of fat roosters. For the third trick, Sister Fox convinces Coyote that there is a round of cheese in the pond, but it is really the reflection of the moon. Finally, Sister Fox gets Coyote to wait for an alleged wedding party while she prepares a fire that finishes Coyote off for good. Compare with *Tale of Rabbit and Coyote* by Tony Johnston and *Borreguita and the Coyote* by Verna Aardema.

Schutz-Gruber, Barbara G. *Trickster Tales from Around the World.* Performed by the author. Ann Arbor, MI: Barbara Schutz-Gruber, 1991. Audiocassette.

Schutz-Gruber tells four tales, recorded before a live audience of children. Her tellings are light, humorous, and well-suited to children. "Coyote and the Blackbirds" is a well-done variant of *Coyote* by Gerald McDermott. "Māui's Gifts" tells how the Pacific-area trickster, Māui, gets the sun to move more slowly across the sky so there will be more daylight. Compare with *Māui and the Sun* by Gavin Bishop. (Note: Transcripts of these stories are found in Schutz-Gruber's book; see page 42 in Chapter 2.)

Sherman, Josepha. *Trickster Tales: Forty Folk Stories from Around the World.* Illustrated by David Boston. Little Rock, AR: August House, 1996.

This extensive collection, accompanied by notes and discussions, is good for storytelling source material or for reading aloud. One strength of this collection is its inclusion of trickster tales from cultures less well-represented, and for finding lesser-known trickster characters. For example, there are tales of Hershele Ostropolier (Eastern European Jewish), Tyl Eulenspiegel (Netherlands), John (African American), Djuba (Morocco), Goha (Egypt), Nasreddin Khoja (Turkey), the lutin (France), Lam-ang (Philippines), and Liar Mvkang (Burma). There are also stories of more well-known tricksters such as Coyote, Raven, Māui, Pedro Urdemalas, Rabbit, and the Leprechaun. Stories in this collection span interest levels from young children through adult.

Sierra, Judy. *Nursery Tales Around the World.* Illustrated by Stefano Vitale. New York: Clarion Books, 1996.

This collection of short tales is organized by such thematic elements as "The Victory of the Smallest," "Slowpokes and Speedsters," and "Fooling the Big Bad Wolf." The three stories in "The Victory of the Smallest" feature small creatures outwitting big bullies. In "Odon the Giant," five small creatures conspire to cure the giant of his stomping around and crushing small creatures. In "The Coyote and the Rabbit," the rabbit challenges the coyote to a race to the four corners of the world. Rabbit wins by using all his look-alike relatives. The three stories in the section on "Fooling the Big

Bad Wolf" feature potential victims who outwit their pursuers. A useful read-aloud source for kindergarten and first grade.

Thornhill, Jan. *Crow and Fox: And Other Animal Legends.* Illustrated by the author. Simon & Schuster Books for Young Readers, 1993.

This collection includes nine tales from six continents. Each tale is about two animals, and, as the author notes, many are based on motifs found in several cultures. Seven tales are trickster tales, and five have pourquoi elements. "Elephant and Hare" uses the moon's reflection in the water as a device to get the elephants to move away and quit trampling the homes of the mice. "Hare and Tortoise" uses the "tar baby" motif to catch Hare, who has been dirtying the water supply. In "Crow and Fox," Fox invites Crow to dinner, but he serves porridge on a rock. Fox uses his tongue to lap it up, but Crow cannot peck enough even for a mouthful. Crow returns the favor by serving Fox a meal of dates, which he drops into a thorn tree, where Fox cannot reach without getting pricked. Each tale is one or two pages of solid text, accompanied by one or two full-page illustrations. A useful collection.

Van Laan, Nancy. *With a Whoop and a Holler.* Illustrated by Scott Cook. New York: Atheneum Books for Young Readers, 1998.

This collection of 50 stories, poems, superstitious sayings, and riddles are told with a down-home Southern style. The contents are organized into three regional groups: the Bayou, the Deep South, and the Mountains. In "The Big Dinin'," Brer Frog outsmarts Brer Rabbit and gets the platter of fish for himself. In "The Watermillion Patch," Brer Rabbit scares off Colonel Tiger and manages to keep most of the watermelons. Numerous other characters populate this chatty volume: Jack, squirrels, roosters, buzzards, and cows. Invite the children to "set a spell" and read these aloud to all ages.

Walker, Paul Robert. *Giants! Stories from Around the World.* Illustrated by James Bernardin. New York: Harcourt Brace, 1995.

This collection of seven stories is accompanied by detailed commentary and source notes. "Coyote and the Giant Sisters," from the Native Americans of the Pacific Northwest, is a trickster tale with transformation elements. Long ago, the animal people could take human form. One day they discover that all the salmon have disappeared. Coyote changes himself into a human baby and floats down the Big River. He is stopped by a dam built by five giant sisters, who are keeping all the salmon for themselves. They rescue the cute little baby and care for it in their lodge. During the days while they are out, Coyote transforms into a man and digs a hole in the dam, returning at night in the form of a baby. One day, the giant sisters discover him digging the hole, but he finishes just in time, releasing all the salmon. Then Coyote lectures the giants and turns them into swallows. He tells them that the people will know the salmon are coming when they see the birds. The swallows herald the salmon even to this day. This collection is an effective read-aloud source for all ages.

———. *Little Folk: Stories from Around the World.* Illustrated by James Bernardin. New York: Harcourt Brace, 1997.

This collection of eight stories about "little people"—leprechauns, fairies, Menehune, etc.—is accompanied by detailed source notes and commentary. "My Friend, the Nisse" (Denmark) tells about a nisse, a little old man who lives in the barn and plays pranks on the farmer. The farmer hires a farmhand who discovers the prankster and matches him prank for prank until they join forces and become friends. "The Capture of Summer," from the Wabanaki people of northeast North America, tells how Glooskap kidnaps a fairy, the queen of Summer, and brings her to the giant of the Winter, thus bringing summer to the north. In "The Red-Ribbon Leprechaun" (Ireland), Bridget Rooney captures a leprechaun and makes him show her where his gold is hidden. She marks the place with her red ribbon while she goes to fetch a shovel, but when she returns, the leprechaun has tied a red ribbon to ten thousand bushes, so that she no longer can find the place. Compare with *Clever Tom and the Leprechaun* by Linda Shute. These stories are most effective as read-alouds to primary and middle grades.

Walker, Richard. *The Barefoot Book of Trickster Tales*. Illustrated by Claudio Muñoz. Brooklyn, NY: Barefoot Books, 1998.

This collection of nine tales provides a variety of cultures and trickster characters. In "Jack and the Wizard" (English), Jack tricks an intimidating wizard into transforming himself repeatedly until he becomes an ant and Jack can gain the upper hand. "The Spirits in the Leather Bag" (Kampuchean) concerns the power of stories. A prince loves stories, so he has his faithful servant tell him one every night. After the tale is told, the spirit of the story goes into a leather bag in his bedchamber. The prince is jealous of the stories and never passes them on to anyone else, but the leather bag gets crowded with discontented spirits who conspire revenge against the prince. Each spirit plans to transform itself on the prince's wedding day to do mischief and harm to him, but the servant overhears their plans, saves the prince, and admonishes the prince to share the stories. "Turtle Goes on the Warpath" (Skidi Pawnee) is a variant of "Turtle Makes War on Man," in *The Boy Who Lived with the Bears* by Joseph Bruchac. Ananse has seldom been as clever as he is in "Ananse and the Impossible Quest" (Ghanaian). The king is tired of Ananse's cleverness, so he devises a task to foil him. He tells Ananse he wants him to go on a special quest for two things but will not tell him what they are. The task is to bring the king two items from the house of Death, from which no one returns, Ananse uses his wits to discover the mission and steal the objects for the king. A light storytelling style and large, well-spaced typeface make this collection suitable as a read-aloud to all ages and for independent reading for middle grades and up.

ORIGINAL TRICKSTER TALES

Banks, Lynne Reid. *The Magic Hare*. Illustrated by Barry Moser. New York: Morrow Junior Books, 1993.

This collection features 10 short stories about a hare with magical powers and a whimsical way of transforming people's lives for the better. They read like fairy tales, full of fantasy and delightful twists of plot. Moser's illustrations are masterful. These are delightful read-alouds for all ages.

Bassett, Jeni. *The Chicks' Trick*. Illustrated by the author. New York: Cobblehill Books, 1995.

Mrs. Heckle and Mrs. Peckle are proud mother hens, always arguing about whose baby chick is better. The two chicks, tired of their mothers' rivalry, secretly switch places. A double-switch maneuver has the moms fooled, and both hens promise their babies to get along with each other from now on.

Berry, James. *First Palm Trees: An Anancy Spiderman Story*. Illustrated by Greg Couch. New York: Simon & Schuster Books for Young Readers, 1997.

In this story, the priest tells the king of a dream he has had, of a wondrous new tree, a palm tree. The king announces a reward for the one who can create the tree of this dream. Anancy, determined to get the reward, enlists the help of the Sun-Spirit; together, he says, they can split the reward. The Sun-Spirit agrees to help. But much to Anancy's dismay, he enlists the help of Water-Spirit, who brings Earth-Spirit, who then brings Air-Spirit, into the plan. Anancy waits for the four spirits to create palm trees, but he hears nothing from his partners. Finally one day, everyone is called to gather at the palace grounds to view the king's new palm trees. Many people step forward to claim credit, including Anancy. The king decides to reward everyone equally with a feast. Anancy, the relentless schemer, is foiled in his quest for riches but is acknowledged as the catalyst for change. This tale is best suited for middle and upper grades.

DeFelice, Cynthia. *Clever Crow*. Illustrated by S. D. Schindler. New York: Atheneum
    Books for Young Readers, 1998.
    This original story, is told in rhyming verse, depicts a mischievous crow that
steals things, including Mama's car keys from the porch of the house. The daughter,
Emma, devises the trick to bring the keys back. She uses her treasured ball of shiny foil
gum wrappers to lure the bird back. The crow drops the keys to grab the shiny ball. This
is a short read-aloud for primary grades.

Hadithi, Mwenye. *Baby Baboon* (1993), *Crafty Chameleon* (1986), *Hungry Hyena* (1994),
    Tricky Tortoise (1988). Illustrated by Adrienne Kennaway. Boston: Little, Brown.
    These brief, original stories are told with the style and motifs of African folktales.
In *Baby Baboon*, a monkey tricks Leopard into tossing a captured Baby Baboon into a
tree, back to safety. *Crafty Chameleon* depicts the tug-of-war trick. In *Hungry Hyena*,
Fish Eagle plots a trick of revenge on the hyenas, who slink away in embarrassment.
Tricky Tortoise shows the trick of using a look-alike brother to feign an impossible
jump. Simple text and bright illustrations provide popular and successful independent
reading for first graders.

Hayes, Joe. *A Spoon for Every Bite*. Illustrated by Rebecca Leer. New York: Orchard,
    1996.
    Drawing on Hispanic folk elements, Hayes creates a story in which a poor young
couple asks their rich neighbor to be the godfather of their baby. They cannot have him
over to dinner because they have only two spoons, but finally, they save their pennies
to buy a third spoon. When they tell the rich man about the third spoon, he laughs at
them and brags that he has a different spoon for every day of the year. The poor woman
counters that they have a friend who has a new spoon for every bite. Not to be outdone,
the rich man buys spoons until he is impoverished, discarding the used spoons at the
poor couple's house. Finally, he meets the couple's friend with a new spoon for every
bite: a Native American who scoops and eats his beans with a tortilla!

Kesey, Ken. *Little Tricker the Squirrel Meets Big Double the Bear*. Illustrated by Barry
    Moser. New York: Viking, 1990.
    Big Double the bear is terrorizing the woodland creatures in his search of enough
food to last him through the winter. Despite his diminutive size, Little Tricker the
squirrel uses his wits to win out over the bear. Told in dramatic mountain storytelling
style, this rollicking and slightly gross tale is sure to amuse.

McDermott, Gerald. *Papagayo the Mischief Maker*. Illustrated by the author. New York:
    Harcourt Brace Jovanovich, 1992.
    This is an original tale based on a trickster character from the Amazon region.
Papagayo the parrot irritates the other animals of the rain forest, especially the nocturnal animals who are trying to sleep in the heat of the day. These nocturnal animals
love to gaze at the moon at night, but one night, a moon-eating monster comes and
takes a bite out of the moon. Each night he takes another bite of the moon. The
creatures get Papagayo to help get rid of the monster. Papagayo keeps watch at night
and gets all the animals to scare the monster away with their screeching and crying.

Meddaugh, Susan. *Hog-Eye*. Illustrated by the author. Boston: Houghton Mifflin, 1995.
    A little pig takes a path through the forest, where a wolf grabs her and takes her
home to make soup of her. She quickly surmises that the wolf can't read, so she "reads"
his recipe book to him. She calls for ingredients that allow her some chances to escape,
but she is unable to do so. Her final, essential ingredient sends the wolf out to a poison
ivy patch. This humorous story is fun for primary and middle grades.

Myers, Walter Dean. *How Mr. Monkey Saw the World.* Illustrated by Synthia Saint James. New York: Doubleday Books for Young Readers, 1996.

This original story is based on the folk elements found in the African American tale *The Cool Ride in the Sky* retold by Diane Wolkstein. During a famine, Mr. Buzzard gets food from the smaller animals by enticing them with a ride in the sky on his back. If they give him a food item, he will take them flying. Once in the air, he frightens them by flying upside down, and he threatens to return them safely only if they give him all the rest of their food. Monkey witnesses this ploy and plays his own trick on Buzzard when his turn comes to ride in the sky. For a young audience, this tale is readable by second graders and up.

Olaleye, Isaac. *Bitter Bananas.* Illustrated by Ed Young. Honesdale, PA: Boyds Mills Press, 1994.

With the look and feel of an African folktale, this is a story of how a boy outwits the baboons who are stealing his sweet palm sap. He mixes palm sap and wormwood, then flavors bananas with the concoction. This bitter-tasting bait cures the baboons of their nuisance behavior. Young children will enjoy joining the refrains of "Oh, no! Oh, no!" and "Oh, yes!" throughout the story.

Root, Phyllis. *Aunt Nancy and Old Man Trouble.* Illustrated by David Parkins. Cambridge, MA: Candlewick Press, 1996.

When Old Man Trouble shows up at Aunt Nancy's door, she lets him in. Things immediately begin to go wrong around her cabin: The stove goes out, she drops and breaks a glass, and her chair breaks. But instead of getting flustered, she comments on how fortunate it is that those things happened, for one reason or another. Old Man Trouble gets discouraged, seeing he can't upset Aunt Nancy. Finally, when she says she's lucky that the spring has dried up, he decides to bring back the spring water and leave. Young children may need a little help catching the subtlety of Aunt Nancy's trickery and the fact that "Aunt Nancy" is a variation of "Anansi." Told in dialect, this is a read-aloud for primary or middle grades.

Schami, Rafik, and Anthea Bell. *Fatima and the Dream Thief.* Illustrated by Els Cools and Oliver Streich. New York: North-South Books, 1996.

Told with the feel of a Middle Eastern folktale, this is the story of how a girl outwits a bullying giant. The son of a poor, sick woman is determined to find work. He finds a castle, where a giant gives him work, but he says he will pay him only if he does not get angry. At the end of the week, as the boy does his chores, the giant inflicts boorish tricks and insults upon the boy, until he does indeed get angry and leave. Next, the boy's sister, Fatima, tries her luck at the same castle. She goes about her work with jaunty self-confidence and finds ways to trick the giant. She finds a room where the giant keeps all the dreams he has stolen from people. Fatima releases the dreams, calls the giant's bluff, and goes home. There, she finds her brother and mother much recovered because their dreams have returned to them.

Wolff, Patricia Rae. *The Toll-Bridge Troll.* Illustrated by Kimberly Bulcken Root. New York: Browndeer Press, 1995.

This is a lighthearted story about a contemporary boy who must face a troll every morning on his way to school. The troll demands a penny to cross the bridge, and the boy proposes a riddle contest instead. The first two days, the boy's quick thinking gets him across. The third day, the boy poses a riddle involving coins, a simple math problem. The troll can't solve it. On the way home from school that same day, the boy learns that the troll's mother wants her son to go to school with the boy, so he can become smart. This story is suitable for primary grades.

Wyllie, Stephen. *A Flea in the Ear*. Illustrated by Ken Brown. New York: Dutton Children's
  Books, 1995.

This is a short, humorous story of double trickery. A wily fox tries to snatch some
hens, but a faithful watchdog rebuffs him. When he learns that the dog is suffering from
fleas, the fox offers a cure. Desperate to obtain relief, the dog, following the fox's
instruction, runs to the pond to drown the fleas. Meanwhile, the fox steals the hens.
When he returns and finds the hens missing, the dog follows their trail to the fox's den.
The dog tells the fox that he couldn't try the cure because the pond is full of fat, juicy
ducks. The fox goes to the pond to eat the ducks, but all he gets is the fleas left behind
by the dog.

Chapter 5

introduction

Children are turned into swans; a man changes into a seal; a woman slips into a dog's skin; a boy becomes a star; the downtrodden youngest son becomes an armor-clad hero. Enchantment, magic spells, spells of punishment or revenge, transformations rewarding honest hard work, transformations to play a trick, shapeshifting—these and more are the wonder of transformation tales. Transformation tales allow us to escape from our everyday, logical, practical world into a world of enchantment, a world in which animals become people and poor people become royalty. Tales of transformation and shapeshifting occur in nearly every culture (Jones 1995, 390). Although these acts of transformation occur for a variety of reasons, they remind us that things can and do change; they sometimes personify our fear of change; and they also fill us with hope that we *can* change and end up happily transformed.

The term "transformation tale," as it is used here, actually covers a range of tales and transformation types. "Transformation" is caused by magic or enchantment; often a transformation is performed on another being by someone such as a sorcerer (in European or Asian tales) or a god (in myths). In Native American folklore, Raven and Coyote are creator/culture-heroes that are both transformers and tricksters. Also, in some Native American cultures, different animals act as transformers of other beings. In contrast to a change caused by a transformer, "shapeshifting" is a voluntary act. Shapeshifters can change their own form and include spirit-beings, animals, ghosts, objects, and interveners. Interveners are mysterious persons or animals who appear to give advice or help, such as the fairy godmother (old man, old woman, etc.) in a Cinderella tale (Leach and Fried 1972, 1004–5). Some shapeshifters achieve their changes through some external object, such as the skin of an animal, as in selkie stories. Sometimes the attributes of a shapeshifter and transformer are present in the same character, such as Raven.

Many of the motifs found in the "Transformation" category of this guide are familiar to Americans because of the strong influence of European culture: stories such as Cinderella, Beauty and the Beast, and The Frog Prince. These are often referred to as "fairy tales." Familiar stories circulating in Europe began to be written down in the sixteenth and seventeenth centuries, and it became popular among upper-class adults to embellish and share these stories. It wasn't until the nineteenth century that these stories came into common use and were written into versions for children (Zipes 1991).

The fairy tale is part of a body of tales from the oral tradition known as "wonder tales," usually involving magic and ending happily. Before these tales came into the body of written fairy tales, they were part of the oral tradition for centuries. Folklore specialist Jack Zipes explains that the transformational elements of these ancient stories contain elements dear to the human heart, causing them to endure: "The early oral tales that served as the basis for the development of the literary fairy tales were closely tied to the rituals, customs, and beliefs of tribes, communities and trades. They fostered a sense of belonging and the hope that miracles involving some kind of magical transformation were possible to bring about a better world" (Zipes 1991, xii).

The European fairy tale usually features transformations that are seemingly impossible events in terms of everyday life. However, transformation tales from other cultures reflect different roots, philosophy, and ethos. Indigenous cultures that have lived close to nature have stories that accept the phenomenon of transformation as a more natural part of living. Many of these cultures view life more holistically; there are few, if any, boundaries between day-to-day life, work, religion, the animal world, the spirit world, and nature. There is a natural flow through the different phases of life, and all people are connected closely with the natural world, which gives the people their life and livelihood. Because of this closeness with nature, it is more commonly accepted that humans can pass easily back and forth into the forms of animals, mountains, stars, and waterfalls. Transformational events are closely associated with geography and the sky. Tales and myths of Native Americans, Maoris, Aboriginals of Australia, and many African cultures reflect this holistic view. A person may change into a dolphin or a star, and while there is a sense of quiet wonder in this happening, it is not an event of impossible magic. Instead, it reflects a kinship with the natural world; it reminds us that everything is connected somehow.

Native American folktales reflect this sense of transformation as an accepted phenomenon of kinship and connectedness with nature. Because Native American cultures and peoples are vastly different in their various traditions and stories, there are few characteristics that apply to *all* Native American traditions and stories. However, some general observations about Native American transformation tales can be noted. In many tales, especially those of the northern Arctic regions, a human's view of the physical world can be temporary, and some beings or objects can change their shape without notice. Traditional Euro-American logic does not apply to these stories. Transformations in Native American tales happen just because they happen, as an accepted phenomenon. Generally, in these tales, humans do not exert the same control over their environment that humans in European tales do. Rather, these stories defer to powers of the natural world, including transformational events. Stories are not just tales about living beings; stories are considered to be living things themselves, and they are told partly to remind people that life is sacred (Norman 1990, xiii). Tales in which animals and people change forms provide a knowledge base about the animal world, and also they reflect a deep empathy with animals (Norman 1990, 145). They reflect a reverence and a range of emotions associated with recognizing the power and bounty of nature.

Transformation can also be seen as the inevitable process of human learning, living, aging, and growing. Storyteller Teresa Pijoan remarks that as a parent, she sees her daughters changing and undergoing transformations as they grow, and she recognizes change in herself. She comments, "In the Indian tradition we are on the path, and endeavoring to stay on the path, when testing comes to us, and we believe that we are on the right path, and that transformation is inevitable" (Young 1992, 12). The concept of change as inevitable marks a difference between Native American and European transformation tales. In European tales, a transformation is sometimes fearful, a thing to be avoided (e.g., a spell by an evil sorcerer that turns a princess into a frog or a prince into a beast). In Native American traditions, transformations are viewed with acceptance, and they reflect a spiritual closeness to the world of animals and nature. In the Native American view, the spirit world and natural world are very close, so it is natural that some beings can pass between them (p. 13).

Criteria for classifying stories as "transformation tales" in this guide are broad and inclusive. The most obvious kind of tale involves a total change of physical form: a princess into a frog, a man into a beast, a boy into a fish, children into stars. But there are other kinds of transformations as well: an enchantment makes an old person young; a certain fruit revives a dying princess; fine clothing from a magical helper transforms a downtrodden servant into a mysterious hero or heroine. In some tales, the outward transformation is accompanied by an interior transformation in a character's thinking or attitudes.

The wonder of transformation tales holds great appeal for children of all ages. They offer an outlet for imagination in an age in which technology and practicality are revered. They offer a totally different spin on life. They invite us into a different world. They fill us with astonishment, not only when we see transformational events occur but also when we see similar story elements occur in other stories from different traditions. These tales offer opportunities for making connections between cultures. They let us dare to hope that anything is possible. As Jack Zipes observes:

"We want to be given opportunities to change, and ultimately we want to be told that we can become kings and queens, or lords of our own destinies. We remember wonder tales and fairy tales to keep our sense of wonderment alive and to nurture our hope that we can seize possibilities and opportunities to transform ourselves and our worlds" (Zipes 1991, xv–xvi).

REFERENCES

Erdoes, Richard, and Alfonzo Ortiz. 1984. Introduction to *American Indian Myths and Legends*. New York: Pantheon Books.

Jones, Alison. 1995. *Larousse Dictionary of World Folklore*. New York: Larousse.

Leach, Maria, and Jerome Fried, eds. 1972. *Funk & Wagnalls Standard Dictionary of Folklore, Mythology and Legend*. New York: Funk & Wagnalls.

Norman, Howard. 1990. *Northern Tales: Traditional Stories of Eskimo and Indian Peoples*. New York: Pantheon Books.

Young, Richard and Judy Dockery. 1992. Introduction to *White Wolf Woman: Native American Transformation Myths*, by Teresa Pijoan. Little Rock, AR: August House.

Zipes, Jack, ed. 1991. Introduction to *Spells of Enchantment: The Wondrous Fairy Tales of Western Culture*. New York: Viking.

Chapter 6

USING TRANSFORMATION TALES WITH CHILDREN

Transformation tales captivate audiences of all ages. These tales are often longer and more complicated than other kinds of folktales published for children, and yet they continue to hold listeners. They are filled with plot twists, enchantment, magic, journeys, adventure, and challenges. These complexities offer something for the older grades, and yet, with a few pauses to check and discuss with the listeners, even first graders follow these tales with passionate purpose. Listeners are held fast by the suspense and drama, the sense of quest, an outrage at the unjust treatment of a character, an identification with the struggle of the protagonist. And they rejoice with the hero or heroine who persists against daunting obstacles. Transformation tales are excellent for story gatherings including a wide age range. Summer library/reading programs and recreation programs in which children show up in unpredictable age combinations can experience success with these tales. And these tales aren't just for children; their elements of conflict, yearning, romance, and irony appeal to adults as well.

Whether they are used in a school setting, a public library, or recreation setting, transformation tales have much to offer, especially when used as a planned grouping of tales followed by creative extension activities. They provide a multicultural context for imaginative thinking, and they help develop listening skills over longer stretches of time. A recreation program could feature a set of three stories followed by an art activity based upon the transformational images in the stories. An instructional team of a teacher and school librarian could lead students through a study using graphic organizers (such as Venn diagrams) for compare-and-contrast activities. Students could write their own transformation tales and make them come alive using a computer multimedia program. A public library could use a transformation theme as the basis for reading incentives or dramatizations or puppet plays. Background on the stories is provided in the annotated bibliography (Chapter 8), and ideas for grouping or linking stories can be found in the story themes and topics chart (Chapter 7). Perusing the chart may spark ideas or suggest new ways to use the tales' conceptual, thematic, and topical elements. The index provides even more information about a title.

The following plans and activities are based on whole-group read-aloud experiences and are not particularly age specific. Most of the tales can be read aloud to a range of ages, and adjustments for the particular group are up to the judgment of the leader or teacher.

These tales are most effective as read-alouds and as catalysts for creative outlets. Many elementary school students, while finding the texts challenging for independent reading, can readily grasp the stories' complexities and express their thinking if the story is read aloud. Adults may use the activities listed below as a menu of options to extend and explore this rich body of literature.

The following types of extensions and explorations are presented in this chapter:

- Compare-and-contrast activities: Questioning strategies and Venn diagrams.

- The Cinderella tale: Comparisons, motifs, charts, and Venn diagrams.

- Student writing and multimedia production: Strategies and planning sheets for students to create their own original transformation stories, in either written or multimedia format.

- Other curricular tie-ins: Transformations in science, biography, and fiction.

- Art activities: Accordion-fold picture, flag book, sliding image, transformation doll, shadow puppet theater.

FOCUS AND GOALS FOR TRANSFORMATION TALE LITERATURE STUDY

Focus Statement: Since times of old, people of different cultures have created and passed on stories with transformation elements. These stories often include aspects of magic and enchantment. Similar kinds of transformations exist across cultures. These stories were told for a variety of purposes, including entertainment, instruction, and perpetuating a sense of quest, wonder, and hope.

Goals:

- The learner will listen to (or read) a variety of transformation tales from different cultures.

- The learner will develop listening skills, focusing on longer and more complicated plots.

- The learner will identify the transformation elements in a story.

- The learner will participate in discussions of transformation tales, identifying aspects of character, plot, and cause-and-effect.

- The learner will participate in compare-and-contrast activities, comparing the similar elements in two or more tales. The learner will identify unique and similar elements in these stories and show his or her understanding in some graphic way.

- The learner will participate in discussions that recognize and identify common themes across different cultures.

- The learner will respond to these stories with a creative project, such as an original story, an art project, or a multimedia production.

COMPARE-AND-CONTRAST ACTIVITIES

When planning a series of stories for storyhours or literature classes, consider reading and discussing a set of stories with common elements. (Consult the story themes and topics chart in Chapter 7 for thematic or topical elements that link stories together.) When listening to a second or third story with similar elements, children will eagerly begin to point out parts of the story that remind them of another story. This is an optimal opportunity to formalize these developing thought processes. Compare-and-contrast activities develop children's higher order thinking skills. When they exercise skills of analysis and comparison, they are using thinking paths that are more advanced than tasks of simple recall. And developing a graphic organizer such as a Venn diagram or a chart helps children to visualize and organize the similarities and differences among stories in terms of plot, character, or cause-and-effect. They also deepen their multicultural understanding as they begin to recognize different cultures of origin, and then recognize commonalties (as well as unique features) that exist across and between cultures.

To get started on compare-and-contrast activities, begin with general discussion questions, to make sure that students have some basic understanding of the story. Then ask some leading questions to bridge into the formal compare-and-contrast activity.

General Discussion Questions

During and after reading aloud, check with students by asking them questions to make sure they are tuned in to the story and understand the plot. This questioning process, especially during the story, is not something to labor over, and it should not be intrusive to the unfolding of the plot. There are some who believe one should never interrupt a story with questions. But if it happens during natural pauses in the story and students are eager to respond, the storyline will not be interrupted. The children will be your best indicators of this; if they are impatient to continue the story, resume reading. With the intricacies of transformation tales, it helps everyone to briefly pause and check for understanding. Some general guidelines for questioning during and after a story include the following:

- What (or who) is being transformed or changed? Why? Do you think another transformation will happen in this story? What and why?

- Is there an enchanter, sorcerer, or other person with magical powers? How does this character use his or her powers?

- Who is the main character, the "good guy," the one we are empathizing with or following? What does this person want and need? Why is this person acting the way he or she is? Do you think this person can achieve his or her goals? How would you feel right now to be that person? Why?

- Are there powers of "good" and "bad" in this story? What or who are they?

- How do other characters influence the main character?

- When there is a long, winding plot, or a series of significant events or transformations, it may help to ask: Where have we been, and where are we going?

- At the end of the story: What other kinds of transformations do you think the magical person could perform? Why would he or she do this?

- At the end of the story: Did any of the characters learn anything in this story? Do you think someone could tell this story and hope someone else would learn a lesson from it? What lesson?

- At the end of the story: What do you think is the most important thing to the main character? What does she or he value most?

A note about "logic" in fairy tales and folktales: Often, during the course of a story, thoughtful students will comment, "Why doesn't the person just do this?" or "That couldn't really happen!" or "How could that be?" These are legitimate questions that sometimes bring the group up short. Students are applying modern-day logical, cause-and-effect questioning and should be recognized for asking good questions. To help students out of this quandary, remind them that for the time being, the group is in the world of folktales and fairy tales. In this world, today's logic often doesn't work. Things are the way they are in a folktale, and listeners just have to accept the world within the story. Wonder and magic are often a part of the folktale world.

Questioning for Compare-and-Contrast Activities

It takes very little questioning to get students started in a Venn diagram activity. Usually, they are eager to bring up points of comparison, including minute details that the teacher hasn't thought of. Prepare a large Venn diagram on a large piece of chart paper, on an overhead projector, or on a computer with graphic capabilities. Label each circle with a story title. Explain to students that each component of the stories will be written somewhere in the circle. If the component exists for two of the stories, it will be written in the space where the two circles overlap. If it exists in just one story, it will be written in the space belonging only to that one story. If the activity is to compare three tales, it may help to start with just two circles, and then add the third once the activity is in full-swing. But be prepared for students who like to start with the ideas that are common to all three stories. And keep in mind the commonalties you want the children to identify, in case they need some questions to lead them in that direction.

To start the process, ask some questions that will get the children to think about the story components. As each component is identified, have the students determine which area of the diagram to write it in: common to two stories, common to all three stories, or found in just one story. Such questions may include the following:

- *Basic plot questions:* What is the problem in Story 1? What happens first? How is this the same or different in Story 2? Is it true for one story, or two, or all three? What other plot elements are important?

- *Transformation questions:* What or who is transformed in Story 1? Into what? How about Stories 2 and 3? Does the person transform himself or herself, or does someone do it to him or her? Is there a magic spell? Is there a magical helper? What would break the spell? Is the transformation helpful, or is it a problem for the character?

- *Cause-and-effect questions:* What causes something to happen in Stories 1, 2, 3? How does each story's plot resolve?

- *Setting questions:* Where do Stories 1, 2, 3 take place?

- *Character questions:* Who is the main character in Stories 1, 2, 3?

- *Cultural questions:* What culture is each story from? What parts of the stories are the same, regardless of culture? What parts are unique to each culture?

On the following pages are two examples of Venn diagrams that are the result of actual student discussions (figs. 6.1 and 6.2, pages 120–21). The story themes and topics chart (Chapter 7) provides additional ideas for linking stories with similar themes and topics. Also provided are blank Venn diagrams for duplication (figs. 6.3 and 6.4, pages 122–23).

Text continues on page 124.

Unique and Overlapping Elements of
The White Cat, The Frog Princess, and *The Princess and the Frog*

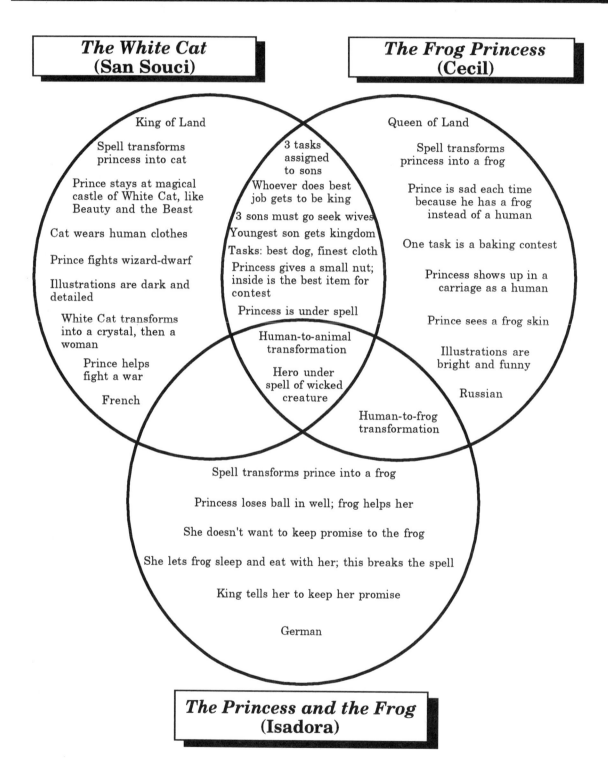

The White Cat (San Souci)

King of Land

Spell transforms princess into cat

Prince stays at magical castle of White Cat, like Beauty and the Beast

Cat wears human clothes

Prince fights wizard-dwarf

Illustrations are dark and detailed

White Cat transforms into a crystal, then a woman

Prince helps fight a war

French

The Frog Princess (Cecil)

Queen of Land

Spell transforms princess into a frog

Prince is sad each time because he has a frog instead of a human

One task is a baking contest

Princess shows up in a carriage as a human

Prince sees a frog skin

Illustrations are bright and funny

Russian

3 tasks assigned to sons

Whoever does best job gets to be king

3 sons must go seek wives

Youngest son gets kingdom

Tasks: best dog, finest cloth

Princess gives a small nut; inside is the best item for contest

Princess is under spell

Human-to-animal transformation

Hero under spell of wicked creature

Human-to-frog transformation

Spell transforms prince into a frog

Princess loses ball in well; frog helps her

She doesn't want to keep promise to the frog

She lets frog sleep and eat with her; this breaks the spell

King tells her to keep her promise

German

The Princess and the Frog (Isadora)

Fig. 6.1.

Unique and Overlapping Elements of
The Selkie Girl, The Enchanted Cap, and *The Seal Prince*

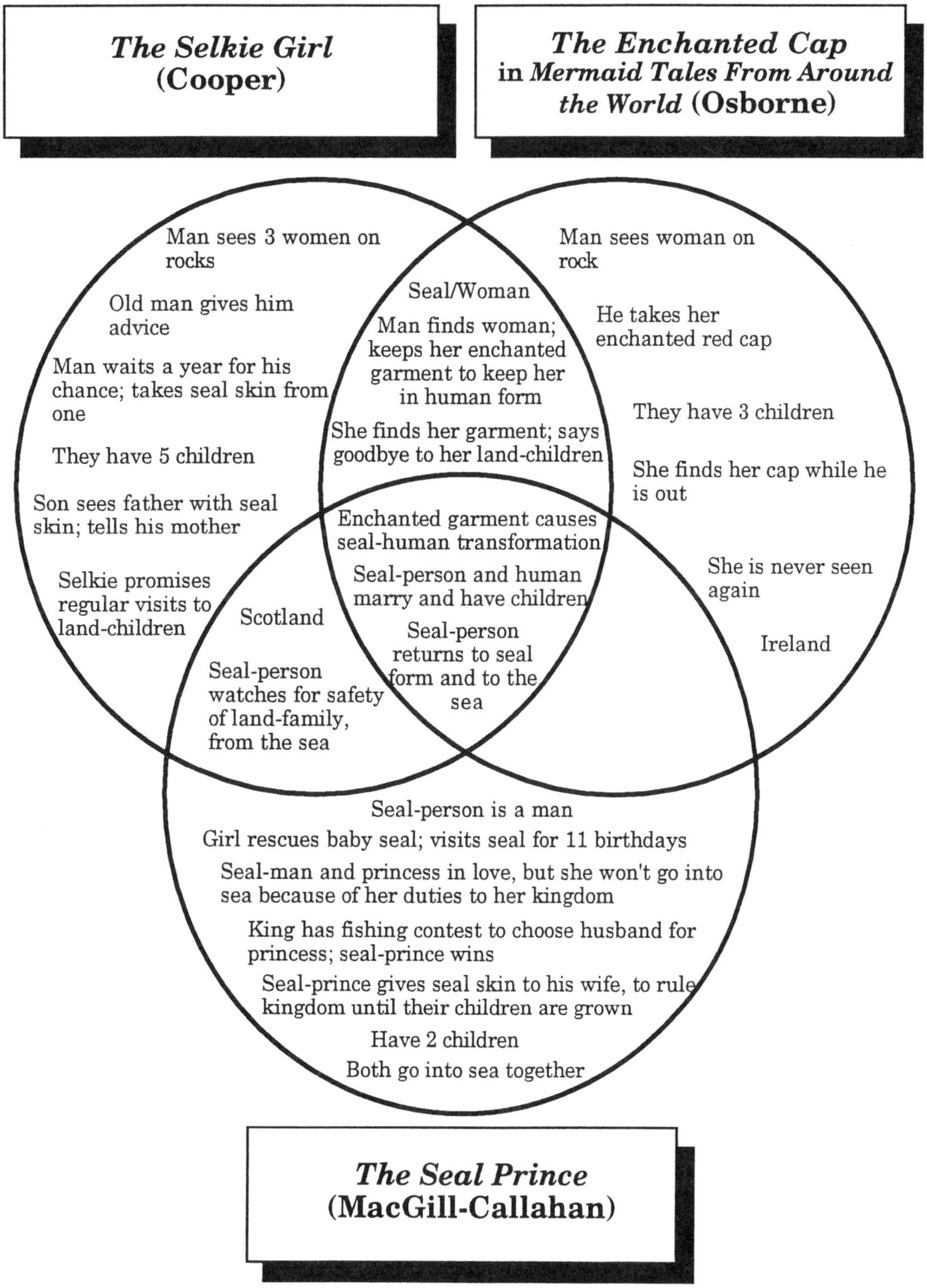

The Selkie Girl
(Cooper)

The Enchanted Cap
in *Mermaid Tales From Around the World* (Osborne)

Man sees 3 women on rocks

Old man gives him advice

Man waits a year for his chance; takes seal skin from one

They have 5 children

Son sees father with seal skin; tells his mother

Selkie promises regular visits to land-children

Seal/Woman
Man finds woman; keeps her enchanted garment to keep her in human form

She finds her garment; says goodbye to her land-children

Enchanted garment causes seal-human transformation

Seal-person and human marry and have children

Seal-person returns to seal form and to the sea

Scotland

Seal-person watches for safety of land-family, from the sea

Man sees woman on rock

He takes her enchanted red cap

They have 3 children

She finds her cap while he is out

She is never seen again

Ireland

Seal-person is a man

Girl rescues baby seal; visits seal for 11 birthdays

Seal-man and princess in love, but she won't go into sea because of her duties to her kingdom

King has fishing contest to choose husband for princess; seal-prince wins

Seal-prince gives seal skin to his wife, to rule kingdom until their children are grown

Have 2 children

Both go into sea together

The Seal Prince
(MacGill-Callahan)

Fig. 6.2.

From *Folktale Themes and Activities for Children, Vol. 2*. © 1999 Anne Marie Kraus. Libraries Unlimited. (800) 237-6124.

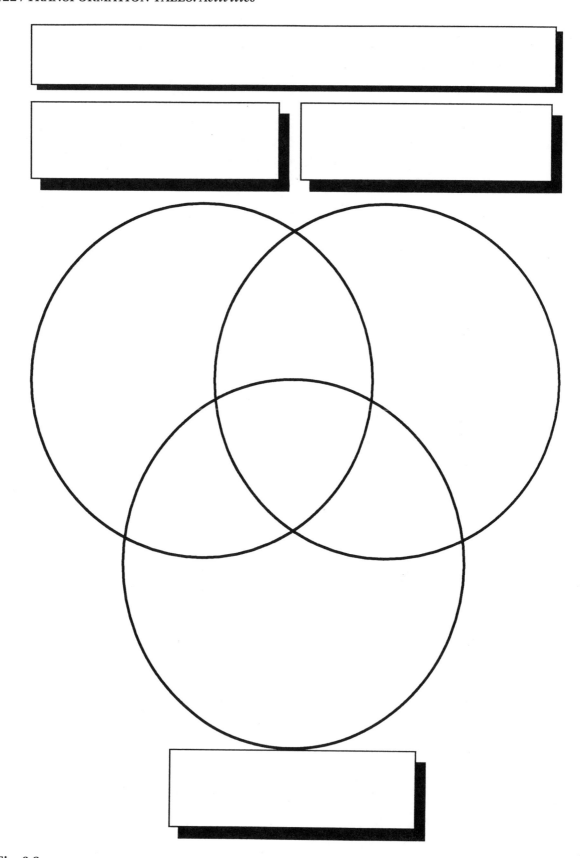

Fig. 6.3.

From *Folktale Themes and Activities for Children, Vol. 2*. © 1999 Anne Marie Kraus. Libraries Unlimited. (800) 237-6124.

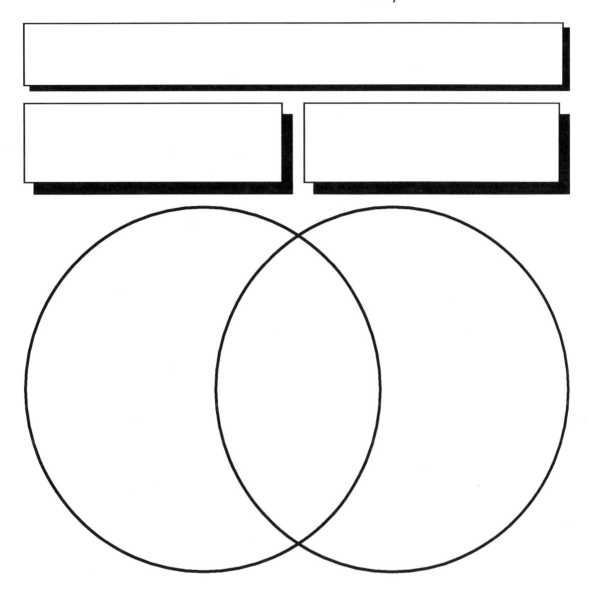

Fig. 6.4.

The Folk Process

Now that the children have discussed stories from different cultures and noted ways in which the same themes or motifs occur across cultures, discuss with them the nature of folktales and how remarkable it is that the same story elements travel across continents and cultural groups. For an explanation of this phenomenon, see "The Folk Process" (pp. 16–18).

THE CINDERELLA TALE:
VARIANTS AND COMPARISONS

A fascinating manifestation of the folk process is the Cinderella tale. Cultures all over the globe have their own versions of this tale. Some Cinderella characters are male while others are female, some have a magical helper while some succeed on their own power, some are rescued while others take a more active role in their destiny. Regardless of the differences, these tales contain some common motifs that identify them as Cinderella variants. The Cinderella character is downtrodden, or is at least written off as someone who won't amount to much. There is usually a family member (e.g., the evil stepmother) who scorns the Cinderella character. There is usually magic or some enchantment, and there is always a transformation. Sometimes the transformation is the physical change from rags to finery, but sometimes it is an attitude transformation of the Cinderella character or a transformation in how others view him or her. The Cinderella is no longer a "nobody," but someone to be reckoned with or admired.

A study of transformation tales would not be complete without a look at Cinderella transformations. More Cinderella variants emerge in picture-book editions every year. For your reference, this guide includes a summary of many of these new picture-book editions of Cinderella tales in chart form (see fig. 6.5 on pp. 127–30). Use this chart as a model for creating your own wall-sized chart for recording and comparing the editions you read. It is a visual way for children to understand how the tradition of storytelling has carried great stories around the globe.

This summary chart is not a comprehensive or authoritative survey of Cinderella tales. Indeed, entire books have been written about this phenomenon. But it is a place to start for group discussion and comparison. On the following pages are a Cinderella bibliography, the summary chart (fig. 6.5 on pp. 127–30), two Venn diagrams (figs. 6.6 and 6.7 on pp. 131–32), and a chart of male Cinderella variants (fig. 6.8 on p. 133).

Variant Tellings of Cinderella

Behan, Brendan. *The King of Ireland's Son*. Illustrated by P. J. Lynch. New York: Orchard, 1997.

Bender, Robert. *Toads and Diamonds*. Illustrated by the author. New York: Lodestar Books, 1995.

Climo, Shirley. *The Egyptian Cinderella*. Illustrated by Ruth Heller. New York: Thomas Y. Crowell, 1989.

———. *The Irish Cinderlad*. Illustrated by Loretta Krupinski. New York: HarperCollins, 1996.

———. *The Korean Cinderella*. Illustrated by Ruth Heller. New York: HarperCollins, 1993.

Coburn, Jewell Reinhart, and Tzexa Cherta Lee. *Jouanah: A Hmong Cinderella*. Illustrated by Anne Sibley O'Brien. Arcadia, CA: Shen's Books, 1996.

Compton, Joanne. *Ashpet: An Appalachian Tale*. Illustrated by Ken Compton. New York: Holiday House, 1994.

DeFelice, Cynthia, and Mary De Marsh. *Three Perfect Peaches: A French Folktale*. Illustrated by Irene Trivas. New York: Orchard, 1995.

Ehrlich, Amy. *Cinderella*. Illustrated by Susan Jeffers. New York: Dial Books for Young Readers, 1985.

Geras, Adèle. "Vipers and Pearls" in *Beauty and the Beast: And Other Stories*. Illustrated by Louise Brierley. New York: Viking, 1996.

Greene, Ellin. *Billy Beg and His Bull: An Irish Tale*. Illustrated by Kimberly Bulken Root. New York: Holiday House, 1994.

Hamilton, Virginia. "Catskinella" in *Her Stories: African American Folktales, Fairy Tales, and True Tales*. Illustrated by Leo and Diane Dillon. New York: Blue Sky Press, 1995.

Han, Oki S., and Stephanie Haboush Plunkett. *Kongi and Potgi: A Cinderella Tale from Korea*. Illustrated by Oki S. Han. New York: Dial Books for Young Readers, 1996.

Hickox, Rebecca. *The Golden Sandal: A Middle Eastern Cinderella Story*. Illustrated by Will Hillenbrand. New York: Holiday House, 1998.

Hogrogian, Nonny. *Cinderella*. Illustrated by the author. New York: Greenwillow Books, 1981.

Hooks, William H. *Moss Gown*. Illustrated by Donald Carrick. New York: Clarion Books, 1987.

Huck, Charlotte. *Princess Furball*. Illustrated by Anita Lobel. New York: Greenwillow Books, 1989.

———. *Toads and Diamonds*. Illustrated by Anita Lobel. New York: Greenwillow Books, 1996.

Kimmel, Eric A. *The Three Princes: A Tale from the Middle East*. Illustrated by Leonard Everett Fisher. New York: Holiday House, 1994.

Louie, Ai-Ling. *Yeh-Shen: A Cinderella Story from China*. Illustrated by Ed Young. New York: Philomel Books, 1982.

Martin, Claire. *Boots and the Glass Mountain*. Illustrated by Gennady Spirin. New York: Dial Press, 1992.

Martin, Rafe. *The Rough-Face Girl*. Illustrated by David Shannon. New York: G. P. Putnam's Sons, 1992.

Mayo, Margaret. "Three Golden Apples" in *Magical Tales from Many Lands*. Illustrated by Jane Ray. New York: Dutton Children's Books, 1993.

Mills, Lauren. *Tatterhood and the Hobgoblins: A Norwegian Folktale*. Illustrated by the author. Boston: Little, Brown, 1993.

Onyefulu, Obi. *Chinye: A West African Folk Tale*. Illustrated by Evie Safarewicz. New York: Viking, 1994.

Pollock, Penny. *The Turkey Girl: A Zuni Cinderella Story*. Illustrated by Ed Young. Boston: Little, Brown, 1996.

San Souci, Robert D. *Cendrillion: A Caribbean Cinderella*. Illustrated by Brian Pinkney. New York: Simon & Schuster Books for Young Readers, 1998.

———. *The Little Seven-Colored Horse: A Spanish American Folktale*. Illustrated by Jan Thompson Dicks. San Francisco: Chronicle Books, 1995.

———. *Sootface: An Ojibwa Cinderella Story*. Illustrated by Daniel San Souci. New York: Doubleday Book for Young Readers, 1994.

———. *The Talking Eggs: A Folktale from the American South*. Illustrated by Jerry Pinkney. New York: Dial Books for Young Readers, 1989.

Schroeder, Alan. *Smoky Mountain Rose: An Appalachian Cinderella*. Illustrated by Brad Sneed. New York: Dial Books for Young Readers, 1997.

Sierra, Judy. *Cinderella*. Illustrated by Joanne Caroselli. Phoenix, AZ: Oryx, 1992. (Note: This is from The Oryx Multicultural Folktale Series, a scholarly compendium of 25 tales, their sources, commentary, and activities for professional use and reading aloud.)

Steel, Flora Annie. *Tattercoats: An Old English Tale*. Illustrated by Diane Goode. Scarsdale, NY: Bradbury Press, 1976.

Steptoe, John. *Mufaro's Beautiful Daughters*. Illustrated by the author. New York: Lothrop, Lee & Shepard, 1987.

Vuong, Lynette Dyer. *The Brocaded Slipper: And Other Vietnamese Tales*. Illustrated by Vo-Dinh Mai. Reading, MA: Addison-Wesley, 1982.

Walker, Paul Robert. "The Giant Who Had No Heart" in *Giants! Stories from Around the World*. Illustrated by James Bernardin. New York: Harcourt Brace, 1995.

Wilson, Barbara Ker. *Wishbones: A Folk Tale from China*. Illustrated by Meilo So. New York: Bradbury Press, 1993.

Winthrop, Elizabeth. *The Little Humpbacked Horse: A Russian Tale*. Illustrated by Alexander Koshkin. New York: Clarion Books, 1997.

———. *Vasilissa the Beautiful: A Russian Folktale*. Illustrated by Alexander Koshkin. New York: HarperCollins, 1991.

Compare-and-Contrast Activities for Cinderella Variants

On the following pages are suggestions for meaningful comparisons among selected Cinderella tales: the reward-and-punishment motif in *The Talking Eggs* and variants (fig. 6.6); the healing fruit theme in *Three Perfect Peaches* and variants (fig. 6.7); and a chart of comparisons of male Cinderellas with animal helpers (fig. 6.8).

Text continues on page 134.

Cinderella Summary Chart

Title/Author/Culture	Heroine's (or Hero's) Name/ *Magical Helper/ Magical Object*	Evil Character(s) (Stepmother)	Ball, Contest, Event, Journey/ *Shoe or Slipper*	Transformation/ *Outcome, Resolution*
Ashpet (Compton) Appalachian (American)	Ashpet (hired girl)/ *Granny over the ridge*/Granny's walking stick	Widow Hooper and her two daughters	Big church meetin'/*Her red shoe*	Undone housework done. Pretty red dress and shoes. *She marries the doctor's son. Widow and girls move away.*
Billy Beg and His Bull (Greene) Irish	Billy Beg/*Bull/* Stick, sword; belt from dead bull's hide	Stepmother	Fight multiheaded dragon and win the princess's hand/*His shoe*	Stick into sword, ordinary strength into superhuman strength. *He marries the princess.*
Boots and the Glass Mountain (Martin) Norwegian	Boots (young man)/*Three enchanted horses/* Steel tinderbox from his mother	Two older brothers	Contest to ride to the top of Glass Mountain and win the princess's hand/*Golden apples from princess*	Ragged commoner into armor-clad hero. *He marries the princess.*
The Brocaded Slipper (Vuong) Vietnamese	Tam/*Fairy*/Fish, fishbones	Stepmother, stepsister Cam	A walk when she loses shoe; a summons from the king to find owner of shoe/*Red brocaded slipper*	Fishbones into jewelry and dress. Tam into princess, bird, tree, loom, persimmon, into Tam again. *Prince and Tam are reunited; live happily married; Cam dies trying to run away.*
"Catskinella" in *Her Stories* (Hamilton) African American	Catskinella/*God-mother, Mother Mattie*/Talking mirror	Father, woodsman who wants to marry her	King's command for all the maidens to bake a cake for his son/*Ring*	Catskin dress into shimmering dress of diamonds. *She marries the prince.*
Cendrillon (San Souci) Caribbean/Creole	Cendrillon/ *Godmother (washerwoman)/* Magic wand	Prospérine (stepmother)	Rich man's birthday ball/*Pink embroidered slipper*	Breadfruit into carriage. Small animals into horses, footmen, coachmen. Rags into gown. *She marries Paul, the wealthy man.*
Chinye: A West African Folk Tale (Onyefulu) African (West)	Chinye/*Old woman*/Gourd	Stepmother, stepsister	Visit to hut with sound of singing/ (*No shoe motif*)	Quiet gourds turn into riches: gold, ivory, etc.; talking gourds turn into thunder and wind. *She uses her riches to help her village.*
Cinderella (Hogrogian) German	Cinderella/*Fairy dove in the hazel tree planted on her mother's grave/* Rustling in the tree	Stepmother, two stepsisters	Ball/festival lasting 3 days and nights/ *Silver slippers, embroidered slippers, gold slippers*	Rags into radiant gown and slippers. *She marries prince; two stepsisters are stricken blind.*
Cinderella (Ehrlich) French	Cinderella/*Fairy godmother*/Magic wand	Stepmother, two stepsisters	Ball at the king's palace/*Glass slipper*	Pumpkin into carriage, mice and rats into horses and coachman. Rags into gown. *She marries prince. She forgives stepsisters, gives them homes and husbands in the palace.*
The Egyptian Cinderella (Climo) Egyptian	Rhodopis/*Falcon/* A sign from the god Horus	Egyptian servant girls	City square, where Pharaoh is holding court/*Slipper with toe of rose-red gold*	Slave girl into queen. *She marries the Pharoah.*

Fig. 6.5.

Fig. 6.5 continues on page 128.

From *Folktale Themes and Activities for Children, Vol. 2.* © 1999 Anne Marie Kraus. Libraries Unlimited. (800) 237-6124.

Title/Author/Culture	Heroine's (or Hero's) Name/ *Magical Helper*/ Magical Object (Wand)	Evil Character(s) (Stepmother)	Ball, Contest, Event, Journey/ *Shoe or Slipper*	Transformation/ Outcome, Resolution
"The Giant Who Had No Heart" in *Giants!* (Walker) Norwegian	Boots/*Raven, salmon, and wolf*/Duck's egg containing the giant's heart	Six brothers, giant	Quest to distant island to locate the giant's heart/ (*No shoe motif*)	Six brothers and their brides from stone to living humans. *He marries his princess.*
The Golden Sandal (Hickox) Middle East/Arab	Maha/*Little red fish*/Fish's magical powers	Stepmother	Wedding preparations for merchant's daughter/*Golden sandal*	Silk gown; foul odor to scent of roses. *She marries Tariq, brother of the bride.*
The Irish Cinderlad (Climo) Irish	Becan (boy), or "Little Bigfoot"/*Bull*/Dead bull's tail as a weapon	Stepmother, three stepsisters	Slay the dragon and rescue the king's daughter/ *Becan's huge boot*	Little Becan becomes powerful enough to fight giant and dragon. *He earns Princess Finola's attentions to see eye-to-eye.*
Jouanah (Coburn) Hmong	Jouanah/*Her dead mother's voice*/ Piece of cowhide in mother's sewing basket	Stepmother, stepsister	New year celebration/*Shoe*	Mother into cow. Magical production of clothes and adornments. *She marries the son of the village elder.*
The King of Ireland's Son (Behan) Irish	Art (man)/*Three old men in cave, stallion*/Stallion's magical powers	Two brothers	Hide and seek contest with fierce giant/(*No shoe motif*)	Full-sized man into miniature size for hiding. *He marries the daughter of the King of Greece; brothers are banished.*
Kongi and Potgi (Han and Plunkett) Korean	Kongi (girl)/*Ox, toad, sparrows, angels from the sky*/(No magic wand motif)	Stepmother, stepsister Potgi	May festival/*Her slipper*	Ragged clothes into fine silks. Chores done. *She marries prince. She forgives and welcomes stepmother and stepsister.*
The Korean Cinderella (Climo) Korean	Pear Blossom/*Frog, sparrows, ox*/The work of *tokgabis*—goblins	Stepmother, stepsister	Village festival/*Her straw sandal*	Jug is mended, rice is hulled, paddies are weeded, turnips changed to treats. *She marries the magistrate.*
The Little Humpbacked Horse (Winthrop) Russian	Ivan/*Little humpbacked horse*/ Horse's magical powers	Two older brothers	Three daunting tasks commanded by the Tsar/(*No shoe motif*)	Simpleton into hero, becomes more handsome, becomes new Tsar. *He marries the Tsarevna and becomes Tsar.*
The Little Seven-Colored Horse (San Souci) Hispanic	Juanito/*The Little Seven-Colored Horse*/Golden sword, horse's magical powers	Two older brothers	Tournament of rings/(*No shoe motif*)	Downtrodden underling into hero of the city. *He marries mayor's daughter. Brothers never return.*
Moss Gown (Hooks) American (tidewater region of North Carolina)	Candace/*Witch woman in the swamp*/Gown and gris-gris chant given by the witch woman	Two older sisters	Three-day frolic with picnics and balls/(*No shoe motif*)	Moss gown into gossamer gown. *She marries the Young Master. The sisters turn their father out, and she reunites with her father.*

Title/Author/ Culture	Heroine's (or Hero's) Name/ *Magical Helper*/ Magical Object (Wand)	Evil Character(s) (Stepmother)	Ball, Contest, Event, Journey/ *Shoe or Slipper*	Transformation/ Outcome, Resolution
Mufaro's Beautiful Daughters (Steptoe) African	Nyasha/*Her own kindness*/The king's magic to transform and keep watch on others	Sister (Manyara)	A summons from the king for eligible women, to choose bride/(*No shoe motif*)	Snake into king. King into boy and woman in forest. *She becomes wife of king; sister becomes servant in king's household.*
Princess Furball (Huck) English	Princess, or "Furball"/*Herself*/ Three nutshells containing three gowns	Father	Three feasts at the palace/*Herbs for soup, thimble, tiny gold spinning wheel*	Dirty fur-clad servant into beautiful gowned princess. *She marries the king.*
The Rough-Face Girl (Martin) Algonquin (Native American)	Rough-Face Girl/ *Her own ability to see with her heart*/Power to see with the heart	Two older sisters	Visit to the dwelling of the Invisible Being/(*No shoe motif*)	Burnt hair and scarred skin into smooth, glossy beauty. *She marries the Invisible Being.*
Smoky Mountain Rose (Schroeder) Appalachian (American)	Rose/*Talking hog*/The hog's magical powers	Stepmother, two stepsisters	Rich feller's fancy party/*Glass slipper*	Clothes into party dress, mushmelon into wagon, mice into horses. *She marries Seb, the rich feller.* *She forgives her stepsisters.*
Sootface (San Souci) Ojibwa (Native American)	Sootface/*Sister of the invisible warrior*/Magic comb and herbed water	Two older sisters	Meeting the invisible warrior/(*No shoe motif*)	Burnt hair and scarred face into smooth and shining beauty. *She becomes wife of invisible warrior; sisters do their own cooking and work.*
The Talking Eggs (San Souci) Creole (American)	Blanche/*Old woman at the well*/Eggs	Mother, older sister (Rose)	Visit at the old woman's home/ (*No shoe motif*)	Plain egg contents into carriage and finery. Fancy egg contents into snakes, etc. *She goes off and lives in the city, well-off but generous.*
Tattercoats (Steel) English	Tattercoats/ *Gooseherd*/Magic power of tune played on gooseherd's pipe	Nobleman grandfather	Royal ball for prince to choose bride/ (*No shoe motif*)	Rag clothing into glowing robes and jewels. *She marries prince; grandfather returns to isolation.*
Tatterhood and the Hobgoblins (Mills) Norwegian	Tatterhood/ *Herself*/Her own powers and wooden spoon	Hobgoblins	Her sister's wedding; becomes hers also/ (*No shoe motif*)	Tattered cloak and weeds into beautiful cloth and flowers. Goat into deer, spoon into wand. *She weds prince and rules "fair and wise."*
"Three Golden Apples" in *Magical Tales from Many Lands* (Mayo) French	Martin/*Old woman on the road*/A whistle to bring all the hares back	Two older brothers	A summons from the king, for the apples to make princess well/ (*No shoe motif*)	Brothers' apples into toads and snakes. Gravely ill princess into healthy one. *He marries the princess.*

Fig. 6.5 continues on page 130.

Title/Author/ Culture	Heroine's (or Hero's) Name/ *Magical Helper/ Magical Object (Wand)*	Evil Character(s) *(Stepmother)*	Ball, Contest, Event, Journey/ *Shoe or Slipper*	Transformation/ Outcome, Resolution
Three Perfect Peaches (DeFelice and De Marsh) French	The youngest brother/*Old woman on the road/A whistle to bring whatever you wish for*	Two older brothers	A summons from the king for the peaches to make princess well/ *(No shoe motif)*	Brothers' peaches into droppings and manure. Gravely ill princess into healthy one. *He marries the princess.*
The Three Princes (Kimmel) Middle Eastern	Prince Mohsen/ *Princess's own wisdom/Crystal ball, magic carpet, healing orange*	(No stepmother motif)	Princess's command to go out into the world and find the greatest wonder/ *(No shoe motif)*	Dying princess into healthy one. Poorest prince into husband of important princess. *Prince Mohsen marries the princess.*
Toads and Dia-monds (Bender) French	Merth (girl)/ *Three-headed troll/Troll's powers*	Widow mother, older sister	Fetch water in the woods/*(No shoe motif)*	Merth's voice into diamonds. Sister's voice into toads. *She uses her wealth with generosity.*
Toads and Dia-monds (Huck) French	Renée/*Old woman at the spring/Old woman's powers*	Stepmother, stepsister (Francine)	Fetch water from the spring/*(No shoe motif)*	Renée's words into jewels. Stepsister's words into toads and snakes. Old woman into other forms. *She marries the prince. Stepsister goes to live in a cave.*
The Turkey Girl (Pollock) Zuni (Native American)	Turkey Girl/*Huge gobbler turkey/ Turkey's magical powers*	Wealthy girls of the village	Dance of the Sacred Bird/*(No shoe motif)*	Rags into white doeskin dress, jewelry. *Because she fails to return by sunset, she reverts to rags; loses her turkey friend forever.*
Vasilissa the Beautiful (Winthrop) Russian	Vasilissa/*Little doll from dead mother/Little doll*	Stepmother, two stepsisters, Baby Yaga the witch	A summons from the Tsar to see the maker of the shirts/ *Shirts woven and sewn by Vasilissa for the Tsar*	Stepmother and sisters into ashes. Wood into loom. *She marries the Tsar. Stepmother and stepsisters are burned to ashes.*
"Vipers and Pearls" in *Beauty and the Beast: And Other Stories* (Geras) French	Rose/*Old woman at the well/Old woman's powers*	Mother, older sister (Ruby)	Fetch water at the well/*(No shoe motif)*	Rose's words into gemstones. Sister's words into vipers. Old woman into fine lady. *She marries prince. Sister is banished to live in a cave.*
Wishbones (Wilson) Chinese	Yeh Hsien/*Old man who explains about the fishbones/ Fish, fishbones*	Stepmother, stepsister	The Cave Festival/ *Violet silk slipper*	Wishes into jewels, silk robes, jade. *She marries king. He wears out the magic of the fishbones.*
Yeh-Shen (Louie) Chinese	Yeh-Shen/*Old man who explains about the fishbones/ Fish, fishbones*	Stepmother, stepsister	Holiday festival/ *Golden shoe*	Rags into beautiful gown and cloak. *She marries king. Stepmother and stepsister are crushed in their cave.*
Cinderella (Sierra)	Collection of 25 Cinderella variants	Several	Several	Several

From *Folktale Themes and Activities for Children, Vol. 2.* © 1999 Anne Marie Kraus. Libraries Unlimited. (800) 237-6124.

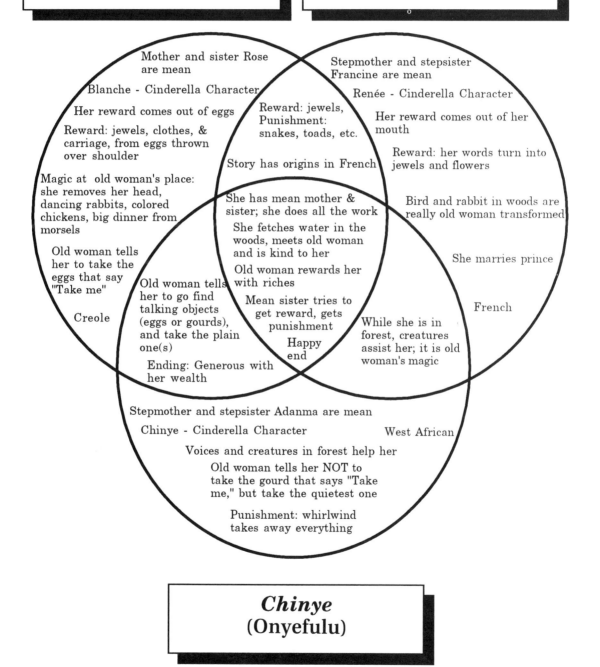

Cinderella Variants: Unique and Overlapping Elements of *The Talking Eggs, Toads and Diamonds,* and *Chinye*

The Talking Eggs (San Souci)

Toads and Diamonds (Huck)

Mother and sister Rose are mean

Blanche - Cinderella Character

Her reward comes out of eggs

Reward: jewels, clothes, & carriage, from eggs thrown over shoulder

Magic at old woman's place: she removes her head, dancing rabbits, colored chickens, big dinner from morsels

Old woman tells her to take the eggs that say "Take me"

Creole

Reward: jewels, Punishment: snakes, toads, etc.

Story has origins in French

She has mean mother & sister; she does all the work

She fetches water in the woods, meets old woman and is kind to her

Old woman rewards her with riches

Mean sister tries to get reward, gets punishment

Happy end

Old woman tells her to go find talking objects (eggs or gourds), and take the plain one(s)

Ending: Generous with her wealth

Stepmother and stepsister Francine are mean

Renée - Cinderella Character

Her reward comes out of her mouth

Reward: her words turn into jewels and flowers

Bird and rabbit in woods are really old woman transformed

She marries prince

French

While she is in forest, creatures assist her; it is old woman's magic

Stepmother and stepsister Adanma are mean

Chinye - Cinderella Character

Voices and creatures in forest help her

West African

Old woman tells her NOT to take the gourd that says "Take me," but take the quietest one

Punishment: whirlwind takes away everything

Chinye (Onyefulu)

Fig. 6.6.

From *Folktale Themes and Activities for Children, Vol. 2.* © 1999 Anne Marie Kraus. Libraries Unlimited. (800) 237-6124.

Cinderella Variants: Healing Fruit Theme in
Three Perfect Peaches, The Three Princes, and *Three Golden Apples*

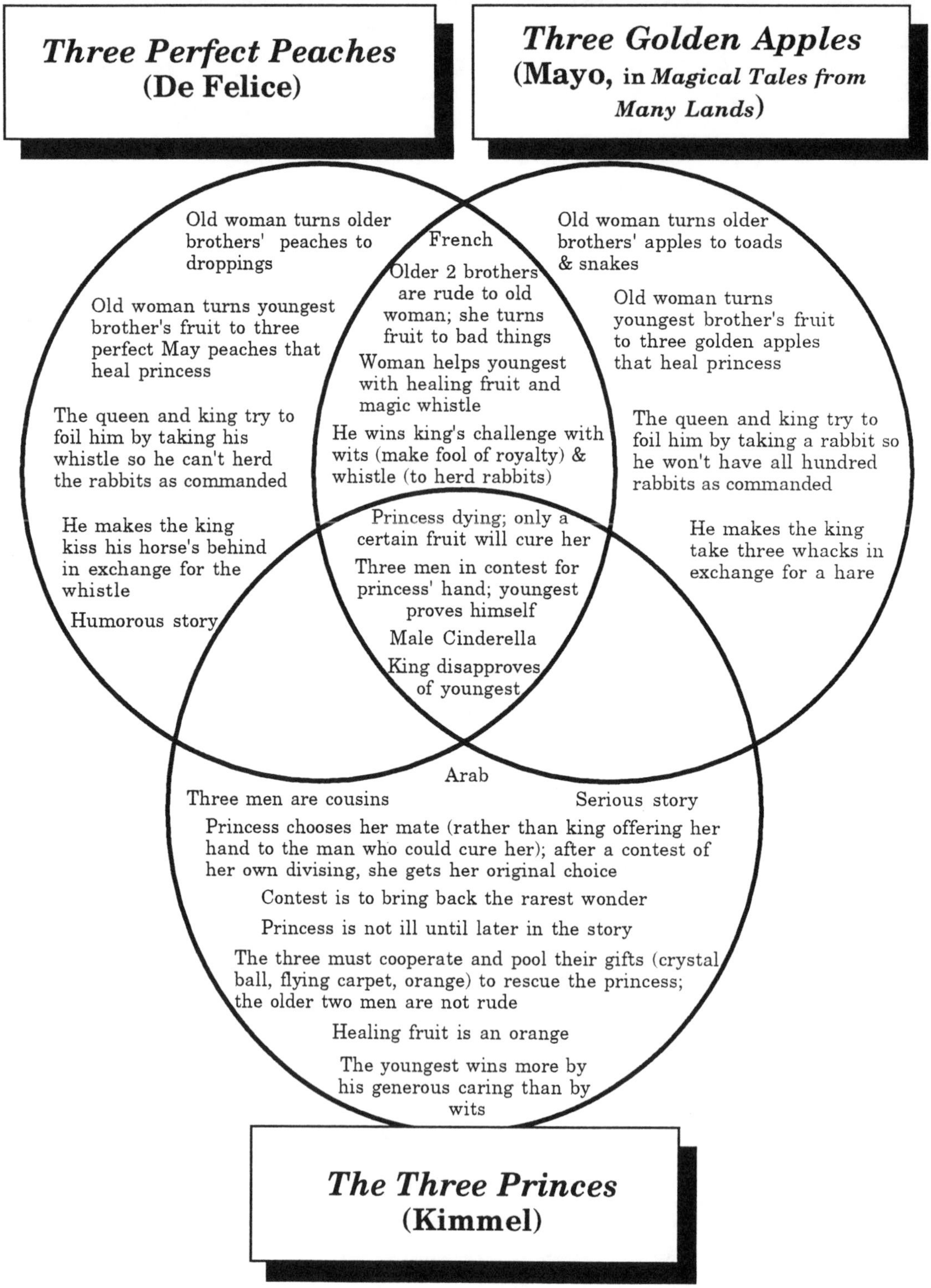

Three Perfect Peaches
(De Felice)

Three Golden Apples
(Mayo, in *Magical Tales from Many Lands*)

Old woman turns older brothers' peaches to droppings

Old woman turns youngest brother's fruit to three perfect May peaches that heal princess

The queen and king try to foil him by taking his whistle so he can't herd the rabbits as commanded

He makes the king kiss his horse's behind in exchange for the whistle

Humorous story

French

Older 2 brothers are rude to old woman; she turns fruit to bad things

Woman helps youngest with healing fruit and magic whistle

He wins king's challenge with wits (make fool of royalty) & whistle (to herd rabbits)

Princess dying; only a certain fruit will cure her

Three men in contest for princess' hand; youngest proves himself

Male Cinderella

King disapproves of youngest

Old woman turns older brothers' apples to toads & snakes

Old woman turns youngest brother's fruit to three golden apples that heal princess

The queen and king try to foil him by taking a rabbit so he won't have all hundred rabbits as commanded

He makes the king take three whacks in exchange for a hare

Arab

Three men are cousins

Serious story

Princess chooses her mate (rather than king offering her hand to the man who could cure her); after a contest of her own divising, she gets her original choice

Contest is to bring back the rarest wonder

Princess is not ill until later in the story

The three must cooperate and pool their gifts (crystal ball, flying carpet, orange) to rescue the princess; the older two men are not rude

Healing fruit is an orange

The youngest wins more by his generous caring than by wits

The Three Princes
(Kimmel)

Fig. 6.7.

Male Cinderellas with Animal Helpers

Title/Author/ Culture	*Character/ Siblings*	*Animal Helper/ Type of Help*	*Character's Situation/ Quest (Test)*	*Transformation/ Outcome with Princess*
Billy Beg and His Bull (Greene) Irish	Billy Beg/(*No sibling motif*)	*Bull* Food and drink in a napkin in ear of bull. Stick/sword in bull's ear. Bull's hide for belt with protective power.	He must make his way on his own in the world. *Fight giants with many heads, fight dragon and rescue princess.*	Common lad to powerful hero. *He marries the princess.*
Boots and the Glass Mountain (Martin) Norwegian	Boots/*Two older brothers scorn and torment him*	*Three wild horses* The three horses carry him up the glass mountain to the princess.	He must find out who is stealing the grain in the barn. *Rescue the princess from glass mountain.*	Common lad to armor-clad hero. *He marries the princess.*
The Irish Cinderlad (Climo) Irish	Becan, or "Little Bigfoot"/*Three sisters want him gone*	*Bull* Food in a tablecloth is inside bull's ear. Dead bull's tail protects as weapon.	He must tend the cows, then survive on his own. *Fight giant and dragon, rescue Princess.*	Becomes powerful to fight giant and dragon. *Princess Finola marries him.*
The King of Ireland's Son (Behan) Irish	Art/*Two older brothers put him in cave, hoping not to see him again*	*Little stallion* Food and drink in a tablecloth are inside stallion's ear. Stallion gives magical help with giant.	He must find out where music is coming from, deal with cave and giant. *Riddles and three-day hide-and-seek contest with giant.*	Full-sized man into miniature size for hiding. *He marries musician, king's daughter.*
The Little Humpbacked Horse (Winthrop) Russian	Ivan/*Two older brothers are lazy, lie, and steal*	*White mare and her colt, 2-humped pony* Horse gives advice and magical power for Tsar's tasks due to jealous men. Protection against jealous men.	He must find out who is stealing the hay in the barn; later must do impossible tasks for the Tsar. *Obtain treasures for Tsar: Golden Sow, Mare, Tsarevna.*	Becomes more handsome; from simple peasant to hero. *He marries the Tsaritsa.*
The Little Seven-Colored Horse (San Souci) Hispanic	Juanito/*His two older brothers scorn him and try to kill him*	*Little Seven-Colored Horse* Horse rescues Juanito, flies, gives advice, wins contest, gives power to do impossible tasks due to jealous men	He must find out who is stealing the corn in the cornfield. *Win contest, obtain treasures for Mayor: bird, ring lost in sea.*	Farm boy to finely clothed hero of contest and quests. *He marries Maria, the Mayor's daughter.*

Fig. 6.8.

STUDENT WRITING AND MULTIMEDIA PRODUCTION

Creative Writing

A logical extension of listening to transformation tales is creative writing. Students may choose to write tales in the style of folktales, with castles, princesses, enchanters, and so on. Or they may wish to take a more contemporary angle, with such elements as rockets, roller blades, or sports stars. The main goal of writing a transformation story is to identify a transformation to take place in the plot. Students must pick an object or character that changes shape or appearance in the course of the story. Students may benefit from a prewriting brainstorming session, to help get the imagination flowing. After picking a basic transformational event, they need to frame the event in a plot, with before-and-after sequencing. An example of a brainstorm list is provided below. Following the list, a student story planning sheet is provided, to help students organize their thoughts prior to writing (fig. 6.9).

**Sample brainstorm list for students'
original transformation stories**

Contemporary stories:

- A book into a butterfly

- Old shoes into new high-top sport shoes

- Shoes into roller blades

- An alien from outer space into a clone of self

- A person into any animal; best friend (parents, siblings, etc.) into an insect or an animal (giraffe, bird, etc.)

- Car into spacecraft

- Dinner into sweet treats

Stories with a folktale or fairy tale style: princess or prince into any animal: swan, insect, anteater, bat, ferret

Habitat-based transformation: person or object into sea otter or whale, polar bear or walrus, cactus or sidewinder snake

Weather-based transformation: animal into cloud, tree into tornado, rain into flowers

Mythical creatures: person or object into dragon, giant, monster

Astronomical transformation: person or object into star, sun, or moon

Object coming alive: doll into girl, wooden toy into animal

Transformation Story Planning Page

My transformation is...

_____ turns into _____

How the story starts:

How the transformation happens:

How the story ends:

The End

Fig. 6.9.

From *Folktale Themes and Activities for Children, Vol. 2*. © 1999 Anne Marie Kraus. Libraries Unlimited. (800) 237-6124.

Multimedia Production

Multimedia computer programs such as The New KidPix and Hyperstudio offer a way for students to publish stories with special visual effects. Students can make multimedia presentations of their original transformation stories, or they can present retellings of existing folktales. A transformation is usually a visual transformation, a before-and-after sequence of images. This changing of images is very effective on a computer screen, especially when enhanced with the computer program's transitions, such as dissolves, wipes, fades, or window blind effects. Creating a multimedia presentation is a way to incorporate new technologies, while still keeping in touch with traditional literature.

A rule in multimedia production is to have the entire project planned out on a story board prior to creating it on the computer. Students must first decide how many screens or slides should be devoted to the project and what the picture and text will be on each slide. They should also decide whether the text of the story will be written on each slide or recorded with a microphone as narrative.

The nuts-and-bolts of specific multimedia applications is not covered in this guide. Access to computers and multimedia programs varies widely, and the technology changes fast. Collaboration between the school's media specialist and the teacher can be the key to success in this endeavor. The media specialist knows the software, hardware, the students, and the literature and can provide direct instruction to students as they plan and produce their transformation stories in multimedia.

This guide does provide a storyboard planning sheet, which may be duplicated for student use (fig. 6.10 on pp. 137–39). A sample plan for a transformation multimedia story is as follows:

- Slide 1: Title and author

- Slide 2: Beginning of the story: "Once upon a time . . ." is a good start

- Slide 3: Middle of the story, with picture of person or object before the transformation

- Slide 4: The transformation to a different image

- Slide 5: End of the story

- Slide 6: Copyright date, school, location

Text continues on page 140.

Multimedia Storyboard

Picture: Text:

Slide #1: Title Screen

(Title)

(Author)

Slide #2: Story Introduction

Fig. 6.10a.

From *Folktale Themes and Activities for Children, Vol. 2* . © 1999 Anne Marie Kraus. Libraries Unlimited. (800) 237-6124.

Multimedia Storyboard

Picture: ## Text:

Slide #3: Person or object before the transformation

Slide #4: The transformation

Fig. 6.10b.

Multimedia Storyboard

Picture: Text:

Slide #5: Ending

_____
_____
_____
_____
_____
_____
_____
_____
_____

Slide #6: Credits

ⓒ **Date, School**
_____
City, State
_____
_____
_____
_____
_____
_____
_____

Fig. 6.10c.

OTHER CURRICULAR TIE-INS

Science

Transformations are not limited to the magic of folktales. Transformations occur every day, in people's moods and appearances, in the technology of television and movie special effects, in the cycles of nature, and in the wonders of chemistry. Children delight in seeing the chemical reaction when vinegar is combined with baking soda or when crystals are grown in the classroom. Classes learn to follow the phases of the moon. Two of the most obvious transformations in nature happen among butterflies and frogs. The metamorphosis from egg to caterpillar to chrysalis to butterfly can be experienced through direct observation and through books. Many books are available on the topics of transformations in science and nature. The books listed below emphasize the step-by-step process:

Hawcock, David. 1995. *The Butterfly: A Circular Pop-Up Book*. Illustrated by Bryan Poole. New York: Hyperion Books for Children.

———. 1995. *The Frog: A Circular Pop-Up Book*. Illustrated by Bryan Poole. New York: Hyperion Books for Children.

Ruiz, Andres Llamas. 1995. *Metamorphosis*. Illustrated by Francisco Arredondo. New York: Sterling.

Biography

There are true biographies as well as folktales of brave young women who donned the clothes and role of a man to achieve a goal. While these stories do not contain magical transformations, the heroine's identity is effectively transformed. Because many of these events (both folk and historical) took place in times and cultures that promoted clearly defined sex roles, often the women had no choice but to assume a male identity to achieve their goal. During a literature study, some interesting comparisons can be made via parallel readings of folktales and biographies. In a broader sense, most biographies show change in a main character as he or she grows and develops in his or her area of expertise and pursuit, an inner transformation. Women who disguise themselves as men show both outer and inner transformations. Listed below are folktales and biographies that demonstrate this theme of gender identity. Detailed annotations for the folktales appear in the annotated bibliography in Chapter 8.

Folktales of Women Disguised As Men

Chin, Charlie. *China's Bravest Girl: The Legend of Hua Mu Lan*. Illustrated by Tomie Arai. Emeryville, CA: Children's Book Press, 1993.

San Souci, Robert D. *Fa Mulan: The Story of a Woman Warrior*. Illustrated by Jean and Mou-Sien Tseng. New York: Hyperion Books for Children, 1998.

Sherman, Josepha. *Vassilisa the Wise: A Tale of Medieval Russia*. Illustrated by Daniel San Souci. New York: Harcourt Brace Jovanovich, 1988.

Biographies of Women Disguised As Men

McGovern, Ann. *The Secret Soldier: The Story of Deborah Sampson*. Illustrated by Harold Goodwin. New York: Scholastic, 1975. This is the story of a young woman who, disguised as a man, fights in the American Revolutionary War.

Reit, Seymour. *Behind Rebel Lines: The Incredible Story of Emma Edmonds, Civil War Spy*. New York: Harcourt Brace Jovanovich, 1988. Not only does Emma Edmonds disguise herself as a man but also as a peddler and a male slave to do her part for the Union as a spy.

Stevens, Bryna. *Deborah Sampson Goes to War*. Illustrated by Florence Hill. New York: Dell, 1984. Deborah Sampson joins the army to fight in the American Revolutionary war, disguised as a man.

———. *Frank Thompson: Her Civil War Story*. New York: Macmillan, 1992. Disguised as a man, Sara Emma Evelyn Edmonds works as a spy for the Union Army, behind Confederate lines, during the Civil War.

Fiction

Transformations are found in full-length fiction books, particularly in fantasy and science fiction. For ideas and titles that explore transformation themes in these longer works, consult the following article:

Bang-Jensen, Valerie. 1998. "Shape-Shifters." *Book Links* 8 (September): 26–28.

ART ACTIVITIES

Because transformations are usually a visual experience, they lend themselves to visual arts projects. Three of the art projects described below fall in the category of "paper engineering," methods of taking two pictures (before and after the transformation) and juxtaposing them so that the viewer sees first one picture, then the other. These activities are listed in order of difficulty; the last one requires adult help. The fourth activity is a fabric art project making a simple stuffed doll or puppet. Finally, there are some ideas for shadow puppet theater.

Accordion-Fold Transformation Pictures

This paper project is easy enough for young children to do with a little adult guidance. Two pictures are drawn and colored, each on a separate piece of paper. Then the pictures are cut into long strips and glued onto a third, larger piece of accordion-folded paper, alternating the strips from the two pictures. The result is a "before" and "after" transformation effect, which changes according to the angle from which it is viewed. This relatively simple paper project produces a dramatic effect, especially when displayed on the wall of a hallway. As people walk down the hall approaching the picture, they first see one image, and then after they pass the picture, they see the other image.

Start by deciding on the two images to be depicted—one before and one after the transformation. This can be the artist's original idea, or it can illustrate a folktale that was read, for example, children turning into swans, as in *The Children of Lir*, or stars into water lilies, as in *Star Maiden*. Then draw or paint each image on a separate 9- by 12-inch piece of paper with the paper in the vertical position. Encourage the artists to completely fill the paper with color, including background color. The effect works best if the drawings have contrasting colors and the images are large. For example, if the children are red and blue in a green background, and the swans are white on a pale blue background, the contrast will be more striking.

Next, cut the two pictures into strips. On the back of each picture, draw six vertical lines spaced one-and-one-half inches apart, and number the strips one through six (this can be prepared before drawing). Then cut the pictures into strips. Next, take a 12- by 18-inch piece of paper (construction paper or white) and fold it like a fan, making the folds one-and-one-half inches apart. Position this larger paper horizontally and make the folds parallel to the 12-inch side. Before gluing the strips to the folded paper, lay out the strips of paper on a desk or table, making sure they are in the right order: first strip #1 from the "before" picture, then strip #1 from the "after" picture, then strip #2 from the "before" picture, then strip #2 from the "after" picture, and so on. Finally, glue the strips in order to the accordion-folded paper (see fig. 6.11). To enjoy the transformation effect, hold it up, tilting it from side to side to change the view. It may help to mount the finished work on another piece of paper, or staple it to a bulletin board. Experiment with the depth of the accordion folds for maximum effect.

Flag Books

This project is a variation on a "pop-up book" design, perhaps more accurately a "pop-down" effect. The element of surprise occurs when the book is opened and pulled outward, creating a picture resulting from the assembly of paper strips, or "flags," inside. To use this idea for a transformation concept, draw the "before" picture on the cover of the book and the "after" image inside on the flags (see fig. 6.12 on p. 145). When the book is opened and the flags fall into place, the image spontaneously, almost magically, appears. With some adult guidance, children of all ages can successfully produce a flag book. However, if doing this with a large group of children, it is most successful with third and fourth graders. Or consider pairing older children with younger children.

Stiff paper, such as construction paper, cardstock, or tagboard, works best for this project. Flag books may be made in a variety of sizes, and with varying number of flags. The model project here is for a small book, 4 by 6 inches when closed.

For each book, assemble the following materials:

- Two 4- by 6-inch stiff papers, for the front and back covers
- One 6- by 8-inch paper, to fold accordion-style, for the spine of the book
- Nine strips of paper, 1¾ by 3½ inches, for the flags
- Glue

Fold the 6- by 8-inch paper accordion-style in 1-inch folds parallel to the 6-inch side. This accordion-folded piece will become the spine of the book. Lay the folded paper on the table so that there are three "hills," plus a "half-hill" on each side sticking up. (Do *not* lay it so that there are four complete "hills." Refer to part A of fig. 6.12). Glue the one-inch-wide strip (the "half-hill") on each side to the 4- by 6-inch covers.

Accordion-Fold Transformation Pictures

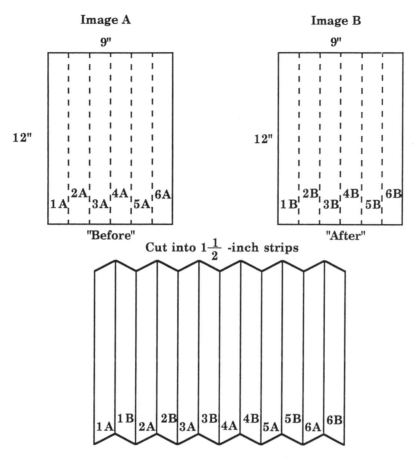

Image A

9"

12"

2A 4A 6A
1A 3A 5A

"Before"

Image B

9"

12"

2B 4B 6B
1B 3B 5B

"After"

Cut into 1½-inch strips

1A 1B 2A 2B 3A 3B 4A 4B 5A 5B 6A 6B

Glue strips onto 12- by 18-inch paper, folded accordion-style

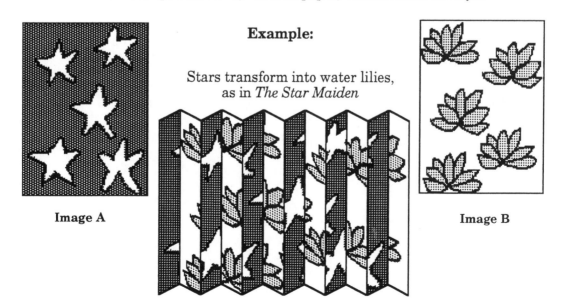

Image A

Example:

Stars transform into water lilies,
as in *The Star Maiden*

Image B

View from different angles to see the transformation.

Fig. 6.11.

From *Folktale Themes and Activities for Children, Vol. 2*. © 1999 Anne Marie Kraus. Libraries Unlimited. (800) 237-6124.

Next, glue the flags to the accordion-folded spine. Start with three flags across the top third of the spine. Glue the end of each flag onto the left side of the "hill," as shown in part B of fig. 6.12. Then take three more flags to glue onto the middle third of the spine; glue these flags to the right side of the "hills." Then glue the last three flags onto the left sides of the hills to complete the bottom third of the book. (The strips are $1\frac{3}{4}$ inches wide to allow for a little bit of space between them, so that they can move freely as the book is opened and closed.)

Now that the book is assembled, draw the pictures. Draw a "before" image on the cover, such as the horse and carriage taking Cinderella to the ball. Then open the book and lay it on the table, until the flags are lying completely flat. Carefully draw the "after" image on the flags. The drawing tool (markers work especially well for this) must be able to pass easily over the uneven surface of the flags. Children should be cautioned to be patient and careful, or else the markers may stray along the edges of the flags. It is best to save a simpler image for the inside picture, such as the pumpkin that Cinderella finds in place of her coach when she leaves the ball too late.

Additional ideas for flag books, pop-ups, and other creative paper effects can be found in:

Swain, Gwenyth. *Bookworks: Making Books by Hand.* Illustrated by Jennifer Hagerman. Photographs by Andy King. Minneapolis, MN: Carolrhoda Books, 1995.

Sliding Images

This slide is a "moveable book" paper-engineering feature that has been around for a hundred years or more as a parlor amusement. It is a sort of window-blind effect; pulling the tab causes one image to be replaced by another. It involves cutting two images on papers into parallel strips or slots with a razor-knife. The children do the drawing, and then an adult does the cutting and assists with the interweaving of the two paper images. Children should be cautioned to pull the tab of the finished product gently and to keep the project flat and wrinkle-free.

Photocopy the two patterns (figs. 6.13 and 6.14, on pp. 147–48) onto light-weight cardstock, or transfer them onto slightly stiff, shiny-quality paper. Draw a "before" and "after" image on the two slotted patterns—for example, a frog and a princess or winter and spring. Draw and color on the back of the patterns, taking care to stay within the slotted area. Leave the one picture on the full sheet (the one with the fold and the two slots). On the picture with the tabs, cut around the outline. An adult now cuts along all the lines with a razor-knife, using a ruler as a guide. Place the cut-out tab image behind the full-sheet image, and lace the strips from back to front. Fold along the fold line of the full-sheet image and glue the folded-over part *carefully* to the cut strips, placing the glue only on the spots indicated by the small boxes. Insert the two tabs into the two slots, and try sliding the image back and forth. See fig. 6.15 on p. 149 for this assembly work.

Flag Book

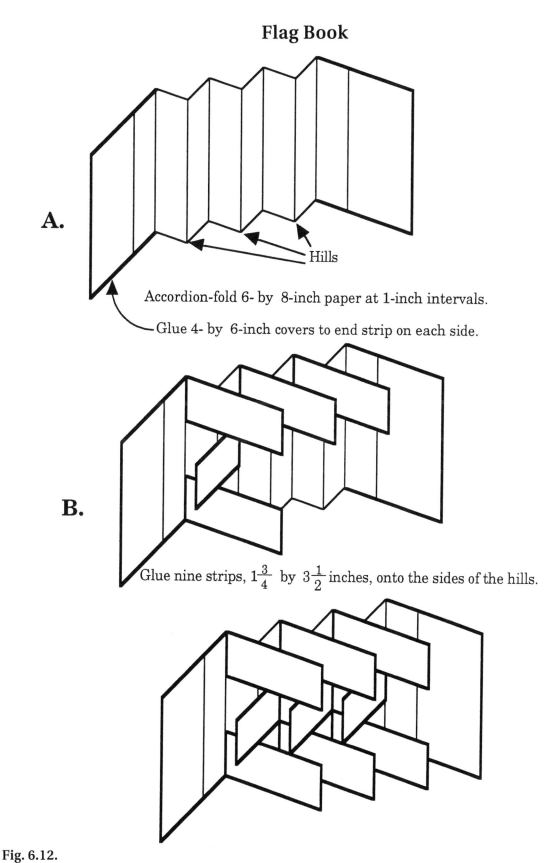

A.

Hills

Accordion-fold 6- by 8-inch paper at 1-inch intervals.

Glue 4- by 6-inch covers to end strip on each side.

B.

Glue nine strips, $1\frac{3}{4}$ by $3\frac{1}{2}$ inches, onto the sides of the hills.

Fig. 6.12.

If it is difficult to get the image to slide freely, consider these troubleshooting possibilities: If any of the razor-knife cutting produces a jagged edge, the sliding image can catch. Try to trim off any jagged edges. Keep the paper smooth and flat; if the paper becomes bent or wrinkled, this will impede the sliding. The paper should be slightly stiff, but not as thick as tagboard. Cardstock from a copy center is an inexpensive paper that works well. If the cardstock has a slick surface, it works even better. Shiny photographic material slides the best. Try using photographs or greeting cards or pictures from glossy calendars. Materials that have glossy surfaces slide the best. Experimentation and a little practice produce some delightful effects.

Transformation Dolls

Dolls or puppets made of fabric and soft fiber materials can be designed to turn inside-out or upside-down to reveal another image or character. Such dolls are enjoyable as toys, as artistic expressions of transformation stories, and as props for storytelling. Some such toys are commercially available. For example, there is a commercially produced soft doll of Sylvester from *Sylvester and the Magic Pebble* by William Steig. One view is of the lovable donkey Sylvester, and by turning him inside-out, he becomes the red pebble. Another commercially available doll is a green caterpillar with a long fastener along its underside; open it up, turn it inside-out, and it becomes a butterfly. There are also human-character dolls (or human-animal) with long skirtlike garments fastened around the waist. Turn the doll upside-down and flip the skirt down, and another head and costume are revealed on the other side. Such upside-down doll designs can easily be created out of materials found in homes or craft closets.

There are two ways to start with the body base. The first is by using an old sock. Use either the entire sock or just the long cuff, tied off at one end with thread or string. Stuff the sock with polyester stuffing or other soft material, not too tightly, and sew the open end shut. Next, tie the middle with string to cinch in the waistline tightly. Now there is a head at either end; the head can be given more definition by using string to cinch in a neck. Decorate the head with facial features using markers, glue-on yarn, buttons, paper, felt, or other materials. A face can also me made with a piece of felt cut in an oval face shape (or animal face shape) and decorated with facial features. Then glue the felt face onto the sock "head." Top the head off with a hat, animal ears, yarn hair, or anything else that gives it personality.

Another way to begin a body base is with two wooden spoons. Turn them so that they face in opposite directions with their handles parallel. Use masking tape to fasten the two handles together. Now the spoons can be decorated as faces, as described above. Experiment with using either the convex side or the concave side of the spoon to give the desired facial effect.

Next, make the doll a skirtlike garment fastened around the "waist." Don't limit the doll design only to female characters just because there is a skirtlike piece attached to it. This piece is only the base for the illusion of the transformation. Attached to the skirt will be whatever creature is involved in the transformation: an animal body, a fish tail, men's pants and boots, etc. Start with a piece of fabric; the size will depend on the size of the doll body base, but a piece approximately 36 inches wide will provide enough fabric to gather and tie around the waist. The length should be approximately 10 to 12 inches, depending on the height of the body base.

Text continues on page 150.

Sliding Image: Image A

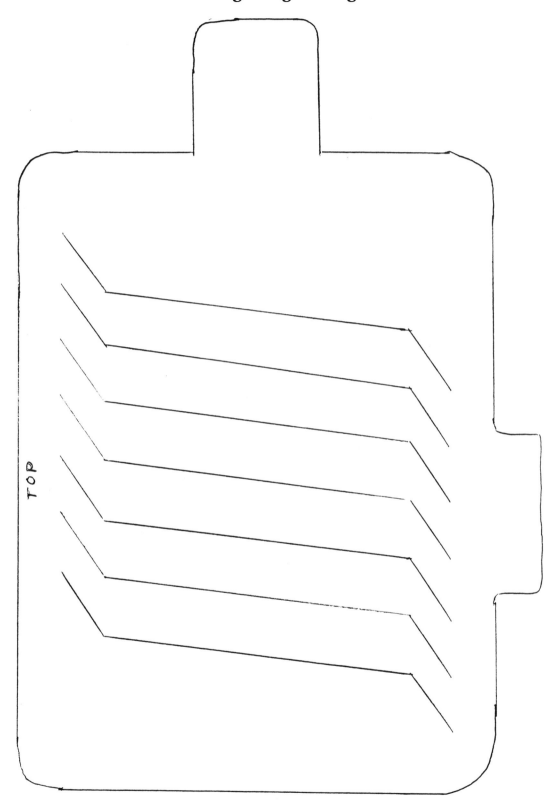

Fig. 6.13.

From *Folktale Themes and Activities for Children, Vol. 2* . © 1999 Anne Marie Kraus. Libraries Unlimited. (800) 237-6124.

Sliding Image: Image B

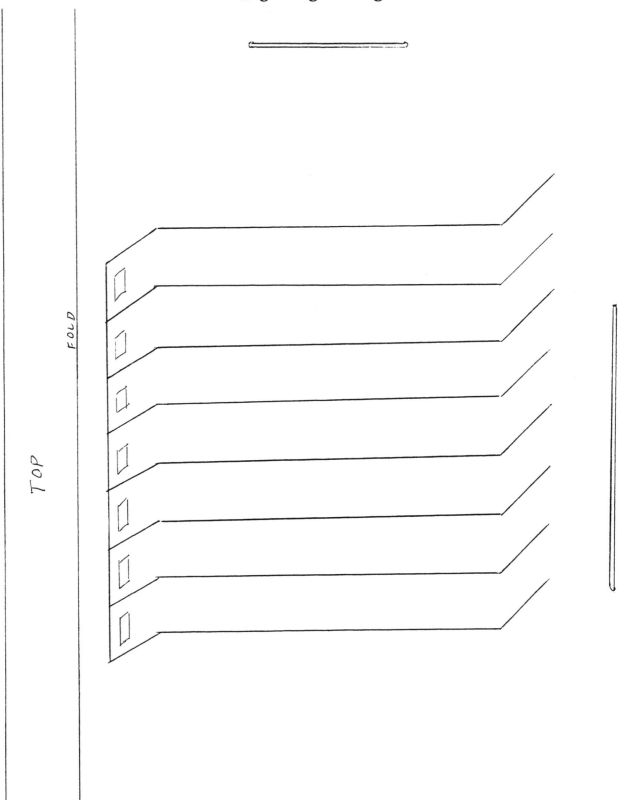

Fig. 6.14.

Sliding Image Assembly

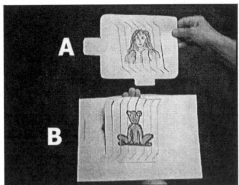

Draw images on fronts and cut along all lines on backs. Then place image A behind image B.

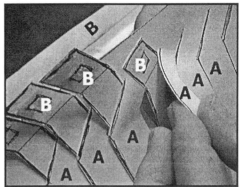

Working on the back side, pull the strips of image B between and through the strips of image A.

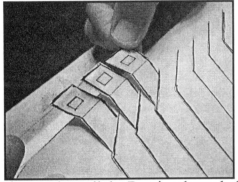

Continue to lace all the B strips through the A strips.

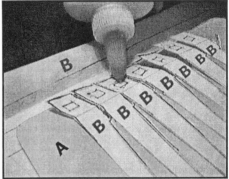

Apply glue carefully and sparingly to the ends of the B strips, in the spaces enclosed by the small boxes.

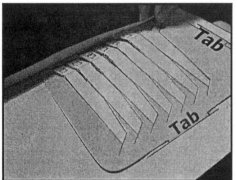

Fold along the fold line, and press onto the glue spots on the B strips. Place the large tabs into the slots.

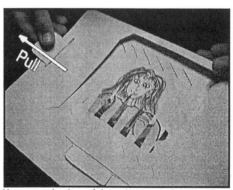

Pull or push the side tab to make the image transform.

Fig. 6.15.

Gathering the skirt material can be done several ways, depending on time, materials, and sewing expertise. If possible, use a needle and a doubled piece of thread to sew a simple running stitch along the long edge of the fabric, about 1/2 inch from the edge. Then knot one end of the thread and push the fabric along the thread toward the knot to gather. Fit the gathered skirt around the waist of the body-base, and tie the two ends of thread to secure the skirt in position. If needed, add some tack-glue or hot glue to keep it in place.

Other methods of gathering the skirt include the following: Use sewing-machine gathering; a volunteer who knows how to use a sewing machine could easily prepare several pieces of fabric using a basting stitch ahead of time for a group of children. Another simple method of gathering is to hand-pinch the fabric into position at the waist, and tie onto the waist with string. Whatever method of gathering is used, experiment with flipping the skirt over, and make adjustments as necessary. In some cases, the skirt will lie smoother on one side and be bulkier on the other, so decide which side will work best for which character.

Finally, decorate the skirt base with the features necessary to represent the character. The best material for creating animal bodies, pants, etc., is felt. It is flexible like fabric but easy to cut and glue. A mermaid transformation doll can be made using the skirt for the land-woman and then gluing a felt fish tail to the flip-side of the skirt. A *Beauty and the Beast* doll can be made by gluing felt pants and boots to one side of the skirt (the prince), and a beastly animal body to the other side. Try a child on one side (boy or girl) and a swan's body and head on the other, as in *The Children of Lir* by Sheila MacGill-Callahan. Another effective doll is a gossipy old woman who turns into an owl as in "Who You!" in *Her Stories* by Virginia Hamilton. Try a princess-to-frog transformation, as in *The Frog Princess*, or a man-to-tree transformation, as in *The Ballad of Belle Dorcas* by William H. Hooks. Consult the story themes and topics chart in Chapter 7 for more transformation ideas.

For final touches, the doll may need arms; try pipe-cleaners, felt, or rolled fabric, and fasten by tying, gluing, sewing, or hot-gluing. Then tell the story behind the transformation expressed by the doll.

Shadow Puppet Theater

For the basics of simple shadow puppet construction and production, see the trickster tales activities chapter of this book (pp. 31–40). Simple shadow puppet dramatizations bring a different dimension to folktales. In addition to the basics of shadow puppet theater, consider the special dramatic effects that can be used to illustrate a transformation event in a story.

Ready-to-use sets of shadow puppets for the following transformation tales are available in these books:

- *The Enchanted Caribou*, by Elizabeth Cleaver; puppets included in the book.

- "Her Seven Brothers," by Paul Goble; puppets in *Folktale Themes and Activities for Children, Volume 1: Pourquoi Tales*, by Anne Marie Kraus.

Transformation tales offer unique opportunities for special effects, because of the magical transition from one object or person to another. In their book *Worlds of Shadow*, David and Donna Wisniewski offer four dramatic but easy techniques for turning one object into another by using the overhead projector and a shadow puppet screen. Refer to their book not only for transformational techniques but also for a wealth of practical and creative ideas for engaging children in shadow puppetry. For more information, consult:

Wisniewski, David, and Donna Wisniewski. 1997. *Worlds of Shadow: Teaching with Shadow Puppetry*. Englewood, CO: Teacher Ideas Press.

REFERENCES

Bang-Jensen, Valerie. 1998. "Shape-Shifters." *Book Links* 8 (September): 26–28.

Hawcock, David. 1995. *The Butterfly: A Circular Pop-Up Book*. Illustrated by Bryan Poole. New York: Hyperion Books for Children.

———. 1995. *The Frog: A Circular Pop-Up Book*. Illustrated by Bryan Poole. New York: Hyperion Books for Children.

Kraus, Anne Marie. 1998. *Folktale Themes and Activities for Children, Volume 1: Pourquoi Tales*. Englewood, CO: Teacher Ideas Press.

McGovern, Ann. 1975. *The Secret Soldier: The Story of Deborah Sampson*. Illustrated by Harold Goodwin. New York: Scholastic.

Reit, Seymour. 1988. *Behind Rebel Lines: The Incredible Story of Emma Edmonds, Civil War Spy*. New York: Harcourt Brace Jovanovich.

Ruiz, Andres Llamas. 1995. *Metamorphosis*. Illustrated by Francisco Arredondo. New York: Sterling.

Stevens, Bryna. 1984. *Deborah Sampson Goes to War*. Illustrated by Florence Hill. New York: Dell.

———. 1992. *Frank Thompson: Her Civil War Story*. New York: Macmillan.

Swain, Gwenyth. 1995. *Bookworks: Making Books by Hand*. Illustrated by Jennifer Hagerman, Photographs by Andy King. Minneapolis, MN: Carolrhoda Books.

Wisniewski, David, and Donna Wisniewski. 1997. *Worlds of Shadow: Teaching with Shadow Puppetry*. Englewood, CO: Teacher Ideas Press.

Chapter 7

This chart groups stories according to their topical and thematic elements. It is a useful tool for planning which tales to group for storytelling/storyhour programs, thematic units for reading classes, or compare-and contrast activities. This chart is also useful for pointing out thematic and topical associations among tales and across cultures. To obtain full bibliographic information on the stories, consult the annotated bibliography in chapter 8. Stories may also be accessed through the index at the end.

Theme/Topic	Transformation	Title/Author/Culture
Human-to-animal transformations		
Human to bird	Children to swans and back	*The Children of Lir* (MacGill-Callahan) European/Irish
	Princess to swan and back	*The Tale of Tsar Saltan* (Pushkin) European/Russian
	Men to storks and back; Princess to owl and back	*The Tale of Caliph Stork* (Hort) Middle Eastern
	Men to storks and back; Princess to woodpecker and back	*The Enchanted Storks* (Shepard) Middle Eastern
	Young women to birds and back	*The Enchanted Book* (Porazinska) European/Polish
	Prince to canary and back	*The Canary Prince* (Nones) European/Italian
	Maidens to ducks and back	*The Tsar's Promise* (San Souci) European/Russian
	Manabozho (man) to hummingbird	"How Manabozho Saved the Rose" in *Manabozho's Gifts* (Greene) Native American/Chippewa
	Eagle to man; Old woman to eagle	The Eagle's Song (Rodanas) Native American/Pacific Northwest
	King Gull to man	"Sedna and King Gull" in *The Dial Book of Animal Tales from Around the World* (Adler) Inuit (in a collection of several cultures)
	Sorcerer to black vulture	"Seven Clever Brothers" in *Magical Tales from Many Lands* (Mayo) Jewish (in a collection of several cultures)
	Witches to owls	"The Halloween Witches" in *Magical Tales from Many Lands* (Mayo) African American (in a collection of several cultures)
	Old women to owls	"Who You!" in *Her Stories* (Hamilton) African American
	Man to crane	*Enora and the Black Crane* (Meeks) Australian/Aboriginal
	Two men to pheasant and kingfisher	*Pheasant and Kingfisher* (Berndt) Australian/Aboriginal
	Boy to raven	"The Wolverine's Secret" in *The Girl Who Dreamed Only Geese* (Norman) Native American/Inuit
	Seagulls to young woman and two uncles	"The Man Who Married a Seagull" in *The Girl Who Dreamed Only Geese* (Norman) Native American/Inuit

Theme/Topic	Transformation	Title/Author/Culture
Human-to-animal transformations		
Human to bird	Man to loon	"The Boy and the Loon" in *Echoes of the Elders* (Smith) Native American/Kwakiutl
	Crane to woman	*The Crane Wife* (Yagawa) Asian/Japanese
	Goose to woman	*Dawn* (Bang) Original
Human to mammal	Boy to koala (marsupial)	"Koala" in *Magical Tales from Many Lands* (Mayo) Australian/Aboriginal (in a collection of several cultures)
	Man to bear	*The Girl Who Lived with the Bears* (Goldin) Native American/Pacific Northwest
	Man to bear	*East o' the Sun and West o' the Moon* (Barlow) European/Norwegian
	Girl's head to sheep's head	"Kate Crackernuts" in *Magical Tales from Many Lands* (Mayo) Scottish (in a collection of several cultures)
	Woman to hare	"The Blue-Eyed Hare" in *Tales Alive!* (Milord) Scottish (in a collection of several cultures)
	Woman to wild deer	"Finn MacCoul" in *Favorite Medieval Tales* (Osborne) Irish (in a collection of several cultures)
	People to guanacos (llamalike animals)	"The Gentle People" in *Tales Alive!* (Milord) Argentinean (in a collection of several cultures)
	Puppy to boy	"The Puppy-Boy" in *The Acorn Tree* (Rockwell) Native American/Inuit (in a collection of several cultures)
	Children to mice	"The Old Owl Witch" in *Echoes of the Elders* (Smith) Native American/Kwakiutl
	Man and woman to buffaloes	*Buffalo Woman* (Goble) Native American/Plains Indians
	Woman to buffalo	*The Return of the Buffaloes* (Goble) Native American/Plains Indians
	Man to walrus	"Why the Rude Visitor Was Flung by Walrus" in *The Girl Who Dreamed Only Geese* (Norman) Native American/Inuit
Human to water creatures	Turtle to undersea princess; Man to crane	"The Kingdom Under the Sea" in *Magical Tales from Many Lands* (Mayo) Japanese (in a collection of several cultures)

Theme/Topic	Transformation	Title/Author/Culture
Human-to-animal transformations		
Human to water creatures	Young men to whales and back	"The Old Man of the Sea" in *Stories from the Sea* (Riordan) Nivkh Siberian (in a collection of several cultures)
	Woman to narwhal	"How the Narwhal Got Its Tusk" in *The Girl Who Dreamed Only Geese* (Norman) Native American/Inuit
	Prince to fish and back	"Marie and Redfish" in *Her Stories* (Hamilton) African American/Creole
Human to water creatures: origin of water creatures	King gull to man to whale	"Sedna and King Gull" in *The Dial Book of Animal Tales from Around the World* (Adler) Native American/Inuit (in a collection of several cultures)
	People to dolphins	*The Rainbow Bridge* (Wood) Native American/Chumash
	Human to water snake	"The Snake That Guards the River" in *The Monster from the Swamp* (Taylor) Native American/Seneca
	Humans to various animals (fish, mammals, birds)	"How Animals Came Back into the World" in *The Monster from the Swamp* (Taylor) Native American/Malecite
Human to water creatures: selkie/ mermaid motif	Woman to seal	"The Selkie Wife" in *Stories from the Sea* (Riordan) Orkney Islands (in a collection of several cultures)
	Merman to man	*Nicholas Pipe* (San Souci) European/British Isles
	Man or woman to mermaid or merman	"Enchanted Cap," "Fish Husband," and others in *Mermaid Tales from Around the World* (Osborne) Various (in a collection of several cultures)
	Woman to seal	*The Selkie Girl* (Cooper) European/British Isles
	Man to seal	*The Seal Prince* (MacGill-Callahan) European/Scottish
	Woman to mermaid, fish, jellyfish, seal	"The Listening Ear," "Pania of the Reef," "Hansi and the Nix," "The Sea Princess and the Sea Witch," and others in *A Treasury of Mermaids* (Climo) Various (in a collection of several cultures)
Human to frog or toad	Princess to toad and back	"The Three Feathers" in *Multicultural Fables and Fairy Tales* (McCarthy) German (in a collection of several cultures)
	Princess to frog and back	*The Frog Princess* (Cecil) European/Russian

Theme/Topic	Transformation	Title/Author/Culture
Human-to-animal transformations		
Human to frog or toad	Princess to frog and back	*The Frog Princess* (Lewis) European/Russian
	Prince to frog and back	*The Frog Prince* (Tarcov; also Ormerod) European/German
	Frogs to prince and princess and back	*Emily and the Enchanted Frog* (Griffith) Original
Human to insect	Woman to bee; Demon and troops into hornets	*The Tsar's Promise* (San Souci) European/Russian
Human to snake	Boy to snake	*Uncle Snake* (Gollub) Central American/Mexican
	Man to water snake	"The Snake That Guards the River" in *The Monster from the Swamp* (Taylor) Native American/Seneca
	Naga to woman, snake, and snake-woman	"Three Fabulous Eggs" in *Mythical Birds and Beasts from Many Lands* (Mayo) Burmese (in a collection of several cultures)
Human/animal transformation using the skin of an animal	Boy to fish	*The Fish Skin* (Oliviero) Native American/Cree
	Boy to fish	*The Day Sun Was Stolen* (Oliviero) Native American/Haida
	Man and twin sons to bears	*The Girl Who Lived with the Bears* (Goldin) Native American/Pacific Northwest
	Woman to seal	*The Selkie Girl* (Cooper) European/British Isles
	Man to seal	*The Seal Prince* (MacGill-Callahan) European/Scottish
	Woman to seal	"The Selkie Wife" in *Stories from the Sea* (Riordan) Orkney Islands (in a collection of several cultures)
	Woman to dog	*The Tree That Rains* (Bernhard) Central American/Mexican
	Princess to ugly green monster	"The Moss-Green Princess" in *The Book of Little Folk* (Mills) Swaziland (in a collection of several cultures)
Human transformational events and motifs		
Human to stone	Stone statues restored to living maidens and men	*The Firebird* (San Souci) European/Russian
	Men to stone	*The Rose's Smile* (Kherdian) Middle Eastern

Theme/Topic	Transformation	Title/Author/Culture
Human transformational events and motifs		
Human to stone	Six princes and brides to stone	"The Giant Who Had No Heart" in *Giants!* (Walker) Norwegian (in a collection of several cultures)
Human to tree	Princess to tree	*The Talking Tree* (Rayevsky) European/Italian
	Humans to leaves on tree	*The Magic Tree* (McDermott) African
	Man to Joshua Tree	*The Ballad of Belle Dorcas* (Hooks) African American
Clothing/disguise female to male	Young woman to male warrior	*China's Bravest Girl* (Chin) Asian/Chinese
	Young woman to male warrior	*Fa Mulan* (San Souci) Asian/Chinese
	Young woman to man	*Vassilisa the Wise* (Sherman) European/Russian
Inanimate being/ object comes alive	Man of semolina to real husband	*Mr. Semolina-Semolinus* (Manna and Mitakidou) European/Greek
	Wooden puppet to boy	*Pinocchio* (Collodi) Original
	Child of snow to real child	*The Little Snowgirl* (Croll) European/Russian
	Child of snow to real child	*First Snow, Magic Snow* (Cech) European/Russian
	Pastry to live character	"The Gingerbread Man," "The Pancake," and "The Bun" in *Nursery Tales Around the World* (Sierra) American, Norwegian, Russian (in a collection of several cultures)
	Clay boy to live clay boy	*Clay Boy* (Ginsburg) European/Russian
	Giant of clay to live giant	*Golem* (Wisniewski) European/Jewish
	Mud pony to live pony	*The Mud Pony* (Cohen) Native American/Skidi Pawnee
	Toy wooden horse to live horse	*A Ride on the Red Mare's Back* (Le Guin) Original
	Painted pictures come to life	*Liang and the Magic Paintbrush* (Demi) Original
	Mud shape of human to Lord of the Animals	*Lord of the Animals* (French) Native American/Miwok

Theme/Topic	Transformation	Title/Author/Culture
Human transformational events and motifs		
Inanimate being/ object comes alive	Cookie to live cookie	*The Gingerbread Boy* (Egielski) Original
	Duckbill dolls to children	"Uteritsoq and the Duckbill Dolls" in *The Girl Who Dreamed Only Geese* (Norman) Native American/Inuit
	Origami doll to live origami doll to human girl	*Little Oh* (Melmed) Original
Transformation of size	Full-sized man to miniature size	*The King of Ireland's Son* (Behan) European/Irish
	Child to 40-foot man and taller; Man to giant that stretches as thin as a spider web	"Kana the Stretching Wonder" in *Giants!* (Walker) Hawaiian (in a collection of several cultures)
	Giant-sized animals to the size they are today	"How Glooskap Made Human Beings" in *How Glooskap Outwits the Ice Giants* (Norman) Native American/Maritime Northeast
	Tiny shepherd and woman to human size	"Little Lella" in *Diane Goode's Book of Giants and Little People* (Goode) Italian (in a collection of several cultures)
Transformation of age	Two young slaves to old people	*Freedom's Fruit* (Hooks) African American
	Old man and woman to young people; Man to wooden figure and back	*The Hired Hand* (San Souci) African American
	Baby to adult giant	*Bawshou Rescues the Sun* (Yeh) Asian/Chinese (Han)
	Young man to old man	*The Girl from the Sky* (Garcia) South American/Incan
	Man to old man	*Miser on the Mountain* (Luenn) Native American/Pacific Northwest (Nisqually)
	Young man to withered old man	"Tír na n-Óg" in *Irish Fairy Tales and Legends* (Leavy) European/British Isles (Irish)
	Old couple to young; Greedy old man to baby	*Magic Spring* (Rhee) Asian/Korean
Strong, independent female character	Man to serpent, lion, searing hot brand, prisoner of the faeries	*Tam Lin* (Yolen) European/Scottish
	Three gifts to large animals	*The Mapmaker's Daughter* (Helldorfer) Original
	Woman to duck, bee, church; Demon and company to hornets	*The Tsar's Promise* (San Souci) European/Russian

Theme/Topic	Transformation	Title/Author/Culture
Human transformational events and motifs		
Strong, independent female character	Man of semolina to real man	*Mr. Semolina-Semolinus* (Manna and Mitakidou) European/Greek
	Objects to deterrents to pursuer: coat to woods, egg to fog, pebbles to high wall	"Susanna and Simon" in *Cut from the Same Cloth* (San Souci) African American (in a collection of several cultures)
Three sons set out; the youngest excels due to transformational events	White Cat to crystal to beautiful princess	*The White Cat* (San Souci) European/French
	Princess to frog	*The Frog Princess* (Cecil) European/Russian
	Princess to frog	*The Frog Princess* (Lewis) European/Russian
	Mouse to beautiful maiden	*The Mouse Bride* (Allen) European/Lap (Finnish)
	Ragged commoner to armor-clad hero	*Boots and the Glass Mountain* (Martin) European/Norwegian
	Full-sized man to miniature size	*The King of Ireland's Son* (Behan) European/Irish
	Simpleton to hero; Object in horse's ear to full meal spread	*The Little Humpbacked Horse* (Winthrop) European/Russian
	Downtrodden underling to hero	*The Little Seven-Colored Horse* (San Souci) Central American/Hispanic
	Brothers' peaches to droppings and manure; Gravely ill princess to healthy one	*Three Perfect Peaches* (DeFelice and De Marsh) European/French
	Brothers' apples to toads and snakes; Gravely ill princess to healthy one	"Three Golden Apples" in *Magical Tales from Many Lands* (Mayo) French (in a collection of several cultures)
Reasons, uses for transformations		
Transformation in order to help others	Coyote to baby to man; Giants to swallows	"Coyote and the Giant Sisters" in *Giants!* (Walker) Native American/Pacific Northwest (in a collection of several cultures)
	Visible man to invisible	*The Twelve Dancing Princesses* (Ray; also Sanderson) European/German
	Raven to pine needle to baby boy to raven	*Raven's Light* (Shetterly) Native American/Pacific Northwest

Theme/Topic	Transformation	Title/Author/Culture
Reasons, uses for transformations		
Transformation in order to help others	Raven to pine needle to baby boy to raven	*Raven* (McDermott) Native American/Pacific Northwest
	Ogre to mouse	*Puss in Boots* (Perrault) European/French
	Manabozho to rabbit	"How Manabozho Stole Fire" in *Manabozho's Gifts* (Greene) Native American/Chippewa
	Animals from giant to normal size	"How Glooskap Made Human Beings" in *How Glooskap Outwits the Ice Giants* (Norman) Native American/Maritime Northeast
	Child to 40-foot man and taller; Man to giant who can stretch as thin as a spider web	"Kana the Stretching Wonder" in *Giants!* (Walker) Hawaiian (in a collection of several cultures)
Transformation as punishment or consequence	Forest giant's ashes to mosquitoes	*The Windigo's Return* (Wood) Native American/Ojibwe
	Forest giant's ashes to mosquitoes	*The Legend of the Windigo* (Ross) Native American/Ojibwe
	Timber Giant's ashes to blackflies, hornets, mosquitoes	"Beaver Face" in *Echoes of the Elders* (Smith) Native American/Kwakiutl
	Giant to mosquitoes	"The Warning of the Gulls" in *The Monster from the Swamp* (Taylor) Native American/Tlingit
	Buffalo to cloud; Buffaloes' shapes to pushed-in heads	*The Great Buffalo Race* (Esbensen) Native American/Seneca
	Plain egg to carriage and finery; Fancy egg to snakes, bees, wolf, etc.	*The Talking Eggs* (San Souci) African American/Creole
	Heroine's words to jewels and flowers; Stepsister's words to toads and snakes	*Toads and Diamonds* (Huck) European/French
	Old women to owls	"Who You!" in *Her Stories* (Hamilton) African American
	Children to mice	"The Old Owl Witch" in *Echoes of the Elders* (Smith) Native American/Kwakiutl
Transformation to play a trick	Rabbit to human forms	*Great Rabbit and the Long-Tailed Wildcat* (Gregg) Native American/Passamaquoddy

Theme/Topic	Transformation	Title/Author/Culture
Reasons, uses for transformations		
Transformation to play a trick	Magic Hare to human forms	*Muwin and the Magic Hare* (Shetterly) Native American/Passamaquoddy
	Raven to pine needle to baby boy to raven	*Raven's Light* (Shetterly) Native American/Pacific Northwest
	Raven to pine needle to baby boy to raven	*Raven* (McDermott) Native American/Pacific Northwest
	Raven to baby	*How Raven Freed the Moon* (Cameron) Native American/Pacific Northwest
	Brothers' peaches to droppings and manure	*Three Perfect Peaches* (DeFelice and De Marsh) European/French
	Brothers' apples to toads and snakes	"Three Golden Apples" in *Magical Tales from Many Lands* (Mayo) French (in a collection of several cultures)
	Coyote to man; Man's appearance unrecognizable	"The Coyote" in *Full Moon Stories* (Eagle Walking Turtle) Native American/Arapaho
	Coyote to baby to man; Giants to swallows	"Coyote and the Giant Sisters" in *Giants!* (Walker) Native American/Pacific Northwest
	Story-spirits transform themselves to harm prince in revenge	"The Spirits in the Leather Bag" in *The Barefoot Book of Trickster Tales* (Walker) Kampuchean (in a collection of several cultures)
	Glooskap to Ice Giant; Stick to skull	*How Glooskap Outwits the Ice Giants* (Norman) Native American/Maritime Indians
	Fox to a series of animals and objects	*Gilly Martin the Fox* (Hunter) European/Scottish
	Animals to sandstone	"Swift Runner and Trickster Tarantula" in *Spider Spins a Story* (Max) Native American/Zuni
Transformation to aid in escape	Three gifts to large animals	*The Mapmaker's Daughter* (Helldorfer) Original
	Maria and Ivan to a river, a bridge, a church, a monk; Their horse to a steeple	*The Tsar's Promise* (San Souci) European/Russian
	Objects to deterrents to pursuer: towel to river, comb to forest	*Baba Yaga and the Little Girl* (Arnold) European/Russian
	Objects to deterrents to pursuer: coat to woods, egg to fog, pebbles to high wall	"Susanna and Simon" in *Cut from the Same Cloth* (San Souci) African American (in a collection of several cultures)

Theme/Topic	Transformation	Title/Author/Culture
Reasons, uses for transformations		
Transformation to aid in escape	Objects to deterrents to pursuer: fork to woods, salt to mountain, drop of water to sea	*Master Maid* (Shepard) European/Norwegian
	Objects to deterrents to pursuer: stone to mountain, comb to ice, breath to fog	"Little Lella" in *Diane Goode's Book of Giants and Little People* (Goode) Italian (in a collection of several cultures)
	Visible Mollie to invisible	*Mollie Whuppie and the Giant* (Muller) European/British
Under spell of evildoer; release from spell by love or honorable deed	White Cat to crystal to beautiful princess	*The White Cat* (San Souci) European/French
	Stone statues to living maidens and men	*The Firebird* (San Souci) European/Russian
	Ugly hag to beautiful princess	*Sir Gawain and the Loathly Lady* (Hastings) European/British
	Swan to beautiful princess	*The Tale of Tsar Saltan* (Pushkin) European/Russian
	Mouse to beautiful maiden	*The Mouse Bride* (Allen) European/Lap (Finnish)
	Beast to prince	*Beauty and the Beast* (Brett, Geras, and others) European/French
	Toad to prince	"The Three Feathers" in *Multicultural Fables and Fairy Tales* (McCarthy) German (in a collection of several cultures)
	Frog to princess	*The Frog Princess* (Cecil) European/Russian
	Frog to princess	*The Frog Princess* (Lewis) European/Russian
	Frog to prince	*The Frog Prince* (Tarcov; also Ormerod) European/German
	Hare to young lass	"The Blue-Eyed Hare" in *Tales Alive!* (Milord) Scottish (in a collection of several cultures)
	Wild deer to woman	"Finn MacCoul" in *Favorite Medieval Tales* (Osborne) Irish (in a collection of several cultures)
	Bear to man	*East o' the Sun and West o' the Moon* (Barlow) European/Norwegian

Theme/Topic	Transformation	Title/Author/Culture
Reasons, uses for transformations		
Under spell of evildoer; release from spell by love or honorable deed	Dog to man	"Feng Zhen-Zhu (The Wind Pearl)" in *Multicultural Plays for Children, Vol. 2* (Gerke) Chinese (in a collection of several cultures)
	White caribou to woman	*The Enchanted Caribou* (Cleaver) Native American/Inuit
	Wild man to knight; Walter-in-the-Mud to golden knight; Objects in spring to gold	*Iron John* (Kimmel) European/German
	Bear to prince	*East o' the Sun and West o' the Moon* (Barlow) European/Norwegian
	Serpent to lion to searing hot brand to man	*Tam Lin* (Yolen) European/Scottish
	Werewolf to man	"The Werewolf" in *Favorite Medieval Tales* (Osborne) French (in a collection of several cultures)
Under spell of evildoer; release from spell by violence	Bear to prince	*Rose Red and Snow White* (Sanderson) European/German
	Bear to prince	*Snow White and Rose Red* (Grimm) European/German
	Tree to princess	*The Talking Tree* (Rayevsky) European/Italian
Transformation of attitude or perception	Solitary lives to community of sharing and celebration; Man and woman to eagles	*The Eagle's Song* (Rodanas) Native American/Pacific Northwest
	Lazy, greedy man to humble, repentant man; Man to wood and back	*The Hired Hand* (San Souci) African American
	Bitter man to accepting, repentant man; Merman to man	*Nicholas Pipe* (San Souci) European/British Isles
	Mean-spirited to caring man; Man to raven	*A Man Called Raven* (Van Camp) Original
	Dark, joyless world to happy world with music, dance, and light	*Musicians of the Sun* (McDermott) South American/Aztec
Test of patience, love, or integrity	Prince to snake, dragon	*The Dragon Prince* (Yep) Asian/Chinese
	Prince to beast	*Beauty and the Beast* (Brett, Geras, and others) European/French

Theme/Topic	Transformation	Title/Author/Culture
Reasons, uses for transformations		
Test of patience, love, or integrity	Prince to snake	*Mufaro's Beautiful Daughters* (Steptoe) African
	Kitchen-cooked man of semolina to real man	*Mr. Semolina-Semolinus* (Manna and Mitakidou) European/Greek
	Tears to pearls; Men to stone	*The Rose's Smile* (Kherdian) Middle Eastern
Transformations in the natural world		
Sky phenomena: origin of stars, planets	Man to morning star	*Bawshou Rescues the Sun* (Yeh) Asian/Chinese (Han)
	Brothers and girl to stars of Big Dipper	*Her Seven Brothers* (Goble) Native American/Cheyenne
	Children and dogs to the Pleiades and nearby stars	*The Lost Children* (Goble) Native American/Siksika
	Woman to image on moon	*The Woman in the Moon* (Rattigan) Hawaiian
	Boy to the morning star (Venus)	*The Orphan Boy* (Mollel) African/Maasai
Sky phenomena: Stars become earth creatures	Stars to water lilies	*Star Maiden* (Esbensen) Native American/Ojibway
	Stars to bear	*When Bear Came Down from the Sky* (de Gerez) European/Finno-Ugric
Sky phenomena: passing between sky world and earth world	Sky people to animals	"The Star Maiden" in *Cut from the Same Cloth* (San Souci) Native American/Chippewa (in a collection of several cultures)
	Raven to pine needle to baby boy to raven	*Raven* (McDermott) Native American/Pacific Northwest
Origin of land formations	Sea serpent to islands, straits, and Iceland	"Jamie and the Biggest, First, and Father of All Sea Serpents" in *Mythical Birds and Beasts from Many Lands* (Mayo) European/Scandinavian (Orkney Islands)
	Woman to Mt. St. Helens	"Loo-Wit, the Firekeeper" in *Keepers of the Earth* (Caduto and Bruchac) Native American/Nisqually
	Woman to Mt. Susitna, Alaska	*The Sleeping Lady* (Dixon) American

Theme/Topic	Transformation	Title/Author/Culture
Transformations in the natural world		
Origin of land formations	Five sisters to Niagara Falls	"The Five Water-Spirits" in *Multicultural Fables and Fairy Tales* (McCarthy) Native American/Canadian (in a collection of several cultures)
Weather influences	Woman to a ray of sunlight, cloud	*Marriage of the Rain Goddess* (Wolfson) African/Zulu
	Buffalo to cloud	*The Great Buffalo Race* (Esbensen) Native American/Seneca
	Snake-boy to lightning	*Uncle Snake* (Gollub) Central American
	Chinese paper cuts to snowflakes, blossoms, fruits of each season	*Lao Lao of Dragon Mountain* (Bateson-Hill) Asian/Chinese
	Sea wind to man, bird, beast	"Sea Wind" in *Stories from the Sea* (Riordan) African/Senegalese
	Music of mouth harp to sea winds	"The Old Man of the Sea" in *Stories from the Sea* (Riordan) Siberian (in a collection of several cultures)
	Sheep and ram to thunder and lightning	*The Story of Lightning and Thunder* (Bryan) African
	January snows to March flowers	*The Month-Brothers* (Marshak) European/Bohemian/Slavic
	Temporary change of seasons: Jan. to March, Jan. to June, Jan. to Sept.	*Marushka and the Month Brothers* (Vojtech) European/Czech and Slovak
Other transformation motifs		
A book holds the secret to the transformation	Young women to birds and back	*The Enchanted Book* (Porazinska) European/Polish
	Boy and man to numerous objects	*Doctor Change* (Cole) European/French
	Prince to canary and back	*The Canary Prince* (Nones) European/Italian
Becoming invisible	Visible man to invisible	*The Twelve Dancing Princesses* (Ray; also Sanderson) European/German
	Visible goblin and man to invisible	"The Goblin's Cap" in *The Book of Little Folk* (Mills) Korean (in a collection of several cultures)
	Visible Mollie to invisible	*Mollie Whuppie and the Giant* (Muller) European/British

Theme/Topic	Transformation	Title/Author/Culture
Other transformation motifs		
Mythical creatures	Fish to dragons; a god to horse	"The Fish at Dragon's Gate" in *Mythical Birds and Beasts from Many Lands* (Mayo) Chinese (in a collection of several cultures)
	Boy to dragon	*The Dragon's Pearl* (Lawson) Asian/Chinese
	Bodach (scruffy man) to sea-god	"The Bodach of the Grey Coat" in *Irish Fairy Tales and Legends* (Leavy) European/British Isles (Irish)
	Naga to woman, snake, and snake-woman	"Three Fabulous Eggs" in *Mythical Birds and Beasts from Many Lands* (Mayo) Burmese (in a collection of several cultures)
Series of transformations	Woman to king to church leader to wish to be God	"Something More . . ." in *Beauty and the Beast and Other Stories* (Geras) European
	Boy and man to numerous objects	*Doctor Change* (Cole) European/French
	Merlin to stag, old woman, wild man, and other forms	*Young Merlin* (San Souci) European/British
	Magic Hare to hunter, woman, chief, boy	*Muwin and the Magic Hare* (Shetterly) Native American/Passamaquoddy
	Wizard to goat to elephant to dinosaur to mouse to ant	"Jack and the Wizard" in *The Barefoot Book of Trickster Tales* (Walker) English (in a collection of several cultures)
	Woman to tiger, elephant, and other forms	*Tiger Woman* (Yep) Asian/Chinese
	Maria to duck, bee, river, church; Prince Ivan to bridge, then monk	*The Tsar's Promise* (San Souci) European/Russian
	Princess to dove, tree, cradle, back to princess	"The Lemon Princess" in *Magical Tales from Many Lands* (Mayo) Arabic/Turkish (in a collection of several cultures
	Fox to boats to sword to horse	*Gilly Martin the Fox* (Hunter) European/Scottish

Chapter 8

This annotated bibliography is arranged by geographic area, and further by cultural group. The overall organization is by continent, with the addition of regions of Central America and the Middle East. Within a continental area, such as Europe or Asia, distinct cultural groups provide subheadings to group tales. Following the continental/cultural headings, there is a section of story collections encompassing tales from many cultures. Finally, there is a section of original stories featuring transformational elements.

Because the majority of these stories are most effective as read-alouds, some annotations do not contain specific age recommendations. These stories appeal to a wide range of ages. The decision to use these tales with any age rests with the reader. The decision should be based on factors such as the read-aloud leader or teacher's skill and preparation, as well as knowledge of the listening audience.

AFRICAN

Bryan, Ashley. *The Story of Lightning and Thunder*. Illustrated by the author. New York: Atheneum, 1993.

Ma Sheep Thunder and Son Ram Lightning bring the rains when needed, especially when a drought comes. Their village honors them with a harvest festival, where Son Ram Lightning gets rambunctious, showing off and making mischief. Because of Son's troublemaking, the King moves Ma Sheep Thunder and Son Ram Lightning out past the edge of town. When Son starts a fire with his sparks, the King decrees that, for safety's sake, Sheep Thunder and Ram Lightning can no longer dwell on earth. They go up the mountain and into the sky, where they become thunder and lightning.

McDermott, Gerald. *The Magic Tree: A Tale from the Congo*. Illustrated by the author. New York: Henry Holt, 1973.

Told in simple language, this tale of rejection, love, and secrets has a sobering ending. A woman has two grown sons but ignores the one named Mavungu. He leaves home, and finding a huge tree, he pulls off the leaves. The leaves turn into people. The last leaf-person is a princess, who thanks Mavungu for breaking the spell. They marry, and she creates a great village, swearing Mavungu to secrecy about their origins. Over time, he starts thinking of his mother and brother, and he sees them. The mother, who still has no love for him, presses him for the secret. Finally he tells, and his village vanishes.

Mollel, Tololwa M. *The Orphan Boy: A Maasai Story*. Illustrated by Paul Morin. New York: Clarion Books, 1990.

Stunning illustrations convey the mood of this sober tale of the origin of the planet Venus. An old man notices a star is missing from the skies. He meets an orphan boy and offers to share his home. When a drought burns up the grass and water supply, the boy tells the old man that he has his father's power over drought, but he must keep it secret. Despite the drought, the old man's herd of cattle remains fat and full of milk. Eventually, the old man's curiosity gives way to betrayal of the trust they shared. He spies on the boy and learns the secret of his power. The boy is instantly transformed into a star. Now there is nothing but a dry, thirsty herd and a separate star in the sky. It is Venus (the "Orphan Boy"), appearing at dawn to take the herd out and again in the evening to bring them back.

Wolfson, Margaret Olivia. *Marriage of the Rain Goddess: A South African Myth*. Illustrated by Clifford Alexander Parms. New York: Marlowe, 1996.

In this Zulu myth, Mbaba Mwana Waresa, the rain goddess, transforms herself into a ray of sunlight, then a cloud, then a woman in rags and ashes to search for and test a man to become her partner. Mbaba Mwana Waresa looks over both gods and mortals. She chooses Thandiwe, a cattle herder, to be her partner, but he must first be tested. He must stand outside the bridal hut he has built during a thunderstorm. A beautiful woman approaches him, and he knows that the lovely woman is not his betrothed (whom he has met only in a dream). So he chooses instead the rain goddess, disguised as a woman in rags and ashes. Interesting details on bead ornament love letters and other Zulu customs are provided in the author's note. This story is best suited to upper grades.

AFRICAN AMERICAN

Bang, Molly. *Wiley and the Hairy Man: Adapted from an American Folk Tale.* Illustrated by the author. New York: Aladdin Books, 1976 (reissued 1996).

The big, ugly, mean Hairy Man lives in the swamp, and he intends to capture Wiley with his magical powers and brutish ways. Wiley and his mother outwit the Hairy Man three times so that he'll never bother them again. Both a trickster and transformation tale, this tale contains frequent shifts of power as Wiley and Hairy Man match wits. The large typeface and easier vocabulary make this a candidate for independent reading by primary students.

Hamilton, Virginia. *Her Stories: African American Folktales, Fairy Tales, and True Tales.* Illustrated by Leo and Diane Dillon. New York: Blue Sky Press, 1995.

This highly acclaimed collection includes a wide range of African American stories "of the female kind," including trickster tales, several transformation tales, pourquoi tales, tales of the supernatural, and biographical stories. The dialect and advanced content make some of these stories better suited to older grades through adult. "Marie and Redfish" is a sad love story of a girl in love with a prince. Her disapproving father gets a wizard to change the prince into a fish, but Marie continues to see him. The father then kills the fish and makes Marie cook it. Afterward, back at the river, Marie's tears open the earth, and she rejoins her lover under the earth. "Lena and Big One Tiger" tells of a girl who marries a handsome man who is really a tiger. "Miz Hattie Gets Some Company" tells of a woman's problem with mice and of a visit from Jesus. He throws his glove on the floor and it turns into a cat to hunt the mice. "Who You!" is a cautionary tale in which the older women fill their time gossiping and ignoring a stranger's plea for help. Finally, a younger girl's response to the stranger makes the older ones feel bad about themselves. They all turn into owls and will remain so until they forget all the bad gossip.

Hooks, William H. *The Ballad of Belle Dorcas.* Illustrated by Brian Pinkney. New York: Alfred A. Knopf, 1990.

This book is classified as fiction but is based on conjure tales heard by the author as a child on the coast of the Carolinas. Belle Dorcas, daughter of a slave mother, is "free issue" because her father is a white master who has signed Belle's papers. Beautiful Belle has many suitors, but she loves only Joshua, the talented fiddler who hopes someday to earn enough money to buy his freedom and then marry Belle. When plans are made to sell Joshua away, Belle turns in desperation to the "cunger woman," Granny Lizard, a woman with knowledge of magic and spells. The old woman assembles a cunger bag that guarantees that Joshua will never leave the plantation. When Belle and Joshua meet secretly that night, Belle is horrified when the spell takes effect and Joshua turns into a tree. Later, Belle learns she can use the cunger bag to turn Joshua into a man every night, but he must return to the form of a tree during the day. One day, the master orders the tree chopped down to build a new smokehouse roof. Belle learns she can still use the cunger bag to have her Joshua every night. When Belle Dorcas dies an old woman, the smokehouse disappears. Pinkney's distinctive scratchboard illustrations combine with Hooks's unique storytelling to create a captivating read-aloud for fourth graders and up.

———. *Freedom's Fruit.* Illustrated by James Ransome. New York: Alfred A. Knopf, 1996.

Although this dramatic story is classified as fiction, it is based on a conjure tale of the slaves of the coastal Carolinas. Mama Marina, a conjure woman, is told by her so-called master to put a spell on the grapes so that the slaves won't eat up his wine profit. She asks for a gold coin for the spell, as she does for all her conjure work. In truth, she is saving the coins to buy freedom for her daughter, Sheba. Sheba and Joe Nathan are in love, and the master is planning to hire Joe out to other plantations. All the slaves are dismayed that Mama Marina works the spell in favor of the master, but Mama has a master plan in mind. One night, Mama makes the two lovers eat the green conjured grapes. The spell makes them sick and transforms them into old, shriveled people. Since the two are now worthless to the master, Mama can afford to buy their freedom papers. She sends the couple to Charleston, promising that the spell will come full circle in the spring, and their youth will be restored. The tale is better suited to middle or upper grades because of the understanding of slavery that is required.

San Souci, Robert D. *The Hired Hand: An African-American Folktale.* Illustrated by Jerry Pinkney. New York: Dial Books for Young Readers, 1997.
    A sawmill in old Virginia is the setting for this tale about integrity. The owner of the sawmill is hardworking, but his son, Young Sam, is lazy and does slipshod work. One day, a shabby-looking man comes and asks to work for a year for free, wanting only to learn the trade. The owner appreciates the help, but Young Sam pushes even more work off now, bossing the Hand around. When an old man comes to buy some wood and complains about his aching body, the New Hand offers to help him. But the others must go away and not watch. Sam pretends to leave but stays to spy. The New Hand tells the man to lie on the saw frame. He then sprinkles sawdust and recites a chant that turns the man into wood. Then the New Hand saws the wooden man into four neat planks, bathes them with water and a chant, and fits them together again. Finally, he pricks his thumb and dabs blood on the wooden man to bring him to life. He is now a young, spry man. Young Sam, who has spied on the process, later tries it himself on the man's old wife. She does not come to life because he doesn't want to prick his finger. He is judged guilty of murder and states his remorse for his greedy and lazy ways. Suddenly, the Hew Hand appears in the courtroom, brings in the woman (alive), and saves Young Sam from jail. But the New Hand is never seen again. It is interesting to note another, subtler transformation in this tale: the transformation of Young Sam's attitude. Beautifully illustrated in well-researched 1700s styles, this is a tale for middle and upper grades.

AMERICAN

Dixon, Ann. *The Sleeping Lady.* Illustrated by Elizabeth Johns. Anchorage, AK: Alaska Northwest Books, 1994.
    Giant people, known for their peaceful ways, used to live near Cook Inlet, Alaska. Two of these giants, a young man and a young woman, are about to be married, but they have to wait because the young man must go to battle. After waiting for him for days, she goes to sleep while sitting on a hill. Her sleeping body then turns into a mountain. This sad tale explains the origin of Alaska's first snowfall and the origin of the mountain still known as "the Sleeping Lady." According to Dixon's research, this is probably a modern folktale, not a native legend. The text is easily accessible to middle grades.

ASIAN

Chinese

Bateson-Hill, Margaret. *Lao Lao of Dragon Mountain.* Illustrated by Francesca Pelizzoli. London: De Agostini Editions, 1996.
    An old woman named Lao Lao earns the admiration of people for miles around for her Chinese papercuts. The greedy emperor hears of her art and imprisons her in a tower on a mountaintop. There, she is to make "jewel" paper cuts from a huge stack of paper. As she toils, fashioning diamond-shaped designs, the Ice Dragon senses something

is wrong. The Dragon picks up the old woman, and she rides on his back, scattering her diamond paper cuts. The paper turns into sparkling snowflakes. She continues to ride on the dragon's back to this day, cutting and scattering papers, which cover springtime trees with flowers, summer fields with flowers, and autumn trees with fruits and nuts. The tower atop the mountain is replaced by three ice pillars, which are the transformed bodies of the emperor and his guards. This tale, containing both pourquoi and transformation elements, is readable by second or third graders, and it works as a read-aloud for all ages.

Chin, Charlie. *China's Bravest Girl: The Legend of Hua Mu Lan.* Translated by Wang Xing Chu. Illustrated by Tomie Arai. Emeryville, CA: Children's Book Press, 1993.

The transformation of this brave young woman is not magical; rather, it is achieved by her wearing men's clothing. Told in rhyming poetry, this is an account of the girl honored in the folk poem from the Soong Dynasty. Hua Mu Lan plans to go to war in her father's place, wishing to repay her father's kindness. She dresses in the clothes of a warrior, leads the troops, becomes a general, and serves for 10 years. The emperor wants to honor her, but she asks instead to be allowed to return home where she is needed. She returns home, changes clothes, and surprises her comrade in arms, who asks her to be his wife. Compare with *Fa Mulan* by Robert D. San Souci.

Lawson, Julie. *The Dragon's Pearl.* Illustrated by Paul Morin. New York: Clarion Books, 1993.

Dramatic events and somber illustrations make this a compelling story for all ages. During a long drought, a boy cuts grass to sell from a green patch of grass that keeps growing back. One day he discovers a pearl in the grass and brings it to his mother. They discover that the pearl is magic: It multiplies the rice in the rice jar and coins in the money box. One night, thieves come demanding coins, and they discover the pearl. To prevent the thieves from getting the pearl, the boy pops it in his mouth and swallows it. The boy is consumed with unquenchable thirst, and is transformed into a dragon. The boy-dragon breathes rain clouds, which end the drought and create the River Min that still flows through the province of Szechuan.

San Souci, Robert D. *Fa Mulan: The Story of a Woman Warrior.* Illustrated by Jean and Mou-Sien Tseng. New York: Hyperion Books for Children, 1998.

This version of the story of Mulan is written by the man who developed the story line for the Disney movie. In this well-researched telling, Mulan is portrayed as an earnest and independent woman who is ready for adventure and a life of duty. When her father is drafted for the Khan's army, Mulan persuades her parents to let her go in his place. Mulan goes through years of battles, and she grows in her fighting techniques, always concealing her womanhood. She learns battle strategy and rises in rank and responsibility. Finally, she develops the plan and leads one of three armies in a decisive battle, resulting in victory. Throughout her years of service, Mulan retains a humble spirit. When the Khan summons her to reward her, Mulan wants only to return to her family. She travels home with an honor guard of companions and then surprises them when she changes into the garb and hairstyle of a woman. The words of her closest comrade hint at a future relationship. This transformation is one of disguise rather than magic and is based on a fifth-century Chinese ballad.

Wolkstein, Diane. *White Wave: A Chinese Tale.* Illustrated by Ed Young. New York: Gulliver Books, 1996.

One day on his way home, a poor young farmer finds a beautiful snail shell. He brings it home, giving it leaves to eat and a jar to live in. When he comes home the next day, he finds dinner waiting for him but no person to thank. Every day, the same thing happens. One day he spies at the window and discovers a beautiful woman emerging from the shell in the jar. He knows she is a moon goddess and that he must never touch her. But one day he rushes into the room while she is there, so she tells him she must leave. Before disappearing into a stormy wind, she tells him that if he ever has a deep need, he can call her name, White Wave, and she will help. When the farmer becomes poor and hungry, he remembers her promise and calls out her name. She responds by sending a torrent of rice from the shell. She never returns, but her story lives on. This tale is a thoughtful offering for middle and upper grades.

Yeh, Chun-Chan, and Allan Baillie. *Bawshou Rescues the Sun: A Han Folktale.* Illustrated by Michelle Powell. New York: Scholastic, 1991.

Both transformational and pourquoi elements are found in this complex plot told with spare, efficient language. As a man and his wife await the birth of their first child, a strong wind comes and steals the sun. The young man decides to find the sun. He journeys for months with a golden phoenix, while at home, his wife gives birth to their son, Bawshou. When the phoenix returns alone, the wife learns that her husband has been transformed into the morning star. Suddenly, the baby Bawshou transforms into a grown giant man. Guided by the phoenix, he embarks on harrowing adventures in search of the sun. Eventually, Bawshou finds the kingdom of the Devils, who have hidden the sun. Bawshou and the phoenix put the sun back in place, and the King of the Devils is burned out of the sky. This tale explains the origin of the morning star, as well as the pink-gold cloud seen at dawn, the Phoenix.

Yep, Laurence. *The Dragon Prince: A Chinese Beauty and the Beast Tale.* Illustrated by Kam Mak. New York: HarperCollins, 1997.

Powerfully told and stunningly illustrated, this is a tale of integrity. Central to this tale is the protagonist's trust in the knowledge of the heart. A poor man has seven daughters. The youngest, Seven, does all the housework and creates exceptional embroidery. One day, her jealous older sister, Three, finds a serpent and tries to kill it. Seven rescues the snake and sets it free. Later, this snake transforms into a large dragon, captures the father, and demands a daughter as a wife, or else he will devour the father. All six of the older daughters refuse to marry the dragon, but Seven gladly spares her father and rides off on the dragon's back. The dragon takes Seven off into the sky, to an underwater kingdom. Seven faces the terrifying dragon, unafraid, and touches his cheek. He asks why she is not afraid. She states, "The eye sees what it will, but the heart sees what it should." The dragon then changes into a handsome prince, and Seven marries him. She lives in luxury, but her spirit wanes as she misses her family. The prince magically transports her back for a visit to her family, where Three knocks her on the head and pushes her into the river. Three returns to the Dragon Prince in place of Seven, but he knows in his heart she is not Seven. Meanwhile, under the river, Seven is rescued and nursed back to health by an old woman. The Dragon Prince searches for Seven, and one day, he discovers a pair of exquisitely embroidered slippers at the market. This clue leads him back to his beloved, and they live happily ever after. All ages will give rapt attention to the quiet power of this story.

———. *The Shell Woman and the King.* Illustrated by Yang Ming-Yi. New York: Dial Books for Young Readers, 1993.

Lonely Uncle Wu sings songs to the sea, and he meets a woman from the sea. She can change into a seashell and back again. After they marry, the jealous king captures Shell and imprisons Wu. Shell refuses to become the king's wife, so he requires her to give him three wonders. With her magical powers, she not only meets the king's demands but also outwits him.

———. *Tiger Woman.* Illustrated by Robert Roth. Mahwah, NJ: BridgeWater Books, 1995.

An old selfish woman refuses to share her food with a beggar who predicts she will become what she says. So each time she states she is as "hungry as a tiger" or "starved as an elephant," her words result in a transformation, accompanied by chaos. Finally, she realizes that her greed has brought on her disastrous transformations, and she learns her lesson to share. Based on a Shantung folk song, the text of this retelling is interspersed with rhyming verse. The book works well as a read-aloud.

Indian

Shepard, Aaron. *The Gifts of Wali Dad: A Tale of India and Pakistan.* Illustrated by Daniel San Souci. New York: Atheneum Books for Young Readers, 1995.
Old Wali Dad is a grass-cutter who lives in a little hut, wanting and needing little. When he counts his coins earned from selling grass, he is astonished at the amount. He buys a bracelet and sends it to a queen who lives to the east. The queen responds by sending him a load of silk fabric. Not knowing what to do with the silk, Wali Dad sends it to a king who lives to the west. The king also sends a gift back. This pattern continues, each time with a more extravagant gift being returned. Each time, Wali Dad bemoans his plight: He wants none of this wealth. Finally, Wali Dad is to meet the king and queen. Before the meeting, two peris (angel-like fairies) change him into a king. Afterward, the king and queen get married, and the peris return to change Wadi Dad back into the poor-but-happy old man he prefers to be.

Japanese

Johnston, Tony. *The Badger and the Magic Fan: A Japanese Folktale.* Illustrated by Tomie dePaola. New York: G. P. Putnam's Sons, 1990.
Goblins, called Tengu, have a magic fan, which can cause noses to grow long and short again. A badger wants the fan, so he transforms himself into a little girl and tricks the Tengu out of the fan. He then turns a wealthy, beautiful young woman into a long-nosed fright. After several failed attempts to cure her, the badger steps in as the hero. However, the Tengu children then turn the trick back on the badger.

San Souci, Robert D. *The Snow Wife.* Illustrated by Stephen T. Johnson. New York: Dial Books for Young Readers, 1993.
Two woodcutters take refuge in a hut during a severe snowstorm. A spiritlike woman appears in the night and speaks to the younger man. She says that she will not forget him, but he must promise never to tell anyone about her. Later, the young man marries and has children. One night, he tells his wife about his experience with the Woman of the Snow. Upset, the wife tells him that it was she. Now that he has broken his promise, she must leave. She transforms into the Woman of the Snow. The man goes on a harrowing quest to get his wife back. Finally, the man promises the Wind God that he will keep an altar in his honor. In return, the Woman of the Snow is brought back to the man in human form. This haunting and sober tale is suitable for middle grades and up.

Yagawa, Sumiko. *The Crane Wife.* Translated by Katherine Paterson. Illustrated by Suekichi Akaba. New York: William Morrow, 1981.
A simple young peasant lives alone. He finds an injured crane in the snow and removes the arrow from its wing. That night, a beautiful woman comes to him and asks to be his wife. The amazed man agrees. Noticing that their food stores are waning, the woman offers to weave cloth to sell, but she makes her husband promise never to look at her while she weaves. The sale of the cloth gets them through part of the winter. When the money runs out again, she says she will weave more cloth, but it must be the last time because each time she weaves, she becomes thinner and paler. However, the man is persuaded by a neighbor to market the fine cloth to the nobility, planting the seeds of greed. The man asks his wife to weave again, thinking of the riches they will

have. While she weaves, the curious husband steals a glance at her, and with horror, he sees a bloody crane, who has plucked out her own feathers to weave the cloth. When his wife discovers the breach of trust, she flies away. Simply told, this is a gentle yet serious tale for all ages. Compare with the story based on this tale: *Dawn* by Molly Bang.

Korean

Rhee, Nami. *Magic Spring: A Korean Folktale.* Illustrated by the author. New York: G. P. Putnam's Sons, 1993.
An old man and his wife, childless, live and work in a village. Their greedy neighbor mocks them for not having a child. One day, the old man follows a bluebird, and then stops to take a drink from a spring. The cold water refreshes and relaxes him, and he sleeps. When he wakes, he feels unusually rejuvenated. When he returns home, his amazed wife sees that he has become young again. He tells her about the spring, and the next day the wife also takes one gulp. The greedy neighbor asks about their transformation. The young couple explain about the spring , telling him he only needs one drink to become young. The greedy man rushes to the spring and slurps up most of the water. When he does not return that evening, the young couple search for him, and they find a little baby; it is the old neighbor transformed by the long drink at the spring. They take the baby home and raise him as their own. This tale, readable by second grade and up, is an appealing read-aloud for primary and middle grades.

AUSTRALIAN/HAWAIIAN

Berndt, Catherine. *Pheasant and Kingfisher.* Illustrated by Arone Raymond Meeks. Greenvale, NY: Mondo, 1994.
Bookbook the Pheasant and Bered-bered the Kingfisher are two men traveling through the land. They find a place to stay by a bamboo-lined stream. But a man warns them that they are on land belonging to a group of men who are coming to kill them. The two defend themselves with spears, but they are outnumbered, so they grow feathers and fly away. Those on the ground turn to stone, where they can be seen today. Told in simple text, this transformation tale also explains the origin of the pheasant and kingfisher.

Meeks, Arone Raymond. *Enora and the Black Crane.* Illustrated by the author. New York: Scholastic, 1991.
A young man named Enora lives with his people in the rain forest. Enora wants to show his family that the birds have magical colors, so he kills a crane as proof and brings it home. Black feathers grow on Enora's body, and he becomes a black crane. Meeks bases this original story on folk elements passed on to him from his Aboriginal grandfather.

Rattigan, Jama Kim. *The Woman in the Moon: A Story from Hawai'i.* Illustrated by Carla Golembe. Boston: Little, Brown, 1996.
This story explains the origin of Hina's image on the moon, as she transforms from human to moon-image. Hina makes the finest tapa cloth in Hawai'i. People stop making their own, wanting Hina's cloth only. She is so busy making tapa, she cannot attend the feasts and festivals. And while most husbands help with the cloth-making and cooking, Hina's husband is too lazy. Tired of her husband's demands and of the fact that many things in the community are *kapu*, or forbidden to women, she starts wandering the island, searching for a place where she will be happier. She tries a mountaintop (too cold), a rainbow (too hot), and finally the moon, where she decides to stay.

CENTRAL AMERICAN

Bernhard, Emery. *The Tree That Rains: The Flood Myth of the Huichol Indians of Mexico.* Illustrated by Durga Bernhard. New York: Holiday House, 1994.

Great-Grandmother Earth, who makes everything grow, warns Watakame that because the people no longer honor the gods, a flood is coming. She instructs him to make a boat and put inside five kernels of each kind of corn, as well as of each kind of bean and squash, five hot coals, and his dog. She rides the boat with Watakame for five years. After the flood, Great-Grandmother Earth goes back to making things grow, and Watakame plants his seeds. A huge fig tree produces water for the crops. Every day, for four days, Watakame comes home to find hot tortillas. He wonders who is making them. The fifth day, he hides and watches his dog. He sees the dog take off its skin and transform into a woman! While she is grinding corn, Watakame steals her dog-skin and throws it in the fire. She then becomes his wife, and they have many children, repopulating the earth. Compare this transformation with *The Seal Prince* by Sheila MacGill-Callahan and *The Day Sun Was Stolen* and *The Fish Skin* by Jamie Oliviero.

Gollub, Matthew. *Uncle Snake.* Illustrated by Leo Vigildo Martinez. New York: Tambourine Books, 1996.

Ignoring his family's warnings, a boy ventures into a cave. The cave is full of snakes, who say they are enchanted children. When the boy returns to his family, his head has changed into the head of a snake. The father takes him to healers and a worker of magic, who say that the boy must always wear a mask. Twenty years later, he is told to stay in the cave for three days and take off the mask. His body turns into that of a snake, but he now has a human head. Then he flies into the sky and becomes lightning. This tale is suitable for middle or upper grades.

EUROPEAN

Geras, Adèle. *Beauty and the Beast: And Other Stories.* Illustrated by Louise Brierley. New York: Viking, 1996.

This collection of eight tales includes the transformation stories of "Beauty and the Beast" and "Vipers and Pearls," a variation of "Toads and Diamonds." In "The Girl Who Stepped on a Loaf," a rude, vain girl gets her comeuppance with Marsh-Wife and the Devil's grandmother. In "Something More . . ." a fisherman's wife is never satisfied, but keeps wishing for more transformations until she wishes to become God. No source notes or information on culture of origin are given. Use this collection for additional comparison material.

Basque

Araujo, Frank P. *Nekane, the Lamiña and the Bear: A Tale of the Basque Pyrenees.* Illustrated by Xiao Jun Li. Windsor, CA: Rayve Productions, 1993.

Nekane's mother gives her a basket of fish and olive oil to take through the woods to her uncle. But she must beware of the lamiña, a forest spirit who loves olive oil and can change into any form. Soon, Nekane finds herself stalked by the lamiña, and then by a bear. The lamiña turns himself into a fog and into the uncle. Using her wits, Nekane sets up the bear and the lamiña to stalk each other. This is an effective read-aloud for all ages.

Bohemian/Slavic

Marshak, Samuel. *The Month-Brothers: A Slavic Tale.* Translated by Thomas P. Whitney. Illustrated by Diane Stanley. New York: William Morrow, 1983.

A mean-spirited woman spoils her own daughter and demands that all the chores be done by her stepdaughter. One day in January, the stepmother orders the girl to go out and pick snowdrop blossoms. The girl sets out on her impossible mission, going into the dark, frozen forest. Her despair turns to hope when she finds a bonfire surrounded by 12 men and boys. When she explains her plight, they decide to help her. The old man January, his brother February, and their young brother March transform the forest clearing from winter to spring. Snowdrops appear all around the girl, and she picks a basketful. When she brings them home, the stepmother and daughter demand an explanation. When the girl tells them of the Month-Brothers, the stepmother sends her daughter to find strawberries, apples, pears, and cucumbers, planning to sell them and get rich. The selfish daughter makes these demands of the Month-Brothers. But January responds with a strong blast of winter. When the girl does not return from the forest, the mother goes to find her. She too freezes. But the stepdaughter grows up to have a home in which the bounties of all the months are found.

Vojtech, Anna, and Philemon Sturges. *Marushka and the Month Brothers: A Folktale.* Illustrated by Anna Vojtech. New York: North-South Books, 1996.

This is a newer telling of the same storyline in Samuel Marshak's book (see entry above). Slightly shorter and gentler, this telling is a recollection of the author from her childhood in Czechoslovakia.

British Isles

Cooper, Susan. *The Selkie Girl.* Illustrated by Warwick Hutton. New York: Margaret K. McElderry, 1986.

Donallan, a fisherman, comes upon three beautiful girls sitting on the rocks by the shore, and he falls in love with one of them. His old neighbor explains that they are selkies, who, once a year in the spring, slip out of their sealskins and take human form. The next year, Donallan steals the sealskin of the selkie he loves and marries her, calling her Mairi. They have five children. One day, one of the children discovers that his father has a sealskin hidden, and he tells his mother. She then dons the sealskin and returns to her family in the sea. But she keeps watch over her land-bound family. This haunting Scottish tale will hold the attention of all ages. Compare with *The Seal Prince* by Sheila MacGill-Callahan and "The Red Cap" in *Mermaid Tales from Around the World* by Mary Pope Osborne.

Hastings, Selina. *Sir Gawain and the Loathly Lady.* Illustrated by Juan Wijngaard. New York: Lothrop, Lee & Shepard, 1985.

King Arthur, out on a holiday hunt, finds himself at the mercy of a treacherous black knight. The villain offers to spare Arthur's life if he will return in three days with the answer to this riddle: What is it that women most desire? On the appointed day, the anxious king, no nearer to the answer, chances upon a hideously grotesque hag. She gives him the answer in return for granting a wish. The grateful Arthur is spared, but he is dismayed to learn that the hag's wish is to be married to one of his knights. Young Sir Gawain gallantly offers himself. Once alone in the wedding bedchamber, Gawain sees that his wife has transformed into a stunning beauty. By marrying her, Gawain has released her in part from a spell. To complete her release, Gawain must answer her trick question: Would he rather have her beautiful at night and ugly during the day, or vice versa? Gawain gives her the answer she seeks. Because of the maturity of the story's content, this tale is best suited to the upper grades.

Hunter, Mollie. *Gilly Martin the Fox*. Illustrated by Dennis McDermott. New York: Hyperion Books for Children, 1994.

In this tale from the Scottish Highlands, the Prince of Alban is under the spell of a witch who requires him to bring her the magical Blue Falcon. Gilly Martin the fox instructs the Prince to be brave and face a five-headed giant who has the falcon. The plot moves on through several fantastic adventures with Gilly Martin giving advice and using his powers as a shape-shifter to help the prince. The prince is ordered to go on a series of quests, first for a sword known as the White Glave of Light, then the Bay Filly of the King of Erin, then the daughter of the King of Lochlan. On each voyage, Gilly Martin changes himself into a sailing vessel to take the Prince of Alban to his next adventure. In the end, Gilly Martin transforms himself into the sword and the filly to fool and foil the giants who want these prizes for themselves. Gilly's tricks of transformation rescue the Prince and secure the princess for the Prince of Alban. This book is suitable for middle grades.

Leavy, Una. *Irish Fairy Tales and Legends*. Illustrated by Susan Field. Boulder, CO: Robert Rinehart, 1996.

This collection includes 10 Irish trickster tales, transformation tales, and legends. "The Giant's Causeway" is the story of how Fionn Mac Cumhail (Finn MacCoul) is saved from the giant's wrath by his quick-thinking wife's trickery. "The Bodach of the Grey Coat" tells of the Bodach, a scruffy, rumpled man, who agrees to run a race against the Prince of Greece to determine whose kingdom will be subservient to the other. The unlikely winner is the Bodach, who is then transformed into Mannán Mac Lir, the sea-god. "The Pot of Gold" is the story of a leprechaun who puts 10,000 red ties on the weeds to disguise which one marks the place where the gold is buried. "Tír na n-Óg" tells of a king who misuses the chief druid's magic stick to change his daughter's head into a pig's head to keep her from marrying. The spell is broken when Oisín, a son of Fionn Mac Cumhail, marries her. They live happily in the land of Tír na n-Óg, where Oisín is unaware of the passing of time in his former land. When he makes a visit to his old world, 300 years have elapsed, and Oisín turns into a withered old man. Authentically told by an Irish author, these stories are good read-alouds for second graders and up.

MacGill-Callahan, Sheila. *The Children of Lir*. Illustrated by Gennady Spirin. New York: Dial Press, 1993.

The king of Ireland's second wife is jealous of the king's love for his four children. The wicked stepmother turns the children into swans, adding the curse that one day of each year, they will resume their human shape, but if they touch the earth they will die. The spell can be broken only if two mountains are joined together. After seven years, the queen, learning of the swans' continued existence, plots their capture and demise. A dramatic rescue ensues, with the help of eagles, Jasconius the whale, and a host of wild swans who join together, end-to-end, connecting the two mountain peaks and breaking the spell. This captivating tale will hold the interest of all ages as a read-aloud.

———. *The Seal Prince*. Illustrated by Kris Waldherr. New York: Dial Books for Young Readers, 1995.

On her eighth birthday, Princess Grainne rescues and releases a trapped baby seal. On her eighteenth birthday, a young man named Deodatus appears on the beach; beside him is a gray cloak. She sees by his eyes that he is the seal. She refuses to go and live in the sea with Deodatus because of her duties to her aging parents and her kingdom, but she continues to meet him on the beach on her birthdays, and she frustrates her parents by refusing to marry the suitors who court her. Finally, her father promises her hand in marriage to any man in the kingdom who can bring in the largest catch of fish. Just as Grainne is about to be married to a homely fisherman, Deodatus appears with the largest catch of fish. The lovers marry, but Deodatus gives her his sealskin, so that he remains on land, allowing Grainne to fulfill her duties to her kingdom. Not until their son's eighteenth birthday do they descend into their ocean life together. This haunting Scottish tale holds the interest of first through sixth graders.

Muller, Robin. *Mollie Whuppie and the Giant*. Illustrated by the author. Buffalo, NY: Firefly Books, 1995.

Echoes of "Hansel and Gretel," strong parallels to "Jack and the Beanstalk," and trickster and transformational elements are all evident in this English tale. Mollie Whuppie, a trickster of British folklore, is the youngest of three daughters abandoned in the forest by their poor parents. The bravest and most cheerful, Mollie leads her sisters to a house, the home of a cruel giant and his wife. A series of harrowing events follow. Mollie leads her sisters in an escape, and they find refuge in a palace. But there, Mollie is asked by the king to go back to the giant three times, once to steal his magic sword, once to take back the purse of gold stolen from the people, and once to snatch his ring that makes him invisible. On the third mission, the giant catches Mollie, but she engineers a clever trick. She gets the giant to hang her in a sack, and while the giant goes off to find a stick to beat the sack, she tricks the giant's wife into switching places with her. To escape Mollie uses the ring to make her invisible, but she goes back to rescue the giant's wife. The giant falls into the river gorge and turns into stone. Mollie and her sisters all get husbands at the palace. Small typeface and long narrative make this better as a read-aloud selection.

Riggio, Anita. *Beware the Brindlebeast*. Illustrated by the author. Honesdale, PA: Boyds Mills Press, 1994.

The villagers in Birdie's hamlet fear the Brindlebeast, who nightly changes himself into fearsome shapes. As Birdie is walking home on All Hallows Eve, she finds a large kettle—full of gold! But when she looks again, it is full of apples. Then it changes into a jack-o'-lantern. Once in Birdie's home, it becomes the terrible Brindlebeast, but Birdie refuses to be intimidated. Then the beast becomes a humble old man, with whom Birdie shares her cozy fire and supper. This "scary story" for young children carries the reassuring message that one need not be afraid of the bogeyman.

San Souci, Robert D. *Nicholas Pipe*. Illustrated by David Shannon. New York: Dial Books for Young Readers, 1997.

Nicholas Pipe is a merman, who can walk on land like a man. He was granted this ability by a sorcerer. Nicholas keeps a low profile in the fishing village, but he always warns people of approaching storms. Margaret is in love with Nicholas, but her father forbids her to speak with him, because her brother drowned, reportedly taken by merfolk. One day, while the father is out fishing, Nicholas warns that a storm is coming. Margaret rows out to find her father, and in a dramatic scene, Nicholas appears and staves off the merfolk long enough for the two to row free. Still, her father forbids Margaret to speak with the merman. While the father is gone, Margaret and Nicholas have a conversation in which he reveals that he must touch the sea every day to stay alive. Some days later, the king's men imprison Nicholas in a cage. (The father is suspected to have had some part in turning him in.) Margaret fears for Nicholas's life because he will not be able to touch the sea. Margaret fills two skins with seawater and sets out to find Nicholas. When she finds him, he is nearly dead, but her tears and the seawater revive him. She brings him back to the sea, where he dives in and swims as a merman again. Her father repents of his bitterness and gives his blessing for the couple's marriage. The father's shift from grudging bitterness into acceptance represents another, subtler kind of transformation. Dramatic, bittersweet, and romantic, this tale will interest readers of all ages.

———. *Young Merlin*. Illustrated by Daniel Horne. New York: Doubleday, 1990.

During his adolescence, Merlin lives alone in the woods, learning about his magical powers, including his ability to change shape. When the new king, Aurelius, hears of Merlin's powers, he sends messengers for him. When they arrive, he jokingly turns into a stag, an old woman, and a wild man. Merlin finally shows his true form to Uther, later to become father of Arthur. The story continues through the death of Aurelius, the crowning of Uther, and Merlin's magical creation of the monument to Aurelius, later known as Stonehenge. This tale, with a legendary tone, is a good choice for upper elementary grades.

Yolen, Jane. *Tam Lin*. Illustrated by Charles Mikolaycak. New York: Harcourt Brace Jovanovich, 1990.

In this retelling of a Scottish ballad, Jennet reclaims the estate of Carterhaugh for the MacKenzie family. The estate has fallen into ruin, ever since the Faeries, the Fey, have taken it over. On her 16th birthday, Jennet goes to Carterhaugh and meets a handsome young man, Tam Lin. He says he is actually 160 years old, taken in his youth by the Queen of the Fey. Jennet vows to reclaim both Tam Lin and Carterhaugh. He tells her what she must do on Hallow's Eve, when the human world and the faery world coexist. During a frightening sequence of events, Jennet speaks out to the Faery Queen, while holding on to Tam Lin. In an attempt to scare Jennet, the Queen changes Tam Lin into a serpent, then a lion's head, then a burning-hot brand. Jennet fends off the attacks with holy water and garden earth. The Queen and her entourage are finally defeated. Jennet and Tam Lin marry and live in happiness. Dramatic in its narrative and its illustrations, this is a tale for middle and upper grades.

Finno-Ugric

de Gerez, Tree. *When Bear Came Down from the Sky*. Illustrated by Lisa Desimini. New York: Viking, 1994.

This story of how Bear came to live on earth is told partially in verse. In this tale from the Finnish and Hungarian languages, Bear is a constellation of stars in the sky. Bear wants to go to earth, and Sky Father warns him that once he goes, he cannot return to the sky. Bear makes a ladder to stretch from the sky to earth, but it is too short, and he make the rest of the trip in a basket. Sky Father reminds him to sleep half the winter. When he arrives, Tellervo, the Lady of the Green Dress, welcomes Bear to the forest. Bear learns about earth, and when the snows come, he remembers to sleep. Simple text and illustrations make this tale appealing to primary grades.

French

Brett, Jan. *Beauty and the Beast*. Illustrated by the author. New York: Clarion Books, 1989.

In this version of the well-known story, the Beast's face is pictured as that of a wild boar. The telling has more detail and narrative than the version by Deborah Hautzig (see below). The Beast is patient and attentive, and when Beauty returns home, she misses him. She returns to him, finding him nearly dead. Her tears and her promise to marry him break the spell, restoring his form to a handsome prince. There are no consequences for her sisters in this version, which has appeal for all ages.

Cole, Joanna. *Doctor Change*. Illustrated by Donald Carrick. New York: William Morrow, 1986.

A constant stream of transformation events makes this a high-action story of wits. Tom, a poor boy, applies for work with Doctor Strange. When Tom admits he can read, the doctor refuses to hire him. Tom goes away, comes back with his jacket turned inside out, and says that he can't read. He gets the job. Tom is told never to go into a certain room where a magic book is kept. Tom spies through the keyhole to the forbidden room and sees the doctor changing into a cat, a princess, a hat, and so on. Then while the master is away on a trip, Tom reads the magic book and learns a few tricks of his own. When the doctor returns, a major showdown ensues, with Tom and the Doctor playing a high-stakes, fast-moving one-upsmanship in transformations. Tom outwits the doctor with the help of his true love, Kate.

Hautzig, Deborah. *Beauty and the Beast.* Illustrated by Kathy Mitchell. New York: Random House, 1995.

   Near the end of this retelling, the Beast changes into a prince because Beauty agrees to marry him. Then a fairy waves her wand, bringing Beauty's sisters before them; she turns them to stone statues in punishment for their wickedness. This straightforward easy-reader version is suitable for late first or second grade independent reading.

Perrault, Charles. *Puss in Boots.* Translated by Malcolm Arthur. Illustrated by Fred Marcellino. New York: Farrar, Straus & Giroux, 1990.

   This is the classic fairy tale of the cat who uses his wits to win riches, prestige, and a princess for his impoverished master. The final in a series of tricks occurs when Puss enters the castle of a wealthy Ogre. Puss inquires about the Ogre's powers to transform himself into any animal. The Ogre shows off by turning into a lion. Then Puss muses that it must be impossible for the Ogre to turn himself into something small, like a mouse. That done, Puss eats the mouse and presents the castle as his master's. This tale is readable by middle grades and suitable listening for all ages. Compare with the Filipino variant, *Pedro and the Monkey* by Robert San Souci.

San Souci, Robert D. *The White Cat: An Old French Fairy Tale.* Illustrated by Gennady Spirin. New York: Orchard, 1990.

   A king announces to his three sons that he will retire and gives them three tasks to determine who is most worthy to succeed him: Bring the prettiest little dog, bring a piece of fine linen, and bring the finest young bride. Each time they set out on a quest for one of these items, the youngest prince has extraordinary adventures in the castle of the White Cat. Each time, she gives the youngest prince a magic object to win the contest with his brothers. In the end, after a fight with a dragon and the transformation of the White Cat into a crystal, the White Cat turns into a beautiful princess. Though this tale is complicated, even young children will sit in rapt attention in a read-aloud session. Compare aspects of this tale with *Beauty and the Beast* and also *The Frog Princess*.

German

Grimm, Jakob, and Wilhelm Grimm. *The Seven Ravens.* Translated by Anthea Bell. Illustrated by Henriette Sauvant. New York: North-South Books, 1995.

   As with many of the Grimm tales, this one contains elements that are a bit gruesome, but it is told smoothly and doesn't dwell on these details. A man and wife have seven sons and a newborn daughter. The baby is frail, so the man sends the sons to fetch water to baptize her. The father, impatient for their return, wishes they would turn into ravens, and they do. When the baby grows into a girl, she goes on a journey to find the ravens and set them free. She takes only a few objects, including her parents' ring. She encounters a frightening sun and moon, but the kind stars help her by sending her to a glass mountain. They give her a little bone with which to unlock the door to the mountain. When she gets to the door, she discovers she has lost the bone, so she cuts off one of her own fingers and opens the lock with it. The ravens are gone, but a dwarf is there, setting out their meal. When the ravens return, she hides. One raven finds the ring in his cup and, recognizing it, hopes his sister is near. She comes out of hiding, and the brothers resume human form. They all embrace and go home.

————. *Snow White and Rose Red*. Illustrated by Gennady Spirin. New York: Philomel Books, 1992.

Two sweet and cheerful sisters live with their mother in a cottage near the woods. A huge bear becomes a friend of the family, playing with the girls. The bear leaves them for the summer because he must guard his treasure from the gnomes who try to steal it. Later, the girls encounter a rude gnome in trouble, and they aid him three times, despite his verbal abuse. When the gnome is found with the bear's treasure, the bear strikes him dead. Immediately, the bear's skin falls away, revealing a prince. Later, the sisters marry the prince and his brother. Glowing, detailed illustrations and cheerful language make this a pleasant read-aloud for primary and middle grades. Another appealing edition of this story is retold and illustrated by Ruth Sanderson (see below).

Isadora, Rachel. *The Princess and the Frog: Adapted from the Frog King and Iron Heinrich by the Brothers Grimm*. Illustrated by the author. New York: Greenwillow Books, 1989.

A princess loses her golden ball down a well. A frog offers to retrieve it for her, if she will take him into her palace. She agrees, not expecting to have to fulfill the promise. When the frog shows up at the palace, the king reminds her to keep her promise. With disdain, she lets the frog eat off her plate and sleep in her bed. After three nights, the spell on the frog is broken, and he becomes a handsome prince. Compare with *The Frog Prince* by Edith Tarcov and also by Jan and David Lloyd Ormerod, noting the various means of breaking the spell.

Kimmel, Eric A. *Iron John: Adapted from the Brothers Grimm*. Illustrated by Trina Schart Hyman. New York: Holiday House, 1994.

Iron John, a "wild man," is kept in a cage in a menagerie. The king's youngest son, Walter, loses his golden ball in the cage and asks for it back. Iron John agrees, on the condition that Walter bring the key for his escape. Walter does so, and he goes with Iron John to live in the forest. Walter grows to manhood in the forest, with Iron John's care and teaching. Walter learns that Iron John's spring turns objects into gold. Later, unfortunately, Iron John must leave Walter, but he promises to help him when he needs it. Walter offers his service to the King, disguising himself as Walter-in-the-Mud. He gets a job helping the garden girl, Elsa. Elsa tells Walter of an upcoming masked ball, and Walter asks Iron John's help to attend it. Iron John provides him a steed and a golden suit of clothes. Walter's mysterious appearance stuns the crowd. Next, there is a tournament, and again Walter gets Iron John to help him attend. Shortly after this, a band of robbers attack and slay many knights and carry off the princesses. Walter follows and fights them but is mortally wounded. A crowned knight takes Walter back to the castle. The crowned knight explains that he is Iron John, who for many years was under a curse that caused him to be a wild man. Now the spell is broken. As for Walter, Iron John says he can be saved only by the tears of a maid who loves him. Elsa pushes her way through the crowd. Her tears heal Walter, who transforms into a golden prince. He marries Elsa.

Ormerod, Jan, and David Lloyd. *The Frog Prince*. Illustrated by Jan Ormerod. New York: Lothrop, Lee & Shepard, 1990.

Basically the same telling of the tale as Isadora's, with the addition of short poems spoken by the frog prince. Once again, the spell is broken by three nights of sleeping on the princess's royal pillow.

Ray, Jane. *The Twelve Dancing Princesses*. Illustrated by the author. New York: Dutton Children's Books, 1996.

This well-known Grimm fairytale, beautifully illustrated, never grows old. Twelve princess sisters awaken tired, their dancing slippers worn out, despite the king's bolting the young women into their chamber every night. To solve the mystery of the princesses' nocturnal activities, the king offers any one of them as a bride to the first man who solves the mystery. A poor wounded soldier decides to try, and meets an old woman who gives him a cloak to make him invisible. One night, he feigns sleep from the sleeping-potion wine, and uses the magic cloak to follow the princesses into a beautiful enchanted kingdom where they dance the night through. When questioned by the king, the prince divulges the princesses' secret, and the king offers him a bride. The prince readily asks for the hand of the eldest, and they reign over the kingdom wisely, making sure that dancing remains a regular event. Compare with the version by Ruth Sanderson (see below).

Sanderson, Ruth. *Rose Red and Snow White*. Illustrated by the author. Boston: Little, Brown, 1997.

The same story line as the Grimm/Spirin edition above, illustrated with dark glowing pictures. A quiet humor underlies the sisters' encounter with the rude and impatient dwarf. The girls assist the dwarf twice by snipping off the end of his beard, which is caught. In a third encounter, they rescue the dwarf from an eagle's talons. A huge bear comes upon the scene, and he swats the dwarf dead. As the fearful girls flee, a voice calls them back. The bear sheds his skin, and a handsome prince stands in its place. He was the bear who had befriended them and lived in their home the previous winter. He had been under the spell of the dwarf, doomed to roam as a bear, and only the dwarf's death would restore him to his original form as a prince. When Rose Red and Snow White are older, they wed the prince and his brother.

———. *The Twelve Dancing Princesses*. Illustrated by the author. Boston: Little, Brown, 1990.

A king is troubled by his 12 beautiful daughters' nightly habit of wearing out their shoes, despite the triple lock on their bedchamber. He offers any one of them as bride to the man who can unlock the secret. A young commoner hopes to try, and he meets an old woman who gives him a magic cloak that makes him invisible. He gets a job as a royal gardener, and soon gains access to the princesses' room with his invisibility. He follows them down a secret staircase, through three magical woods, across a lake in a swan-shaped boat, and into a palace where the 12 dance all night with princes under a spell. The young man solves the mystery and gains the hand of the youngest princess. This retelling of the familiar Grimm fairy tale works as a read-aloud for all ages. Compare with the version by Jane Ray (see above).

Tarcov, Edith H. *The Frog Prince*. Illustrated by James Marshall. New York: Scholastic, 1974.

This is a straightforward retelling of the familiar tale, suitable for independent reading by second grade and up. An interesting point of comparison is the method of breaking the spell: The princess throws the frog against the wall. Also available as a book-and-cassette kit from Scholastic Cassettes.

Greek

Manna, Anthony L., and Christodoula Mitakidou. *Mr. Semolina-Semolinus: A Greek Folktale*. Illustrated by Giselle Potter. New York: Atheneum Books for Young Readers, 1997.

A princess named Areti does not care for her suitors. Instead, she makes a man herself, in the kitchen. She mixes semolina with almonds and sugar and prays for 40 days. Then the "man" comes to life. Mr. Semolina-Semolinus becomes known all over the world for being "five times beautiful and ten times kind." A queen in a distant land hears of him and desires him for herself. She sends her men to capture him. Areti sets out to find him, ordering three pairs of iron shoes. She walks to the ends of the world, asking the Moon, the Sun, and the Stars. Each time, Areti is given a nut, with the instructions to break it when she most needs it. The smallest star sends Areti to the wicked queen's home. Areti cracks the first nut, which contains a golden spinning wheel. She barters her spinning wheel for a night with Mr. Semolina-Semolinus. However, the evil queen gives him a drink that causes him to sleep, so Areti isn't able to speak with him. The second and third nights, Areti cracks the other two nuts, again bargaining her treasures for a night with Mr. Semolina-Semolinus. The third night, a tailor tells Mr. Semolina-Semolinus that his beloved is searching for him. He only pretends to drink the sleeping potion, so he is conscious when Areti meets him. After a tender reunion, they ride off together. The selfish queen then attempts to concoct a man of her own, but the ingredients spoil. Charmingly told and winsomely illustrated, this tender tale will appeal to a wide audience.

Italian

Nones, Eric Jon. *The Canary Prince*. Illustrated by the author. New York: Farrar, Straus & Giroux, 1991.

A princess is banished to a distant castle by a jealous stepmother. A prince sees her gazing out the window, and they wish to meet each other. A witch enables this by giving the girl a book and telling her that if she turns the pages forward, the prince will transform into a canary and fly into the princess's room. Turning the pages backward will transform him into a man. The stepmother suspects something and devises a method to mortally wound the prince. As he lies dying in his castle, the princess overhears some witches reveal the cure. The princess makes her way to his castle, cures the prince, and flees. Eventually the prince learns of the circumstances of his cure and marries the princess. This tale works as an interesting read-aloud for all ages.

Rayevsky, Inna. *The Talking Tree: An Old Italian Tale*. Illustrated by Robert Rayevsky. New York: G. P. Putnam's Sons, 1990.

A king, on a quest to collect all the rarest things, searches for a talking tree. He finds it, discovering that the tree is really a princess under the spell of a witch. He learns that to break the spell, he must cut the tree down with the magic ax belonging to a cruel ogre. The king's search leads him to the ogre's daughter, who gives him the ax. He uses the ax to break the spell and to cut off the witch's head. However, the princess is still wooden to the touch because there is magic oil on the ax. The king cleverly gets the jealous ogre's daughter to provide the antidote for the magic oil. The king and princess marry. This tale is best suited to middle grades.

Jewish

Wisniewski, David. *Golem*. Illustrated by the author. New York: Clarion Books, 1996.

This Caldecott award-winner is set during the persecution of the Jews in Prague in the year 1580. Angry mobs were perpetuating the "Blood Lie," accusing Jews of mixing the matzoh with the blood of Christian children. Judah Loew ben Bezalel, a prominent rabbi in Prague at the time, receives a sign that it is time for the Golem. The legend of the Golem is that of an inanimate being, which is brought to life through a solemn religious ritual, invoking the name of God. The Rabbi and two assistants sneak out of the ghetto and dig up a mass of clay. The Rabbi shapes it into a huge, crude body, then recites chants. Golem comes to life. The rabbi brings the Golem into the ghetto where the Jews live and instructs him to protect the Jews and capture those who are persecuting them. One day, a mob storms the ghetto, and Golem unleashes too much violence against them. The rabbi agrees to destroy Golem only after receiving assurance of his people's safety. The rabbi changes him back to clay, and performs the prayer for the dead.

Lap/Finnish

Allen, Linda. *The Mouse Bride: A Tale from Finland*. Illustrated by the author. New York: Philomel Books, 1992.

In the far north, an old Laplander woman tells a woodman's fortune. She tells him he will have three sons; he should plant a tree for each one; and when the boys are grown, each should cut his tree down. The direction it falls will lead each to his wife. While this works for the first two sons, the youngest, Jukka, is led only to a cottage inhabited by a mouse. When the father tells each son to bring back a loaf of bread made by his new wife, Jukka's mouse bride summons the aid of a thousand mice. Together, they bake a superior loaf, impressing the other brothers. Next, the father tells his sons to have their wives weave cloth. Again, Jukka returns with the most impressive cloth. Finally, the woodsman tells his sons to bring their wives for a Midsummer celebration. Jukka worries when he sees his mouse bride in a miniature carriage drawn by mice. On the way to the celebration, a peasant boy kicks the carriage off a bridge into the river, and Jukka finds that his bride is now a beautiful maiden driving five sleek horses. She explains that she had been a king's daughter, and a Lapland witch had turned her and her servants into mice. This straightforward telling is accessible to all ages. Compare with *The Frog Princess* by J. Patrick Lewis.

Norwegian

Barlow, Gillian. *East o' the Sun and West o' the Moon*. Illustrated by the author. Translated by Sir George Webbe Dasent. New York: Philomel Books, 1988.

A poor man with many children has an especially pretty youngest daughter. One night, a huge White Bear asks the man for his youngest daughter in exchange for wealth. The White Bear takes her to a castle filled with finery. She lives there, but each night after she extinguishes the light, a man comes into her room and sleeps beside her. The girl becomes lonely for her family, and the bear agrees to take her home for a visit, but tells her she mustn't have a talk alone with her mother. She tries to avoid this talk, but her mother gets her alone, so she tells all, and tells how lonely her days are. Her mother declares that the man who sleeps beside her might be a troll. She instructs her daughter to smuggle a candle into her bedroom and, when the man is asleep next to her, to light the candle to see who he is, but she must be careful not to drop any wax on him. When she does this, she discovers a handsome man and falls in love with him. However, she accidentally drips wax on him. He awakens and, lamenting that all is ruined, says he must go away to his stepmother's castle and marry a long-nosed princess. (He is under the stepmother's spell, which causes him to be a bear by day.) When the girl awakens the next day, the castle and finery are all gone. She embarks on a long and perilous journey East o' the Sun and West o' the Moon, to find her beloved. Eventually, she finds the castle and outsmarts the stepmother and long-nosed princess. The spell is broken, and the lovers reunite. This variant of "Beauty and the Beast" is a standard Norwegian tale.

Shepard, Aaron. *Master Maid: A Tale of Norway*. Illustrated by Pauline Ellison. New York: Dial Books for Young Readers, 1997.

A young man named Leif goes off to make his way in the world. He always does things his own way, so it is a big step when he takes instructions from a maiden who is held captive in the house of a cruel troll. Leif asks the troll for a job and is given seemingly easy tasks. Disobeying the troll's warning, Leif finds a beautiful maiden working in the kitchen. She gives Leif crucial information to make him successful in his jobs for the troll. Finally, the couple flee from the troll, and their escape is made possible by the Master Maid's three objects. First, she throws a wooden fork over her shoulder, and it becomes a thick woodland to deter the troll. Next, she throws a lump of salt, which becomes a mountain in the troll's path. Finally, she pours a drop of water from a flask, and a sea is created, across which they boat to safety. The tale ends with Leif's acknowledging that it is best to defer to the maiden. This is a short but delightful tale for all ages.

Polish

Porazińska, Janina. *The Enchanted Book: A Tale from Krakow.* Translated by Bożena Smith. Illustrated by Jan Brett. New York: Harcourt Brace Jovanovich, 1987.

The miller's daughters are beautiful, and they want different things. The eldest wants beauty and fine things; the middle one wants to dance; the youngest loves work and learning. An old beggar woman is invited to stay the winter with the miller and his daughters. She is to teach the three sisters to read, but only the youngest learns. Each daughter is then approached by an enchanter in disguise. He takes each to his castle, where entry to one room is forbidden. Each girl goes into the room, and finds caged birds with drooping wings; these birds are really other young women who have been put under the enchanter's spell. When the youngest daughter goes into the room, the transformed birds tell her that she can break the spells of the castle by reading a magic book. She does so and breaks several spells, restoring the birds to women, and effecting their escape and the enchanter's demise. Though long for a single picture book, this tale will be enjoyed even by primary-age children.

Russian

Aksakov, Sergei. *The Scarlet Flower: A Russian Folk Tale.* New York: Harcourt Brace Jovanovich, 1989.

A Russian version of *Beauty and the Beast,* this tale's story line is similar to the well-known French telling. Small differences occur in details such as the gifts the three daughters ask of their father as he departs on his journey. The youngest daughter, the favorite, asks for a scarlet flower unequaled by any other in the world. Other such details make for interesting comparisons between tellings. This version is rather long, with small, dense text, but is accessible to upper grades for independent reading and to younger grades for reading aloud.

Arnold, Katya. *Baba Yaga and the Little Girl: A Russian Folktale.* Illustrated by the author. New York: North-South Books, 1994.

A little girl's stepmother sends her to Baba Yaga, the witch, for a needle and thread. Before going to Baba Yaga, the girl receives three cryptic instructions from her aunt: Tie the birch branch, oil the hinges, and feed the dog. These three actions later aid in the girl's escape from the witch. While the witch prepares to eat the little girl, the witch's cat gives the girl a towel and a comb to help her escape. As the girl flees, the birch, the gate, and the dog let her pass. Then she uses the cat's gifts: She throws down the towel, which turns into a river to deter the witch. Then she throws down a comb, which turns into a forest. The girl escapes to her father, who throws out the cruel stepmother. Compare this escape with the escape from the troll in *Master Maid* by Aaron Shepard.

Ayres, Becky Hickox. *Matreshka*. Illustrated Alexi Natchev. New York: Doubleday Book for Young Readers, 1992.

A woman gives Kata a wooden doll named Matreshka. Later, when the evil witch Baba Yaga captures Kata, Matreshka repeatedly rescues Kata from dangerous situations. Each time, Matreshka transforms herself into a smaller creature (as in Russian nesting dolls). At the climax, Matreshka confuses Baba Yaga's magic spell so that Baba Yaga turns herself into a frog. Young children will enjoy this tale.

Cech, John. *First Snow, Magic Snow*. Illustrated by Sharon McGinley-Nally. New York: Four Winds Press, 1992.

A woodsman and his wife have no children. During the first snow of the season, he shapes a baby out of snow and brings her home, where she comes alive. The child, Snowflake, grows; she learns to walk and talk and makes up a song about the magic snow. But as the spring thaw progresses, Snowflake begins to fade in spirit. Finally, at a spring celebration she vanishes, and the parents go north to find her. After an arduous journey, they find Grandfather Frost and Snowflake. Grandfather Frost tells them that Snowflake must stay with him. He tells the parents to sleep. When they wake, they are in their own bed at home, and the first snow of the new season is falling. They get their Snowflake back until the next spring. Compare with *The Little Snowgirl* by Carolyn Croll.

Cecil, Laura. *The Frog Princess*. Illustrated by Emma Chichester Clark. New York: Greenwillow Books, 1994.

This tale features a princess under a spell that has turned her into a frog. The queen has three sons, and she instructs them to find brides by shooting an arrow. The two older brothers find suitable women; the youngest finds a frog. The queen assigns each bride-to-be three tasks to determine who will inherit the kingdom: baking, weaving, and training a dog. For each task, the frog princess performs a stellar job. Finally, when it is time for the youngest prince to marry the frog, the spell on her is broken, and she transforms into a beautiful princess. Compare with *The Frog Princess* by J. Patrick Lewis and *The White Cat* by Robert D. San Souci.

Croll, Carolyn. *The Little Snowgirl: An Old Russian Tale*. Illustrated by the author. New York: G. P. Putnam's Sons, 1989.

A hardworking couple want more than anything to have a child. At Christmastime, the husband fashions a child out of snow. She comes alive, but she will not come inside or eat warm food. The parents feel guilty about her sleeping out in the snow, especially on Christmas Eve, when Babushka comes and grants good children their greatest wish. On Christmas morning, the snowgirl's greatest wish has come true: She is a real, warm, little girl. This tale is suitable for independent, primary-student reading. Compare with *First Snow, Magic Snow* by John Cech.

Ginsburg, Mirra. *Clay Boy*. Illustrated by Jos. A. Smith. New York: Greenwillow Books, 1997.

Freely adapted from Russian folk sources, this is a variation on the "gingerbread boy" theme. An old Grandpa and Grandma are alone, as their children are grown and gone. Grandpa takes a piece of clay and forms a little boy as their new child. The clay boy dries on the hearth and comes alive, announcing his hunger. The grandma and grandpa feed him, and he asks for more and more. He grows to giant size, eating the chickens and pets, Grandma and Grandpa, and some of the villagers. Finally, a little goat appears and runs right into the clay boy's big belly. The impact shatters the clay boy, and all the people and animals spill out. Everyone dances and sings the praises of the little goat. The large typeface, simple text, and lively illustrations make this tale well-suited to young children.

Lewis, J. Patrick. *The Frog Princess: A Russian Folktale*. Illustrated by Gennady Spirin. New York: Dial Press, 1994.

In this more in-depth telling than the version by Laura Cecil, the tsar tells his three sons to find brides by shooting an arrow. The youngest prince finds a frog for a bride. Each time the tsar assigns a task of skill to his sons' wives, the frog wife produces dazzling results. Then when the tsar hosts a ball, the frog wife arrives as Vasilisa the Wise, and she performs some stunning transformations. Her prince finds her frog skin and burns it; this turns out to be a grave error, for she disappears. This leads to a number of seemingly impossible tasks and adventures, including a visit with Baba Yaga. The prince succeeds and breaks the spell over Vasilisa. This is a suitable read-aloud for first graders and up.

Pushkin, Alexander. *The Tale of Tsar Saltan*. Illustrated by Gennady Spirin. New York: Dial Press, 1996.

Tsar Saltan marries one of three sisters, and the other two jealously conspire throughout the story to work malicious acts against the Tsar's wife. While the Tsar is away at war, the sisters send him a message that his wife (the Tsarina) and son are drowned. Then they put the wife and child in a barrel and roll it into the sea. The Tsarina and her son land on an island, where they are aided by a swan who is really an enchanted princess. Three times, a ship visits the island on its way to trade with Tsar Saltan. Each time, the son, who has become a prince wants to go along to see his father, and each time, the swan helps him by changing him into an insect so he can travel unnoticed. While in the kingdom of Tsar Saltan, the disguised prince seeks vengeance by stinging the treacherous aunts in the eye. The prince hears of a beautiful princess whom he wishes to marry. When he tells this to the swan, she changes into a radiant maiden, and they marry.

San Souci, Robert D. *The Firebird*. Illustrated by Kris Waldherr. New York: Dial Books for Young Readers, 1992.

Prince Ivan captures and releases the magical Firebird, who gives him a feather as a talisman. Then Ivan meets Elena and other maidens who are imprisoned by the evil wizard Katchei. Other would-be rescuers are also there, turned to stone. Ivan uses his feather (summoning the Firebird's help), and the Firebird directs him and Elena to go into three chambers guarded by multiheaded dragons. In the third room, Ivan and Elena open a casket from which a hare flees. The hare turns into a duck, and the duck into a crystal egg. Ivan shatters the egg, which destroys the wizard.

——. *The Tsar's Promise: A Russian Tale*. Illustrated by Lauren Mills. New York: Philomel Books, 1992.

Clever Maria has magical powers to help Prince Ivan outwit the demon under the lake. Ivan first sees Maria and her 29 sisters as white ducks on a lake. When they emerge from the water, they transform into human form. Maria is commanded to turn Ivan over to the demon, but her love for Ivan moves her to help him instead. The demon gives Ivan three impossible tasks, in exchange for his freedom. Maria accomplishes the first two for Ivan by transforming into a bee to give him instructions. For the third task, the lovers' escape is aided by Maria transforming into a river and Ivan transforming into a bridge. Their final success is ensured when Maria turns herself into a church, Ivan becomes a monk, and their horse becomes the steeple. The demon and his company, in anger, turn into hornets. This tale is full of detail, plot twists, and suspense, and holds the interest of all grade levels as a read-aloud.

Sherman, Josepha. *Vassilisa the Wise: A Tale of Medieval Russia*. Illustrated by Daniel San Souci. New York: Harcourt Brace Jovanovich, 1988.

This is a tale of transformation, not by magic, but by changing clothes to the opposite gender in order to effect a rescue. Vassilisa the Wise appears in many Russian folktales. In this one, her husband, the merchant Staver, has been imprisoned by Prince

Vladimir. Disguised as a Tartar nobleman, Vassili, Vassilisa goes to the palace to try to free her husband. The prince's niece tries to convince Vladimir that Vassili is a woman, so he gives the nobleman a number of tests to challenge his masculine powers. Vassili wins at wrestling, archery, and chess. At the evening's feast, Vassili gets Vladimir to let Staver out of prison to sing and play the *gusla* for them. Vassili then uses a chess game to get Vladimir to turn Staver over to her. Only now does she reveal her female identity. It is refreshing to read a story, out of the past, in which a woman is so clearly in command of a situation, despite the political advantage of men in the society.

MIDDLE EASTERN

Hort, Lenny. *The Tale of Caliph Stork*. Illustrated by Friso Henstra. New York: Dial Books for Young Readers, 1989.

Caliph Chasid, who is with his Vizier, buys a snuffbox with an inscription. The inscription has a magic word that can change them into animals and warns that if they laugh, they will forget the magic word to change back into humans. They turn themselves into storks and have a good laugh at the dancing of another stork. But then they can't remember the magic word. They fly back to Baghdad and discover that Chasid's evil cousin, a sorcerer, has taken over the city. The two then set out for the holy city of Medina, but they tire and land at a ruined castle, where they meet an owl. She explains that she is a princess of India under the sorcerer's spell. The spell can be broken only if a man freely proposes marriage. The two storks have an argument about who would marry an owl. Then the owl leads the two storks to spy on a banquet of the sorcerer. They learn the magic word, change themselves back into men, free the princess of her spell, and return to Baghdad, where they are welcomed back. The sorcerer is changed into a caged peacock. Compare with *The Enchanted Storks* by Aaron Shepard.

Kherdian, David. *The Rose's Smile: Farizad of the Arabian Nights*. Illustrated by Stefano Vitale. New York: Henry Holt, 1997.

A kind sultan overhears the wishes of three sisters. He grants the desired marriages to the two older sisters and marries the youngest sister himself. Her wish is to marry the sultan and give him a good son and a beautiful daughter with the smile of a rose and tears that turn into pearls. She does indeed give birth to both wonderful children, but her jealous sisters take the babies and send them in a basket downstream. The kingdom's gardener finds the babies and he and his wife raise them. Meanwhile, the queen and sultan grieve. The children, Farizad and her brother, grow to adulthood with beauty and integrity. One day, an old woman visits Farizad and tells her she must take a journey of 20 days and seek three things: the Talking Bird, the Singing Tree, and the Water of Gold. Her brother offers to make the quest for her, but he is turned into stone. Farizad sets out on the quest herself. Her single-mindedness of purpose protects her from the hazards of the journey. She obtains the three objects and asks the Talking Bird to release her brother. In so doing, many other young men are released from the same fate and are changed back from stone into men. Later, the Talking Bird helps the sultan realize that Farizad and her brother are his two lost children. Together they return to the palace and reunite with the queen. This tale will appeal to all ages.

Shepard, Aaron. *The Enchanted Storks: A Tale of Bagdad*. Illustrated by Alisher Dianov. New York: Clarion Books, 1995.

The Calif and his Vizier are sold a snuffbox by a peddler. The box contains a short verse, indicating that it can work a magic transformation. The two inhale the powder and are turned into storks. But then they cannot reverse the spell. They return to the city, where they discover that the Calif's brother is taking over the kingdom. Then they fly to a forest, where they meet a woodpecker, who tells them she is a princess under the spell of the evil sorcerer Khadur. She leads the storks to spy on a night meeting of the sorcerer and the Calif's brother. There they learn the magic word necessary to turn back into men. Then, the Calif proposes marriage to the woodpecker, which breaks her spell. The author's notes explain that while this tale is told in the Middle East (and is set in Bagdad), it was originally written by the German author Wilhelm Hauff. Compare with *The Tale of Caliph Stork* by Lenny Hort.

NATIVE AMERICAN

Caduto, Michael J., and Joseph Bruchac. *Keepers of the Earth: Native American Stories and Environmental Activities for Children.* Illustrated by John Kahionhes Fadden and Carol Wood. Golden, CO: Fulcrum, 1989. J P T 398. 208 997 Cad

These 24 tales are accompanied by discussion and nature activity ideas. A notable tale is "Loo-Wit, The Fire-Keeper," the story of a beautiful woman who keeps and shares fire with the people. When two chiefs fight over her, Loo-Wit is heartbroken and does not want to be among humans anymore. The creator transforms her into Mt. St. Helens. It is said that if people do not take proper care of the earth, Loo-Wit will awaken and show her displeasure. And this is just what happened when Mt. St. Helens erupted. The same stories in this collection, minus the discussions and activity ideas, can be found in *Native American Stories* by Joseph Bruchac. This author team has also collaborated on *Keepers of the Animals* (1991), *Keepers of Life* (plant stories and discussions; 1994), and the *Keepers of the Night* (1994). These tales are suitable read-alouds for middle and upper grades; some work well with lower grades as well.

Cleaver, Elizabeth. *The Enchanted Caribou.* Illustrated by the author. New York: Atheneum, 1985.

The black-and-white silhouette illustrations are actually photographs of Cleaver's shadow puppet theater. This book includes complete instructions and patterns so that students can act out this story with shadow puppets. In this tale from Canadian native peoples, a young woman named Tyya goes to collect driftwood. She gets lost and is found by a young man. He welcomes her to his summer tent, where he lives with two brothers. The three brothers go out the next day to hunt caribou, instructing Tyya not to let anyone in the tent. An old woman comes and says she is a shaman, so Tyya lets her in. The shaman combs Tyya's hair, and she turns into a white caribou. The brothers come home to find Tyya missing. A dream reveals to the men what happened to Tyya and how to break her spell. To this day, hunters are kind to white caribou because they may be enchanted.

Cohen, Caron Lee. *The Mud Pony: A Traditional Skidi Pawnee Tale.* Illustrated by Shonto Begay. New York: Scholastic, 1988.

A boy wishes for a pony of his own, and he shapes one out of mud. While he is off playing with his mud pony, the camp moves to follow the buffalo. When the boy returns, he finds that everyone has gone. In his sorrow, he falls asleep and dreams that his mud pony is alive. When he wakes, the boy discovers that his pony is indeed alive, and he takes him to the new camp. Later the boy is asked to go into battle against enemies who are preventing his people from hunting buffalo. He distinguishes himself in battle and in the hunt. Years later, the boy is made a chief. One night he dreams that his pony tells him it is time for him to return to Mother Earth. Simple and solemn, this story will appeal to all ages.

Ø Eagle Walking Turtle. *Full Moon Stories: Thirteen Native American Legends*. Illustrated by the author. New York: Hyperion Books for Children, 1997.

In this collection are 13 stories, one for each moon of the year, as told by the author's Arapaho grandfather. "The Coyote" presents Coyote at his malicious worst, transforming himself into a man called White Smoke. He takes White Smoke's place as husband and father of a family and plays destructive tricks on White Smoke in order to keep him away. One trick transforms White Smoke's appearance so that his family would not recognize him, although his youngest son intuitively knows it is his father. "The Moose" is a gentle story-within-the-story that effects a transformation in attitude. A man with medicine powers watches a moose family patiently teaching its calf how to find food. Then he relates this event to the woman who is chief. When she hears this story, she recognizes its message and becomes a new person, changing from a bad-tempered chief into a considerate ruler who sets a fine example. This collection is most effective as a read-aloud to primary and middle grades.

Esbensen, Barbara Juster. *The Great Buffalo Race: How the Buffalo Got Its Hump*. Illustrated by Helen K. Davie. Boston: Little, Brown, 1994.

In this Seneca tale, there is a great drought and the buffaloes are starving. Young Buffalo wants to travel to find new grasslands. Old Buffalo says they should wait for the rain that is coming and they shouldn't eat the grass of other herds. They have a fight, and Young Buffalo wins, so he and Old Buffalo take two groups westward. A third group stays behind. Old Buffalo's group steps carefully, watching for small creatures and nests, but Young Buffalo's group is not so careful. All the buffaloes who go westward drop and die from thirst. The Great Spirit scolds Young Buffalo and Old Buffalo and gives them a hump as a way to remember their mistake. Then the Great Spirit pushes the buffaloes' heads in and down, to make sure they watch out for the small creatures on the ground. Finally, the Great Spirit transforms Old Buffalo into a cloud to watch over the other buffaloes, and Young Buffalo is transformed into the Red Buffalo of the under-earth. This tale is best suited to middle and upper grades.

———. *The Star Maiden: An Ojibway Tale*. Illustrated by Helen K. Davie. Boston: Little, Brown, 1988.

One night, the people see a bright star that seems to fall to earth. A man is sent to investigate. He has a dream in which a shining silver maiden tells him that she wants to live on earth. The chief says she may choose the form she will become. She becomes a hillside flower, and then a prairie flower, but these are not satisfactory. Finally, she calls to all her star sisters to settle in the waters of the lake. The next morning, the people find the lake scattered with water lilies. This gentle tale is appealing to first grade and up.

French, Fiona. *Lord of the Animals: A Miwok Indian Creation Myth*. Illustrated by the author. Brookfield, CT: Millbrook Press, 1997.

This is a simple, short tale, featuring pourquoi, trickster, and transformation elements. Coyote is a creator in this story, having just created the world and its creatures. He calls a meeting to decide how they will make the Lord of the Animals. The animals each speak up in turn, stating that one of their own traits is the most important attribute for the Lord of the Animals. Finally, Coyote tells them to each shape a model of the Lord of the Animals from a lump of mud from the river, and then choose one of them to be their ruler. The animals start the project, but nighttime comes, and they all fall asleep. This is part of Coyote's plan. He stays awake and finishes his model, allowing the others to melt away in the river. Coyote incorporates many of the characteristics suggested by the other animals, but he assembles them in a new way: He shapes a man and gives him life as Lord of the Animals. This tale is suitable for primary and middle grades.

Goble, Paul. *Buffalo Woman*. Illustrated by the author. Scarsdale, NY: Bradbury Press, 1984.

In this Plains Indian tale, a great hunter sees a buffalo cow that transforms into a woman. She offers to marry the man as a sign of trust between the people and the Buffalo Nation. They marry and have a child, but the man's relatives treat her so badly that she finally leaves and returns to the Buffalo Nation. The hunter pursues his wife and Calf Boy, passing several tests from the Buffalo Nation to prove his worthiness. The buffalo transform the man into one of them, symbolic of the special relationship between them.

———. *Her Seven Brothers*. Illustrated by the author. New York: Bradbury Press, 1988.

A young girl is skilled at decorating clothes with porcupine quills. One day, the girl makes clothes for her seven brothers from the north, whom she has seen only in her mind. Then she makes the long journey to the north, where she finds a little boy with special powers and his six older brothers. One day, the brothers refuse the buffaloes' demand to give them their sister, so the buffalo stampede. The seven brothers and their sister flee up a tree, which grows taller until it takes them into the sky. There they are transformed into the stars of the Big Dipper. This pourquoi/transformation tale from the Cheyenne people is suitable for second graders and up. (A complete set of patterns for shadow puppets for this tale are included in *Folktale Themes and Activities for Children, Volume 1: Pourquoi Tales*, by Anne Marie Kraus.)

———. *The Lost Children: The Boys Who Were Neglected*. Illustrated by the author. New York: Bradbury, 1993.

Six children are orphans, and they are neglected by the tribe. Only the camp dogs like them. In their sadness, they decide they don't want to be human anymore, and they discuss what they would like to be. They decide to be stars because stars endure. One child leads the way into the sky, warning the others not to look back. One looks back and turns into Smoking Star, a comet. In the sky world, Sun Man and Moon Woman take care of the orphans. They become the Pleiades. The camp dogs, missing the children, howl at the sky. So they are reunited with the children and become hundreds of small stars near the Pleiades. Large typeface and a simple telling makes this Siksika tale readable by second graders and up.

———. *The Return of the Buffaloes: A Plains Indian Story About Famine and Renewal of the Earth*. Illustrated by the author. Washington, D.C.: National Geographic Society, 1996.

When the buffalo do not return in the spring and the people are in danger of starving, two young men are sent out to search for food. On their journey, they suddenly smell buffaloes and turn to find a mysterious woman standing at the door to a cave, which is her dwelling. Although it is not clear from the plot, the author's note states that this woman is one of the Buffalo People, transformed into human form. She tells the men she will send the buffalo. Later, back in the camp, the people are awakened by the thundering of a buffalo stampede. The people give thanks and offer gifts. Goble ends with the information about modern day tours of Wind Cave in the Black Hills, where the breath of the buffaloes can still be felt. This tale is suitable reading for third graders and up.

———. *Star Boy*. Illustrated by the author. Scarsdale, NY: Bradbury Press, 1983.

In this tale from the Blackfeet people, a young woman admires Morning Star in the sky, and he transforms into a handsome man. He takes her to the Sky World to meet his father the Sun and his mother the Moon. They marry and have a child. Later, the woman disobeys an instruction and is punished. The people see a falling star as she is sent to earth with her son. The son grows up, goes on a quest for forgiveness, and lives an honorable life. When he dies, he is taken into the Sky World as a star, traveling with the Morning Star and the Evening Star low over the horizon.

Goldin, Barbara Diamond. *The Girl Who Lived with the Bears.* Illustrated by Andrew Plewes. New York: Gulliver Books, 1997.

In this tale from the Pacific Northwest, the daughter of a chief has a spoiled and complaining nature. She complains about the bears' presence in the woods as she gathers berries, despite her friends' warnings not to anger the bears with her comments. Two men approach her, offering to help her to her home at dark. They take her to a village that is not her own and keep her there. She learns that she is being held as a slave by the Bear People. The man who has brought her there is the nephew of the bear chief. Mouse Woman teaches her a trick that helps her escape from her slave quarters, but then she must marry the chief's nephew. In time, she grows to love her husband, but she does not like to see him don his bearskin; she prefers his human form. She has two children: twins who have a human form, but can become bears by wearing bear-skins. The bear-husband senses that the young woman's brother is coming to kill him. The young woman wants to intervene, but her bear-husband instructs her to allow the killing, so that his bear-spirit can be released to watch over her. He teaches her songs and rituals to perform after he is dead. He tells her that every time a human kills a bear, these rituals must be performed, so that the Bear People will not get angry at humans.

Greene, Jacqueline Dembar. *Manabozho's Gifts: Three Chippewa Tales.* Illustrated by Jennifer Hewitson. Boston: Houghton Mifflin, 1994.

Manabozho, great-grandson of the moon, has powers beyond humans, yet he is not a god. He uses his powers of transformation to solve problems and help people. In "How Manabozho Stole Fire," he turns into a rabbit to gain access to a magician's wigwam to bring fire to the people. In "How Manabozho Saved the Rose," he turns into a hummingbird to locate the last rose and save it from extinction. These three tales are suitable for fourth grade and up.

Gregg, Andy. *Great Rabbit and the Long-Tailed Wildcat.* Illustrated by Gat Bowman Smith. Morton Grove, IL: Albert Whitman, 1993.

Wildcat wants to eat Rabbit, not just any rabbit, but Great Rabbit. Wildcat pursues him and is repeatedly tormented by Great Rabbit's tricks of transformation. Following Great Rabbit's tracks, Wildcat comes upon the dwelling of a medicine man, who offers him some roast rabbit and a night's sleep. The next morning, Wildcat wakes to find that he is out in the snow and has eaten squash, not rabbit! The same deception happens two more nights, first at the lodge of an old woman and then at the home of a warrior. Each time, Wildcat comments that the host looks as though she or he has rabbit ears. Wildcat howls with aggravation when he realizes that he has been eluded and made a fool of. Great Rabbit also cuts off Wildcat's tail, and that is why wildcats have short tails today. This Passamaquoddy/Algonquian legend works with second grade and up. Compare with *Muwin and the Magic Hare* by Susan Shetterly.

Luenn, Nancy. *Miser on the Mountain: A Nisqually Legend of Mount Rainier.* Illustrated by Pierr Morgan. Seattle, WA: Sasquatch Books, 1997.

This tale from the Pacific Northwest teaches the meaning of wealth and depicts spirits as the bringers of snow, thunder, and wind. At the base of the mountain Ta-co-bet (Mt. Rainier) lives a miserly man, Latsut, who is obsessed with acquiring barter shells called *hiaqua*. He has a vision in which his totem, Elk, advises him to journey to the summit of the mountain to seek hidden wealth. Latsut, single-minded and inconsiderate, leaves his family for the dangerous climb. At the summit, he finds the three rock formations that Elk had mentioned. At the base of the elk-shaped peak, Latsut digs and finds a bottomless cache of *hiaqua* shells. He grabs all he can carry, ignoring the giant thumping otters that surround him. He leaves no thanks or gift for the mountain, vowing to return for more. The spirits of wind, thunder, and snow bellow and lash at Latsut, trying to make him realize his blind greed. Frozen and exhausted, he begins to leave strings of shells for the otters and the spirits. Finally he realizes his foolishness, recognizing that life is more important, giving up the rest of his shells. He sleeps in a lodge built by Elk and awakens a white-haired old man. He returns to his wife, gathers his people to him in a feast, and explains to his descendants the true meaning of wealth. This tale is suitable for middle and upper grades.

Martin, Rafe. *The Boy Who Lived with the Seals.* Illustrated by David Shannon. New York: G. P. Putnam's Sons, 1993.

This tale of the Chinook people of the Pacific Northwest takes place near the mouth of the Columbia River. The People are camped near the River, and one young boy disappears. Sometime later, the boy's parents meet an old woman from another tribe who tells of seeing seals on an island in the sea, and with them is a boy. The parents travel to the island and find their boy. They take him home and re-teach him the way of humans. But he is never quite the same. He becomes skilled at making canoes and paddles with beautiful carvings, but he prefers to work alone at the shore. One day, he rejoins the seals. Compare with *The Selkie Girl* by Susan Cooper and *The Seal Prince* by Sheila MacGill-Callahan.

Max, Jill, ed. *Spider Spins a Story: Fourteen Legends from Native North America.* Illustrated by six Native American artists. Flagstaff, AZ: Rising Moon, 1997.

This collection of 14 tales from various tribal traditions all feature the spider. In the different tales, Spider acts variously as helper, magical agent, trickster, and Grandmother of the Earth. The Zuni legend "Swift Runner and Trickster Tarantula" features both helper Spider Woman and malicious trickster Tarantula. Huge Tarantula tricks Swift Runner, the son of a Zuni priest, out of his ceremonial clothing. Attempts by the people to retrieve the regalia fail, until the elders instruct the people to seek the help of the two war gods and their grandmother, Spider Woman. They create shapes of animals out of flour and ground sandstone. These shapes come alive, and they are placed where Tarantula will want to hunt them. Once Tarantula kills them and starts to haul them home, the animals transform back to piles of flour and sandstone, and Tarantula is defeated by the Zuni warriors. The story ends with the people roasting Tarantula, but he has one trick left: He explodes into millions of little tarantulas. These tellings are sophisticated, and typeface is small, so this collection is best suited as a read-aloud source for middle and upper grades.

McDermott, Gerald. *Raven: A Trickster Tale from the Pacific Northwest.* Illustrated by the author. New York: Harcourt Brace Jovanovich, 1993.

In this classic tale of the Native Americans of the Pacific Northwest, Raven decides to bring the gift of light to the creatures of earth. He uses his powers of transformation to become a pine needle and later a human baby in the lodge of the Sky Chief. Behaving like any child who insists on his own way, Raven grabs the Sky Chief's light and brings it to earth. After introducing students to this simpler telling, compare it with *Raven's Light* by Susan Shetterly. This tale is best suited to primary grades.

Norman, Howard. *The Girl Who Dreamed Only Geese: And Other Tales of the Far North.* Illustrated by Leo and Diane Dillon. New York: Gulliver Books, 1997.

In this collection of 10 tales drawn from the oral tradition of the Inuit and Eskimo peoples of North America, "Why the Rude Visitor Was Flung by Walrus" tells of a village shaman who enjoys turning into a walrus and spending time with the walruses. When a rude visitor insults and annoys the village, the shaman changes into a walrus and seeks the advice of his ancestors beneath the sea. The subsequent confrontations and dealings with the rude visitor are humorously told. "Uteritsoq and the Duckbill Dolls" tells of Uteritsoq and his wife, who is mourning for their lost son. Disregarding the tribal rules for a mourning mother, Uteritsoq selfishly demands that his wife mend his kayak. She stitches the kayak, but her needle and thread turn into a giant dog. The dog brings Moon Man to reprimand Uteritsoq and take him to the moon world for a while.

Back on earth, the woman moon spirit is with Uteritsoq's wife, creating duckbill dolls. The dolls turn into real children. When Uteritsoq returns home, he finds a house full of children that he must provide food for. In "The Wolverine's Secret," an orphan boy, who can turn into a raven, is falsely accused of stealing the sun and moon. He sets out to find and expose the wolverine, the real culprit. "The Man Who Married a Seagull" features a seagull who is turned into a young woman. In "How the Narwhal Got Its Tusk," also notable as a pourquoi tale, a boy's aunt is transformed into a narwhal, and his harpoon becomes her tusk. These stories, with their twists and turns of the supernatural, are for upper grades through adult.

———. *How Glooskap Outwits the Ice Giants: And Other Tales of the Maritime Indians.* Boston: Little, Brown, 1989.

This is a collection of six stories from Native Americans on the coast of New England and Canada. Glooskap is a giant who creates human beings, and he performs amazing feats of strength and endurance to protect the humans. In "How Glooskap Made Human Beings," Glooskap realizes that despite his enjoyment of nature, he is lonely, and he decides to create human beings. But the animals, who were giant-sized at that time, say they will overpower the humans. So Glooskap goes from one animal to the next, changing each from a giant into the size it is today. These tales are best suited to middle and upper grades.

Oliviero, Jamie. *The Day Sun Was Stolen.* Illustrated by Sharon Hitchcock. New York: Hyperion Books for Children, 1995.

This Haida (Pacific Northwest) legend contains elements of the pourquoi, trickster, and transformation tale. Illustrated with Haida totem symbols by a Haida artist, this simply told tale recounts how Bear hides Sun and how a boy disguises himself as a fish to get Sun back. Bear, deciding he is too hot, hides Sun in a hole. The boy dons a fish skin, gets himself caught by Bear, and waits for Bear to sleep. He shaves off some of Bear's fur so he, too, will know what it's like to be cold. The boy leaves Bear's cave with the fur in a sack, but the sack has a hole through which some fur scatters. Bear becomes cold and releases Sun for warmth. Some of the other animals use the scattered fur for their own warmth, which is why some animals grow extra fur in the winter. This tale is a very successful, easy to read, easy to understand example of Haida folklore. It is suitable for second grade and up.

———. *The Fish Skin.* Illustrated by Brent Morrisseau. New York: Hyperion Books for Children, 1993.

In this Cree story from northern Canada, the people are tired of the clouds. When they ask the sun to stay, it gets hot and dry, and everything begins to die. A boy wants to help, so he visits the Great Spirit in the forest. The Spirit gives him a fish skin. When he dons the fish skin, he is transformed into a fish. He drinks up volumes of water, until he becomes huge. Then he calls to a cloud and blows all his water at the cloud. The water falls back to earth as rain.

Rodanas, Kristina. *The Eagle's Song: A Tale from the Pacific Northwest.* Illustrated by the author. Boston: Little, Brown, 1995.

Long ago, the people lived in isolated dwellings, never gathering or conversing together. Three brothers live in one home and have plenty of provisions because two of the brothers are skilled hunters, but it never occurs to them to share with others. The youngest brother, Ermine, does not hunt, but carves and decorates boxes and bowls. When the two brothers fail to return from a hunting trip one day, Ermine goes to look for them. An eagle approaches, and it turns into a young man. The eagle then takes Ermine on his back and flies to the home of his old eagle-mother. She teaches Ermine music, drumming, singing, dancing, and the joy of being together. Ermine returns to his village, and teaches his people the joy of celebration and music. During a festival, Ermine's brothers return, escorted by the eagle-man. Ermine discovers that the people's learning how to share and celebrate has restored the old eagle-mother's youth.

Ross, Gayle. *The Legend of the Windigo: A Tale from Native North America.* Illustrated by Murv Jacob. New York: Dial Books for Young Readers, 1996.

When members of the community disappear, the people suspect the Windigo, a terrible monster that is made of stone. A boy has an idea: If stones in a fire-pit can get hot enough to crack, maybe the Windigo can be burned and cracked as well. The people dig a pit and cover it with branches to trap the Windigo. When he falls in, they cast firewood and hot coals in and burn him until he cracks. They hear him scream, and then they hear another, tiny sound. The Windigo has transformed himself into mosquitoes, to torment people forever in revenge. This story is suitable for all ages. Compare with *The Windigo's Return* by Douglas Wood.

Rubalcaba, Jill. *Uncegila's Seventh Spot: A Lakota Legend.* Illustrated by Irving Toddy. New York: Clarion Books, 1995.

Uncegila is a huge, evil, serpentine creature with spots down her back. If a warrior can shoot an arrow into the seventh spot, the tribe will know no hunger or fear. Two brothers, one blind, set out on the mission, aided by Ugly-Old-Woman. When Blind-Twin embraces Ugly-Old-Woman, she is transformed into Beautiful-Young-Girl, and she equips the men with magic arrows. The woman's instructions and arrows are successful, and the monster dies. The brothers cut out Uncegila's heart; the heart speaks to them with many instructions for rituals. These rituals cause transformations, including restoring Blind-Twin's sight and bringing prosperity to the village. However, the people tire of the heart's demands and miss the challenge of hunting. They decide to give up the protection of Uncegila's heart. Now they face life's uncertainties with their own self-confidence. This tale is suitable for middle grades and up.

Seymour, Tryntje Van Ness. *The Gift of Changing Woman.* New York: Henry Holt, 1993.

This is actually a nonfiction book describing the Apache Changing Woman ceremony, a traditional coming-of-age ritual for girls still practiced by Apache people to celebrate a girl's transformation from childhood to womanhood. The ceremony reenacts the story of Changing Woman, the person who was the sole survivor of a great flood and the one from whom all Apache people have descended. Excerpts of the legends of Changing Woman, as well as a description of the four-day ceremony, are included. On the last day of the ceremony, the honored girl is painted with clay to represent White Painted Lady (another name for Changing Woman). Painted with this clay, she symbolizes the fourth stage of human life, the transformation into old age. The richness of this symbolic ceremony is told with respect and honor. This book offers students a real-life example of how the cyclical transformations of life are honored and reenacted.

Shetterly, Susan Hand. *Muwin and the Magic Hare.* Illustrated by Robert Shetterly. New York: Atheneum, 1993.

In this tale from the Passamaquoddy Indians, a bear (Muwin) is in pursuit of a snowshoe hare. He comes upon a hunter, then an old woman, and finally a chief. At each of these stops in his journey, the host feeds the bear and tells him a story. There are verbal and visual clues that these three hosts, plus the boy at the end, are really the magic hare, who transforms himself. Because there are several stories within the story, students may need help mapping it as they go, so they don't lose the main story framework. Compare with *Great Rabbit and the Long-Tailed Wildcat* by Andy Gregg.

———. *Raven's Light: A Myth from the People of the Northwest Coast.* Illustrated by Robert Shetterly. Atheneum, 1991.

Using the sources of the Tlingit, Kwakiutl, Haida, and Tsimshian peoples of the Pacific Northwest, Shetterly tells an extended version of how Raven brings light to the earth. Raven transforms himself to steal light from the lodge of the Great Chief of the Sky World. This is a more extensive telling than *Raven* by Gerald McDermott; it includes the concept of parallel worlds in the sky and the earth, and it begins with Raven creating earth and the creatures in it.

Smith, Don Lelooska. *Echoes of the Elders: The Stories and Paintings of Chief Lelooska.* Illustrated by the author. Edited by Christine Normandin. New York: DK Ink, 1997. Book and compact disc recording.

Of the five Kwakiutl tales in this multimedia collection, three feature transformation elements. "The Old Owl Witch" tells of a strange creature whom the children taunt, despite warnings to leave her alone. In the end, she turns the disobedient children into mice. The melancholy "Boy and the Loon" tells of a lifelong alliance between a boy and a loon. Each in his turn provides help and support for the other and leadership for his people. In the end, the boy, now an old man, flies off to become one of the loon people. "Beaver Face" is the name given by taunting peers to a girl who was born with a cleft lip. One day, while playing near the forest's edge, the children are all snatched up by Tsonoqua the Timber Giant. The giant plans to devour the children, but Beaver Face helps them all escape, bravely faces Tsonoqua, and kills her. But after the villagers burn the giant's house, the ashes of Tsonoqua transform into biting blackflies, hornets, and mosquitoes. This collection is a tribute to Chief Lelooska for all ages.

Steptoe, John. *The Story of Jumping Mouse.* Illustrated by the author. New York: Lothrop, Lee & Shepard, 1984.

In this tale from the Plains Indians, a young mouse wants to go to the far-off land he has heard about in stories. On his journey, he meets Magic Frog, who gives him powerful legs like a frog to jump high. Later, he meets a bison who is blind. Jumping Mouse tries the same magic the frog used to give the bison his eyesight. Now the bison can see, but the mouse is blind. The bison protects the mouse until they come to the mountains, where Jumping Mouse meets a wolf who has lost his sense of smell. The mouse gives his sense of smell to the wolf, who happily protects him for a time. Without sight or smell, Jumping Mouse wonders how he will survive. Magic Frog appears again and commends the mouse's selflessness. He tells him to jump high, and Jumping Mouse then becomes Eagle. This story is well suited to primary and middle grades.

Stevens, Janet. *Old Bag of Bones: A Coyote Tale.* Illustrated by the author. New York: Holiday House, 1996.

Coyote is complaining that he is nothing but an old, hungry bag of bones. When he sees the magical Young Buffalo, he persuades him to give him youth, strength, and power. Young Buffalo agrees to transform Coyote into a buffalo, but warns him that only a real buffalo has true power. Now a "Buffote," Coyote brags about his powers, but he ends up back where he was—a decrepit bag of bones. But he hasn't learned his lesson yet! By the last page, he is on the make for another creature to mooch from.

Taylor, C. J. *The Monster from the Swamp: Native Legends of Monsters, Demons and Other Creatures.* Illustrated by the author. Plattsburgh, NY: Tundra Books, 1995.

These eight tales are about fearsome monsters, most of whom who are challenged and overcome by people for the good of all. "The Snake that Guards the River" tells of a man who eats some giant eggs, and then his legs become paralyzed. Then his legs become joined and covered with scaly skin, and he begs his friend to take him to water. Finally, he ends up in a huge river with his whole body transformed into that of a snake. This tale explains why the Cheyenne people make an offering to the snakeman before crossing the Mississippi River. "The Revenge of the Blood Thirsty Giant" is a violent telling of the legend of the Windigo, in which the evil monster is burned but returns to torment humans in the form of mosquitoes. In "How Animals Came Back into the World," the bravest humans jump into a lake and become transformed into animals, birds, and fish, so that animals are restored to the earth.

Van Laan, Nancy. *Shingebiss: An Ojibwe Legend.* Illustrated by Betsy Bowen. Boston: Houghton Mifflin, 1997.
    This tale features Shingebiss, a diver-duck who is also a "spirit teacher" who can transform himself from spirit to man to duck. Winter Maker tries repeatedly to defeat the little duck's attempts to break the ice of Lake Superior and find fish to eat. Finally, Shingebiss sings a song inviting Winter Maker either to come into his wigwam or leave him alone. Winter Maker comes in, thinking he will freeze Shingebiss out, but the warmth of the wigwam melts Winter Maker a little bit. Winter Maker then decides to leave Shingebiss alone. The story ends with a reminder that people who follow Shingebiss's example will find enough food and warmth to last the frigid winters of the Lake Superior region. This tale is suitable for all ages.

Wood, Audrey. *The Rainbow Bridge: Inspired by a Chumash Tale.* Illustrated by Robert Florczak. New York: Harcourt Brace, 1995.
    This creation myth takes place on an island off the California coast. The earth goddess, Hutash, wants to share life with other beings, so she creates the Chumash people by scattering seeds from a sacred plant. Over time, the number of people grows until the island is too crowded. Hutash arranges for some of the people to move to the mainland; she constructs a rainbow bridge for the people to cross. Some of the people fall off the bridge, and Hutash, hearing their cries, turns them into dolphins. The Chumash believe to this day that the dolphins are their brothers and sisters.

Wood, Douglas. *The Windigo's Return: A North Woods Story.* Illustrated by Greg Couch. New York: Simon & Schuster Books for Young Readers, 1996.
    In this Ojibwe (Anishinabe) tale, the People are faring well, until something strange starts to happen. One by one, people go out to the woods, but they do not return. The People gather, fearing that the others have been taken by the Windigo, the forest giant who can turn himself into anything. A girl suggests that they dig a deep pit in the ground, covered with branches, to trap the Windigo. The trap works, and the People throw hot coals into the pit, burning the Windigo to ashes. They take the ashes and throw them into the wind from a high hill. The People are relieved, the seasons pass, and the Windigo does not return. But one evening the next summer, the air fills up with a cloud of ashes. The ash-beings land on the people's skin, bite them, and make them itch. The girl declares the Windigo has returned to torment them—in the form of mosquitoes.

SOUTH AMERICAN

Garcia, Anamarie. *The Girl from the Sky: An Inca Folktale from South America.* Adventures in Storytelling Series. Performed by the author. Illustrated by Janice Skivington. Chicago: Childrens Press, 1992. Book and audiocassette kit.
    This kit contains a wordless book with illustrations of the story's events and an audiocassette of the narrative. In this South American tale, a potato farmer falls in love with a star maiden. After she returns to the sky, he grows impatient to see her again and goes to the sky world to find her. He does not realize that going to the sky will result in his coming back to earth as an old man. This kit will be useful to nonreaders and students in ESL classes.

McDermott, Gerald. *Musicians of the Sun*. Illustrated by the author. New York: Simon & Schuster Books for Young Readers, 1997.

This brief, somber tale from the Aztecs relates the transformation of the world from a dark, silent, joyless place to a world filled with light and music. The Lord of the Night is determined to give the people the joy of dancing, light, laughter, and music. He sends Wind to the house of Sun to rescue the four musicians Red, Yellow, Blue, and Green. Wind is afraid of Sun, a warrior who uses fire against others, so the Lord of the Night gives Wind three objects (a shield, thunder, and clouds) to protect himself on his quest. Wind confronts Sun and finally gains the advantage by unleashing clouds and thunder. The musicians are brought to earth, and they bring such happiness that Sun pours down its light on the world. This tale is suitable for all ages.

MANY CULTURES IN A COLLECTION

Adler, Naomi. *The Dial Book of Animal Tales from Around the World*. Illustrated by Amanda Hall. New York: Dial Books for Young Readers, 1996.

This is a useful collection of nine stories (one transformation, four trickster, and four pourquoi tales). In "Sedna and King Gull" (Inuit), Sedna loves King Gull, who transforms himself into a man; Sedna's father agrees to their marriage. One day, King Gull sees hunters killing birds needlessly, and in an effort to stop them, he himself is mortally wounded. His dying wish is to have his body thrown into the ocean. When Sedna does so, King Gull transforms into a whale, and Sedna's tears transform into sea creatures: seals, dolphins, walruses, and more. Sedna becomes queen of the sea, and she rules that hunters may take only as much as they need, or else she will cause storms. This collection is suitable for reading aloud or for independent reading by middle grades.

Climo, Shirley. *A Treasury of Mermaids: Mermaid Tales from Around the World*. Illustrated by Jean and Mou-sien Tseng. HarperCollins, 1997.

In this collection of eight mermaid tales, "Hansi and the Nix" (Switzerland) tells of a nix, a creature who has a mermaid tail while in the sea and human legs and feet while on land. Hansi becomes friends with the nix, who wants him to teach her how to yodel. She takes him to live with her under the sea, and whenever he becomes homesick for his life on land, she brings his land-things to him. "The Listening Ear" (Japan) is the story of a second son who accepts whatever comes his way. He catches a red snapper in shallow water, but when it looks at him with anguished eyes, he releases it. It turns into a lovely maiden, who takes him to her undersea kingdom and gives him the "listening ear" as a reward. Although it appears to be nothing more than a broken shell, the "listening ear" has special powers that ensure his happy fate. In "The Sea Princess and the Sea Witch," a sea witch forces the princess to eat a yellow sea grape, which turns her into a seal. "Pania of the Reef" (Maori/New Zealand) tells of a mermaid who charms a handsome warrior, and they marry. But she can stay with him only in the dark night, and she must return every day to the sea. After they have a child, he tries to keep her on land, but she flees to the sea. "Mrs. Fitzgerald the Merrow" (Irish) and "Odysseus and the Sirens" (Greek) also feature transformations.

―――. *A Treasury of Princesses: Princess Tales from Around the World*. Illustrated by Ruth Sanderson. New York: HarperCollins, 1996.

The seven tales in this collection include "The Moon Maidens" from China and "Prince Ivan and the Frog Princess" from Russia. While the source notes are useful, other tellings may be more accessible. Use for additional material or for comparisons.

Gerke, Pamela. *Multicultural Plays for Children: Volume 1: Grades K-3*, and *Volume 2: Grades 4-6*. Young Actors Series. Lyme, NH: Smith and Kraus, 1996.

These two volumes contain both general and specific instructions for producing plays derived from folktales. The 10 plays in each volume are introduced with cultural and literary information. The scripts include a sprinkling of words in other languages. Volume 1 includes "Ma Lien and the Magic Paintbrush," both a trickster and transformation tale, in which a girl is given a magic paintbrush. Everything she paints is transformed into a real object. When a greedy ruler commands her powers for his own use, she paints a scene in which he willingly participates in his own demise. Also in Volume 1 is "I Dodici Mesi (The Twelve Months)," in which a girl is saved from her stepmother's wrath by 12 sisters who control the 12 months. When she is commanded to fetch items such as violets and apples during January, the month-characters temporarily transform a bit of the forest into the appropriate months to help her. Volume 2 includes a science fiction interpretation of "East of the Sun and West of the Moon," featuring a prince under a spell that transforms him into a bear by day. The Chinese story "The Wind Pearl" features a man who is transformed into a dog and is saved by the love of a woman.

Goode, Diane. *Diane Goode's Book of Giants and Little People*. Illustrated by the author. New York: Dutton Children's Books, 1997.

This collection of 17 tales and poems includes "Little Lella" (Italian), which tells of a tiny shepherd who lives under a curse that he will never grow until he finds "lovely Little Lella of the three singing apples." His quest to find her includes encounters with three different tiny ladies in walnut shells who give him advice and objects to help him. Upon finding and stealing the cage with the three apples from an old woman, the shepherd is aided in his escape by transformations: The stone he tosses behind him turns into a mountain; the comb he throws down becomes an ice pond, and the old woman's breath (which he collected in a bag) turns into a fog, all deterring his pursuers. When at last he finds Little Lella, they fall in love, grow, and get married. Compare this escape with those in *Master Maid* by Aaron Shepard and *Baba Yaga and the Little Girl* by Katya Arnold.

Mayo, Margaret. *Magical Tales from Many Lands*. Illustrated by Jane Ray. New York: Dutton Children's Books, 1993.

This useful collection includes 14 tales. In "The Lemon Princess," the beautiful Lemon Princess undergoes a series of transformations because a greedy servant girl is trying to take her place; however, with a final transformation and clever planning, she secures Prince Omar's affections. In the melancholy "Kingdom Under the Sea," a beautiful sea princess takes the form of a turtle when traveling to the surface, and a man turns into a crane because he does not keep a promise to leave a gift box unopened. "Kate Crackernuts" tells of a princess under a spell that gives her a sheep's head. In "Three Golden Apples," an old woman turns a rude man's golden apples into slimy toads and another's into slithery snakes. In "The Seven Clever Brothers," each brother acquires a special power, which is used against a sorcerer who changes into a black vulture. Two stories feature transformations that provide pourquoi explanations: "The Halloween Witches" explains the origins of owls, and "Koala" explains the creation of the first koala.

———. *Mythical Birds and Beasts from Many Lands*. Illustrated by Jane Ray. New York: Dutton Children's Books, 1996.

Some of these well-illustrated stories contain transformation elements. In "The Fish at Dragon's Gate" (Chinese), Kun, the grandson of the supreme god, changes himself into a horse to try to avoid being struck by lightning. Kun dies, but he gives life to the Golden Dragon, now the rain god. The Golden Dragon creates the Yellow River, where some of the fish swimming upstream leap and turn into dragons. In the humorously told "Jamie and the Biggest, First, and Father of All Sea Serpents" (Scandinavian/Orkney Islands), Jamie defeats the huge serpent by boating into its mouth and setting the serpent's liver ablaze with a glowing peat pot. The serpent's thrashing creates the straits between Denmark and Sweden; his teeth become the Orkney, Shetland, and Faroe Islands; and his dead, burning body becomes Iceland. "Three Fabulous Eggs" (Burma) features a Naga (shape-changer) princess. In this story, she changes shapes from woman to snake to snake-woman.

McCarthy, Tara. *Multicultural Fables and Fairy Tales: Stories and Activities to Promote Literacy and Cultural Awareness*. New York: Scholastic Professional Books, 1993.
    In the format of a professional teacher resource book, this collection contains short tellings of four folktale genres for reading aloud. Each tale has a page of preparatory suggestions for the teacher and one page of student activities. Included are seven pour-quoi tales, five trickster tales, and six fairy tales, some of which include transformations. The pourquoi story "The Five Water-Spirits" ends with the transformation of five sisters into Niagara Falls. "The Three Feathers" and "The Frog Prince" feature an enchanted princess (or prince) transformed into a toad (or frog). In the trickster tale "The Teapot Badger," a badger turns himself into a pot of tea, and back again, as a form of trickery.

Mills, Lauren. *The Book of Little Folk: Faery Stories and Poems from Around the World*. Illustrated by the author. New York: Dial Books, 1997.
    This is a collection of 29 folktales, original stories, and poems about faeries and little people. In "The Moss-Green Princess" (Swaziland), the father of a princess, Kitila, has died, and the new king has married her mother. But he has another daughter of his own, whom he favors. To ensure that Kitila's beauty does not overshadow his daughter's, he plots to force Kitila to wear the skin of a grotesque monster. The king's men kill the monster and skin it. Because the monster is really a faery-being, the skin conforms to Kitila's body, and she cannot take it off. Years later, an old man gives Kitila a stick with special powers. When Kitila wades into water with the stick, the ugly monster skin comes off, and she returns to her human form. When a prince comes seeking a wife, he is shown the ugly moss-green princess, and he is horrified. But two children who know Katila's secret take him to hide and watch her enter the pool with the magic stick. He prepares to marry Kitila, and as she bathes in the water, birds take her ugly skin away forever. In "Little One Inch" (Japanese), a childless couple pray for a baby, even if he is as small as a thumb. Later, they have a tiny child, Little One Inch. When he is "grown," he gets a job in the lord's palace as bodyguard to the princess. One day, she is accosted by a monster, and Little One Inch repeatedly stabs the monster with his needle-sword, chasing him away. Afterward, Little One Inch is transformed into a full-sized man, and he and the princess marry. In "Tom Thumb" (England), the Fairy Queen's daughter helps Tom out of a scrape by transforming into a butterfly. "The Goblin's Cap" (Korea) tells of a couple that hides in the night to discover who is eating their food. They wait with a stick, which they use to lift off the cap of an invisible goblin. Now that his cap is off, the goblin becomes visible. The man decides to use the cap himself, to make himself invisible so that he can steal things. This he does, until one day, a jeweler discovers him and teaches him a lesson. These stories are best suited for read-aloud sessions for first through sixth grade children.

Milord, Susan. *Tales Alive! Ten Multicultural Folktales with Activities*. Charlotte, VT: Williamson, 1995.
    Four of the ten tales in this collection are transformation tales. "The Gentle People," from the Patagonian region of Argentina, describes how a community chooses transformation into guanacos (llamalike creatures), to remain peaceful and avoid fighting a war. "The Blue-Eyed Hare" features a Scottish girl who is under the spell of a witch, which turns her into a hare. In "Lighting the Way," an Aboriginal girl asks a magician to turn her into the morning star so she can help her friends on a journey. "Urashima the Fisherman" is a Japanese tale of a fisherman whose turtle turns into a goddess of the sky world. This is a good source for read-alouds for middle and upper grades.

Osborne, Mary Pope. *Favorite Medieval Tales*. Illustrated by Troy Nowell. New York: Scholastic, 1998.

This collection of nine legends is a good sample of varied tales and topics. "Finn MacCoul" (Irish) is an introductory overview of the life of one of Ireland's most beloved legendary heroes. In this telling, Finn meets his wife Saba, who is under a spell transforming her into a deer. Finn's hounds and his fellow warriors, the Fianna, help her resume human form. Later, she again comes under the evil spell and once more becomes a doe. "The Sword in the Stone" (English) tells of the coming of Merlin and his powers, which include his powers of sight and of transformation. "The Werewolf" (French) tells a classic story of a knight named Sir Marrok who is under an evil spell causing him to transform into a werewolf for three days every week. His treacherous wife learns that the secret to his human form is his clothing, and she steals his clothes from their hiding place to be rid of him. This is a useful collection for upper grades.

———. *Mermaid Tales from Around the World*. Illustrated by Troy Howell. New York: Scholastic, 1993.

In this collection of 12 tales, transformations from human to sea creature occur in "Fish Husband" and "The Enchanted Cap." Primary and middle grades will enjoy comparing "The Enchanted Cap" with *The Selkie Girl* by Susan Cooper. Other tales are more appropriate for upper grades.

Riordan, James. *Stories from the Sea: An Abbeville Anthology*. Illustrated by Amanda Hall. New York: Abbeville Press, 1996.

This collection of nine tales includes transformation and pourquoi tales. "Sea Wind" (Senegalese) is a story of love between a woman, Aminata, and Sea Wind, who can take the shape of a man, gull, or other creature. Sea Wind comes to Aminata's village and marries her, but he never stays for long. They have three children: Sea Breeze, Flower Wind, and Breath of Mercy. Aminata dies, and Breath of Mercy provides comfort to those in mourning. In "The Old Man of the Sea" (Siberian), a young man named Azmun travels up river to find the Old Man of the Sea to tell him that his people are starving for lack of fish. He encounters young men having sword fights; they turn into small whales, and one takes him to the Old Man. When Azmun finds him, the Old Man is fast asleep, and it is his oversleeping that has caused the lack of fish. He wakes and sends an abundance of fish to the people. Azmun thanks the Old Man by giving him his mouth harp, which can be heard to this day in the sound of gale winds. The "Selkie Wife" (Scottish) is the haunting story of a seal who transforms into a woman and lives on land for seven years. Compare with *Selkie Girl* by Susan Cooper.

Rockwell, Anne. *The Acorn Tree: And Other Folktales*. Illustrated by the author. New York: Greenwillow Books, 1995.

In this collection of ten tales illustrated and told for young listeners, there are three transformation tales. In "The Acorn Tree" (European), a magic mill turns acorns into pancakes and pie, providing for an elderly couple. In "The Flower Children" (African), a woman stops chopping a tree, learning that its flowers are really transformed children. She may have the children as hers, but she must promise never to scold them. One day, she gets cross with them, and they turn back into flowers. The "Puppy-Boy" (Inuit) starts with the appearance of a puppy at the home of an old childless couple. They take care of the puppy, and it grows. One day, they find a baby at their door, but when they hold it, it turns back into the puppy. This happens again, but later, the baby remains in human form. The puppy-boy asks his father to make him a toy whaleboat and spear, which he uses to catch a real whale. Now the old couple have enough to eat, and they live happily.

San Souci, Robert D. *Cut from the Same Cloth: American Women of Myth, Legend, and Tall Tale*. Introduction by Jane Yolen. Illustrated by Brian Pinkney. New York: Philomel Books, 1993.

This collection of 15 tales spotlights the power and cleverness of women. In the Chippewa tale "The Star Maiden," a young hunter witnesses the descent of a basket from the sky. The basket contains women chanting a song of power. He falls in love with the youngest, but the women may not stay or talk with earth people. The young hunter goes to a medicine woman who gives him a medicine bag, which will change him into a mouse so that he can sneak into the basket the next time the women come. When the youngest woman discovers the mouse, he changes back into his human form. The woman consents to become his wife and live on earth; later, the couple and their baby live in the sky world. Because of their yearning to see the earth world again, the sky ruler tells them to gather objects representing the animals. Each object gives sky people the power to transform into those animals so that they can visit the earth. In the African American tale "Susanna and Simon," Susanna uses her conjuring skills to escape with her sweetheart. While her angry father chases them, determined to kill Simon, the couple drops objects behind them to deter their pursuer. First, Simon drops his coat, and it becomes a thick forest. Then Susanna drops an egg, which becomes a fog, and a sack, which becomes a pond. Later, she drops a pebble, which turns into a mountain. The father continues to surmount these and other obstacles, until Simon casts down a sack of pebbles. They become a long, high wall, which Susanna's father cannot get over or around.

Sierra, Judy. *Nursery Tales Around the World*. Illustrated by Stefano Vitale. New York: Clarion Books, 1996.

This collection of short tales is organized by thematic elements, e.g., "Runaway Cookies" and "Fooling the Big Bad Wolf." The "Runaway Cookies" stories include "The Gingerbread Man" and two other variations on this theme: "The Pancake" (Norway) and "The Bun" (Russia). These stories embody the motif in which pastry comes alive and takes on a life of its own. This collection is suitable for kindergarten and first grade.

Walker, Paul Robert. *Giants! Stories from Around the World*. Illustrated by James Bernardin. New York: Harcourt Brace, 1995.

This collection of seven stories is accompanied by detailed commentary and source notes. "Kana the Stretching Wonder" (Hawaiian) describes the works of Kana, brother to ten giants and one dwarf, all sons of the chief and his wife Hina. Kana is a *kapua*, a hero who is part divine and part human with the ability to change shape. Kana is born in the shape of a rope and is thrown in the pigpen. His wise grandmother retrieves him and raises him. He changes into the shape of a child, but in 40 days, he is 40 feet long and growing longer. One day, the princess Hina is kidnapped. Kana is asked to help rescue her. Her rescue is successful, thanks to Kana's ability to stretch taller and higher, until he is as thin as a spider web. "The Giant Who Had No Heart" (Norwegian) tells of a king who sends six sons out into the world to find wives, but keeps the youngest, Boots, home with him. The giant then turns the six sons and their brides into stone. Boots sets out to find them and has amazing adventures that lead to their rescue and restoration to human form. Transformation elements are also found in the trickster tale "Coyote and the Giant Sisters," a story from the Native Americans of the Pacific Northwest. Long ago, the animal people could take human form. One day they discover that all the salmon have disappeared. Coyote changes himself into a human baby and floats down the Big River. He is stopped by a dam built by five giant sisters, who are keeping all the salmon for themselves. They rescue the cute little baby and care for it in their lodge. During the days while they are out, Coyote transforms into a man and digs a hole in the dam, returning at night in the form of a baby. One day, the giant sisters discover him digging the hole, but he finishes just in time, releasing all the salmon. Then Coyote lectures the giants and turns them into swallows.

He tells them that the people will know the salmon are coming when they see the birds. The swallows herald the salmon even to this day. This collection is an effective read-aloud source for all ages.

Walker, Richard. *The Barefoot Book of Trickster Tales*. Illustrated by Claudio Muñoz. Brooklyn, NY: Barefoot Books, 1998.

This collection of nine tales provides a variety of cultures and trickster characters. In "Jack and the Wizard" (English), Jack tricks an intimidating wizard into transforming himself repeatedly until he becomes an ant and Jack gains the upper hand. "The Spirits in the Leather Bag" (Kampuchean) concerns the power of stories. A prince loves stories, so he has his faithful servant tell him one every night. After the tale is told, the spirit of the story goes into a leather bag in his bedchamber. The prince is jealous of the stories and never passes them on to anyone else, but the leather bag gets crowded with discontented spirits who conspire revenge against the prince. Each spirit plans to transform itself on the prince's wedding day to do mischief and harm to him, but the servant overhears their plans, saves the prince, and admonishes the prince to share the stories. "Turtle Goes on the Warpath" (Skidi Pawnee) is a variant of "Turtle Makes War on Man," in *The Boy Who Lived with the Bears* by Joseph Bruchac. Ananse has seldom been as clever as he is in "Ananse and the Impossible Quest" (Ghanaian). The king is tired of Ananse's cleverness, so he devises a task to foil him. He tells Ananse he wants him to go on a special quest for two things but will not tell him what they are. The task is to bring the king two items from the house of Death, from which no one returns, Ananse uses his wits to discover the mission and steal the objects for the king. A light storytelling style and large, well-spaced typeface make this collection suitable as a read-aloud to all ages and for independent reading for middle grades and up.

ORIGINAL TRANSFORMATION STORIES

Bang, Molly. *Dawn*. Illustrated by the author. New York: William Morrow, 1983.

This is an original adaptation of the Japanese folktale *The Crane Wife*. One day, a shipbuilder comes upon a wounded Canada goose and nurses it back to health. Later, a woman comes to the shipyard in search of work as a sailmaker. She weaves superior sails, marries the ship builder, and bears a daughter. She weaves a set of sails for her husband's own sailboat of extraordinary lightness and strength. Then the shipbuilder gets the biggest job of his life. The customer wants the same kind of sails as the shipbuilder's own, but his wife says she cannot produce them. The husband becomes angry, and the wife relents, but she makes him promise not to watch her weave the sails. However, the builder does look, and he finds a Canada goose who has plucked all the feathers from her breast to make the cloth. The story is told with the deep regret of the bereft husband and the hopefulness of the daughter. This tale is suitable for middle and upper grades.

———. *The Paper Crane*. Illustrated by the author. New York: Greenwillow Books, 1985.

A man owns a restaurant, and all is well until a new highway is built. Now no one comes to the restaurant anymore. One day, a poor-looking stranger comes into the restaurant, and the owner serves him. The stranger says he cannot pay in money, but he will pay in his own way. He folds a paper crane and tells the owner that if he claps his hands, the crane will come to life. The owner tries it, and indeed the paper crane becomes a live bird that dances. People come from all over to see the bird and eat at the restaurant. After months pass, the stranger returns. He plays a flute, the crane dances, and he rides out of the restaurant on the crane's back. He is never seen again. This story is suitable for independent reading by second graders.

Browne, Anthony. *Changes.* Illustrated by the author. New York: Alfred A. Knopf, 1990.

    With spare text and Browne's characteristic surreal illustrations, this book captures the unsettling imagination of a boy. In this tale, the boy is told to expect that things will change. The boy looks around, and sees things changing before his eyes: a slipper into a bird, the sofa into an alligator, a cushion into a gorilla, a bike wheel into an apple. As it turns out, the "changes" are the product of his anxiety over the new baby that has just come home.

Collodi, Carlo. *Pinocchio.* Adapted from the translation by M. A. Murray. Illustrated by Ed Young. New York: Philomel Books, 1996.

    This is the familiar story of the mischievous wooden puppet who comes alive and whose nose grows every time he is not truthful. This newly illustrated version features paper collage to accompany the long, dense text. This book is best suited to reading aloud.

Demi. *Liang and the Magic Paintbrush.* Illustrated by the author. New York: Holt, Rinehart and Winston, 1980.

    Based on a Chinese folktale, this story is about a boy named Liang, who wants to paint but is too poor to afford a brush. One night, a man riding a phoenix gives Liang a magic paintbrush. Everything Liang paints comes alive. A greedy emperor then orders Liang to paint him things that will bring him wealth and power. Eventually, Liang paints a boat on a sea in a storm, and the emperor drowns.

Egielski, Richard. *The Gingerbread Boy.* Illustrated by the author. New York: Harper-Collins, 1997.

    Although this is a retelling of a traditional folktale, it is classified as an original tale, probably due to its contemporary urban setting and characters. The text remains very close to traditional tellings, but the illustrations bring a fresh appeal to this new version.

Griffith, Helen. *Emily and the Enchanted Frog.* Illustrated by Susan Condie Lamb. New York: Greenwillow Books, 1989.

    The first of three stories in this book is a modern spin-off of the "frog prince" motif. Emily finds a frog near a pond and thinks it is a handsome prince wanting to be kissed to break his spell. She kisses the frog, and it indeed becomes a handsome prince. But the prince is disturbed by the transformation. He tells her she has it backward: He liked being a frog. The morose prince gets on Emily's nerves. He tells Emily she must help him by finding another frog who is under the same spell and, if kissed by a human, will become a princess. Then if the two kiss each other, they will both become frogs again. Emily reluctantly begins kissing frog after frog, until finally one becomes a grouchy princess. The two resentful frog-humans kiss, and then they hop off as frogs once more. This amusing story is suitable for primary and middle grades.

Harrison, Joanna. *When Mom Turned into a Monster.* Illustrated by the author. Minneapolis: Carolrhoda Books, 1996.

    A typical family scene, with a messy house, messy children, and a frazzled mom, strikes a familiar note with many families. The phone rings, and Mom finds out that relatives are coming in a few hours for a visit. Efforts to clean up and run errands are complicated by several mishaps of the children. Mom's frantic pace escalates, and in each illustration, Mom is growing ugly green hands, ears, tail, etc., as she slowly turns into a monster. Apologies by both Mom and the kids restore both peace and Mom's human appearance. When the cousins come, they are so unmannerly that *their* mom begins to turn into a monster. A reassuring family story, this story is suitable for primary and middle grades.

Helldorfer, M. C. *The Mapmaker's Daughter.* Illustrated by Jonathan Hunt. New York: Bradbury, 1991.

A mapmaker's daughter, Suchen, yearns to go to a place called Turnings, said to be under a spell. One night, she aids a prince who is escaping to Turnings. The next morning, the king comes to arrest the mapmaker and Suchen for helping his son flee to Turnings. Suchen begs the king to be allowed to search for the prince. She leaves on her journey with three gifts from her father: her mother's cape, a map, and a lock of her father's hair. Once she reaches Turnings, Suchen gets inside the witch's castle where the prince is being held. As Suchen and the prince flee, the objects her father gave her are transformed and come to their aid: The snake (her father's hair) helps them over the wall, the birds (map) take them over the mountains, and the fish (her mother's cape) carries them across the river. When they arrive in their home kingdom, the prince gives Suchen a horse and cape for her next adventure. This story will appeal to students from first through fourth grades.

Heller, Nicholas. *A Troll Story.* Illustrated by the author. New York: Greenwillow Books, 1990.

This is the simple story of a boy, Lewis, who can change himself into a troll at will. Despite the temptations to do so, he refrains from transforming himself during the day. But after his family is asleep at night, Lewis transforms himself into a troll and plays with the other trolls. This story is suitable for primary grades.

Kraft, Erik. *Chocolatina.* Illustrated by Denise Brunkus. Mahwah, NJ: BridgeWater Books, 1998.

In this slightly zany original story, Tina (nicknamed Chocolatina) loves eating chocolate to excess. Her scary-looking health teacher always chants, "You are what you eat." One night, Tina wishes that were true, and she wakes to find herself transformed into a solid piece of chocolate. Her school day is a miserable experience, and that night, Tina wishes herself back to normal. This story is light entertainment for primary grades.

Lattimore, Deborah Nourse. *Punga the Goddess of Ugly.* Illustrated by the author. New York: Harcourt Brace, 1993.

This fictional account of twin Maori sisters combines fiction with information about the traditional Maori customs, especially a dance called the haka, still done in New Zealand. Twin sisters are learning traditional weaving, songs, stories and haka dance from their grandmother. Grandmother tells them they need to practice their haka dance, a dance done with the tongue sticking out. One sister gets silly as she dances and runs into the forest, where she is captured by Punga, the Goddess of Ugly, and is transformed into a wooden image on Punga's roof pole. The remaining sister dances a fierce haka dance, and convinces Punga to release her sister to dance with her. They dance their best, and magically receive a moko, a chin tattoo as a mark of coming of age.

Le Guin, Ursula K. *A Ride on the Red Mare's Back.* Illustrated by Julie Downing. New York: Orchard, 1992.

A father and his little boy go out hunting, but only the father returns, saying only that the trolls got the boy. The boy's older sister sets out to find him, taking only a scarf, knitting needles, yarn, bread, and her little toy wooden horse. From under a bridge, a huge arm thrusts up to grab the girl. Suddenly, her toy horse squirms and turns into a red, full-sized mare. The horse talks to the troll and to the girl, and the girl, appeasing the troll with the bread, finds out that her brother is being kept at the High House. The horse tells the girl it has only that one night to help the girl. The mare carries the girl to the High House, where she finds her brother among other ill-behaved troll-children. She has trouble convincing her brother to come with her, until she wraps him in the scarf she has made for him. Dawn is approaching, the hour when the mare's time is up, and also the time when sunlight comes, which trolls cannot tolerate. When the first rays of sunlight appear, the trolls turn into a ring of stones, and the mare turns back into a tiny toy. Narrative and pictures have the feel of a folktale, and the drama keeps younger children at the edge of their seats.

Meddaugh, Susan. *Cinderella's Rat.* Illustrated by the author. Boston: Houghton Mifflin, 1997.

This spin-off of the Cinderella story is a winner, due to point of view, and humor in both text and illustrations. A rat narrates the strange events that happen the day he and his sister are caught in a trap. The fairy godmother's wand zaps him, turning him into a coachman for Cinderella, while his sister Ruth remains a rat. The coachman, seeking to rescue his rat-sister Ruth, finds a boy, who helps him locate a wizard, who tries to change Ruth into a girl, with several botched attempts. Meanwhile, the clock strikes midnight, the coachman turns back into a rat, but Ruth remains a girl who says "woof." At least the rat's life is easier now, with a part-human sister to protect him. This story is entertaining for primary and middle grades.

Melmed, Laura Krauss. *Little Oh.* Illustrated by Jim Lamarche. New York: Lothrop, Lee & Shepard, 1997.

This delightful tale, filled with adventure, gentleness and love, keeps up a lively pace due to its turns in plot and its glowing, expressive illustrations. A Japanese woman makes an origami girl, paints a face on her, and puts her in a box. The next morning, the paper doll comes alive, though still in origami form. The delighted woman takes care of her and calls her Little Oh. One day, on a trip to the market, a dog upsets the woman's basket, and Little Oh is lost. She has a harrowing adventure down a river, gets help from a crane, and ends up on the doorstep of a man in her neighborhood. When the man returns Little Oh to her home, she turns into a flesh-and-blood girl, and the man and woman fall in love. This story is engaging for primary and middle grades.

Shaw-MacKinnon, Margaret. *Tiktala.* Illustrated by László Gál. New York: Holiday House, 1996.

In this story, an Inuit girl seeks to become a great soapstone carver. She is told that her time has not come yet and that she must travel alone for three days to find a spirit helper. Out in the wilderness, she hears a voice. After telling the voice that she wants to carve the image of a harp seal, she turns into a one. She learns about seal life from another seal, who has been instructed to be her helper. She doesn't understand the anger of the animals toward human beings, until she sees a man start to club a baby seal to death. Tiktala stops the man and turns back into a human being. She returns home as an expert carver.

Smith, Janice Lee. *Wizard and Wart.* An I Can Read Book. Illustrated by Paul Meisel. HarperCollins, 1994.

A humorous easy-reader featuring episodes in which Wizard works his magic with the companionship and commentary of his dog, Wart. Wizard sets up his magic business and gets animal customers who want to be transformed into the same species as their true loves. Then, in *Wizard and Wart at Sea* (1995), Wizard and his dog, Wart, take a vacation. While at the beach, the two are bothered by birds, so Wizard changes the beach birds to goats, the water birds into whales, and the pool birds into monkeys. Now the entire resort is a mess. Responding to protests, Wizard turns all the previous transformations into songbirds, and everyone is happy.

Steig, William. *Sylvester and the Magic Pebble.* Illustrated by the author. New York: Windmill Books, 1969.

This beloved and enduring story of Sylvester the donkey evokes empathy, as he and his family experience heartache resulting from an unintentional transformation.

Sylvester the donkey finds a magic pebble, which, he discovers, has the power to grant wishes. On his way home with the pebble, he meets a lion, and in a panic, he wishes he were a rock. As a rock, Sylvester cannot grasp the pebble to wish himself a donkey again, and he is very lonely. His loving parents search in vain for him for a year. The following spring, his parents try to cheer up with a picnic on the very rock that is Sylvester. Sylvester's father finds the pebble and places it on the Sylvester-rock. The next time Sylvester wishes to be himself again, his wish comes true. Their joyful reunion is tenderly communicated through the text and illustrations. This story is suitable for primary grades.

Van Camp, Richard. *A Man Called Raven.* Illustrated by George Littlechild. San Francisco: Children's Book Press, 1997.

Written and illustrated by men of the Dogrib and Plains Cree Nations, this contemporary story has a haunting link to the legendary Raven. Two boys are trying to corner and harm a raven, when a fierce-looking man suddenly appears and scolds them. He then tells the boys the story of a mean man who used to shoot ravens just to harm them. An injured raven started to follow the man everywhere until the man could barely ever sleep. One day, the man fell from a tree and changed into a raven. The raven-man flew back to his village to spy on the people. He saw a funeral—his own. When he saw how the people cared about him, his attitude changed. He began to guard his people and even saved some lives. After telling this story, the man is asked by the boys if the raven ever got to become a man again. He replies that it happens once in a while, when the people need a reminder about caring for the Earth and its creatures. When the man leaves, the reader realizes that this visitor *is* the raven-man. The message of this story is appropriate for middle grades and up.

Index